◇◇◇◇◇

Married to a Pastor's Wife

◇◇◇◇◇

MARRIED TO A

H.B. London, Jr.
& Neil B. Wiseman

PASTOR'S WIFE

 VICTOR BOOKS

A DIVISION OF SCRIPTURE PRESS PUBLICATIONS INC.
USA CANADA ENGLAND

Editors: Ron Durham and Barbara Williams
Design: Paul Higdon

Library of Congress Cataloging-in-Publication Data

London, H.B.
  Married to a pastor's wife / by H.B. London, Jr. & Neil B. Wiseman.
    p.   cm.
  ISBN: 1-56476-392-7
  1. Spouses of clergy.   I. Wiseman, Neil B.   II. Title.
  BV4395.L66   1995
  253'.2 — dc20   95-16079
                                                                          CIP

© 1995 by Victor Books/SP Publications, Inc. All rights reserved.

Printed in the United States of America.

1 2 3 4 5 6 7 8 9 10 Printing/Year 99 98 97 96 95

CONTENTS

SECTION 2

FACING REALITIES TOGETHER

SECTION 3

HOW TO BE YOURSELF AND
A MINISTER'S WIFE TOO

COULD YOU FIND
TWO HIGHLIGHTERS?

Having finished writing this book, we did what you are about to do. We read it. Or, we should say, we read it again. We smiled at the right places and prayed at others—for ourselves and for you. We even laughed at the apparent audacity of two male pastors trying to write a book mostly for women. Some of our best friends hooted when they learned about our subject: "You are going to write *what?*"

We are pleased with the book, and we hope you will be. We tried to make it distinctive, unique, and to the point. We want everyone to know we think pastors' wives are heroines of contemporary Christianity. We admire their faith, commitment, and grit.

We have an unusual request to make. Before you start reading this book, would you locate two highlighter pens? Any color will do, just so you have two different colors. Maybe you'll choose yellow and orange, or pink and green. Two highlighters—because we suggest that pastors' wives and their husbands read this book together, though not necessarily at the same time. Let each partner read a chapter or even finish the book, marking important points with his/her own highlighter color as he/she reads. Then somewhere along the way stop to ask your spouse, "Why did you mark this idea or sentence?" We believe your relationship will be energized and deepened each time one of you says, "I didn't know you thought that way."

Thanks for allowing us to share a small part of your journey with God. Our thanks to pastor friends who wrote inspiring salutes to their wives. We have enjoyed visiting old familiar places with you. We have been stimulated by this adventure of getting acquainted with new ways of sharing ministry in these new times. And we are grateful to the Victor Books team who, with their customary efficiency, will see that thousands know about this book.

We love being married to a pastor's wife.

H.B. AND NEIL

Introduction
A TWENTY-ONE GUN SALUTE

Hats off to all women married to pastors. These ladies of faith deserve many twenty-one-gun salutes, thunderous applause, and stunning bouquets. Let's celebrate their faithfulness — light the fireworks, strike up the band, call out the cheerleaders, organize 10,000 parades, and buy out all the confetti in every store. Let's cheer and whistle as these unheralded heroines of Christianity take their well-deserved bows.

Without these women's spunk and tenacity, many pastors would quit before next Sunday. Without many of them working in the secular marketplace as breadwinners, pastors' families could not survive financially — so they would have to leave the ministry. And without their kingdom involvement, many congregations would lose their most dynamic spark plug for getting a lot of good done in the name of Christ.

Ladies, we celebrate the amazing vigor you bring to the work of God. Though many ministry settings are difficult, the whole church is not in flames. All the wonderful work being done in local congregations does not appear on the front pages of newspapers or in lead articles of clergy magazines. In a thousand and one places, women married to ministers are making miraculous contributions to the well-being of the church and the salvation of the world.

We know every pastor needs a special lady at his side as his wife. His ministry needs to be enriched by a satisfying marriage like the one Mrs. Norman Vincent Peale pictures:

> I agree that any woman might have other stimulating jobs, but no one is so difficult and demanding, so exciting and potentially rewarding as the job of living with a man, studying him, supporting him, liberating his strength, compensating for his weak-

nesses, making his whole being sing and soar the way it was designed to do.[1]

Such stimulating, happy, at-home relationships are a rich resource for enabling a man of God to do noble work for his Lord.

Those who live in ministry marriages know how much a pastor depends on his spouse to prop him up, to validate his ministry, and to challenge the mistaken assumptions he often makes about himself and others. Poet Alfred Tennyson's lines especially apply to ministry marriage partnerships:

> The woman's cause is the man's; they rise or sink
> Together, dwarfed or godliness, bond or free.[2]

Although more and more women are entering the ministry, it is still the rule for more men than women to be called by churches, and for their wives to find themselves playing a supportive role. While that more-common situation is usually assumed in this book, the authors cordially invite female ministers to reverse the assumed gender perspective as they read.

We would not presume to write a book primarily for pastors' wives without having experienced a ministry marriage, as well as having listened to hundreds of ministry wives tell of their joys and heartaches, opportunities and frustrations. A word about our experience is therefore in order.

H.B. LONDON was most recently pastor in Pasadena, California, at a congregation with more than 3,000 members. He pastored churches of all sizes for thirty-one years. Now he uses this experience to serve as a pastor to pastors through his work as vice president of ministry outreach and pastoral ministries at Focus on the Family in Colorado Springs, Colorado.

As founder and director of the Pastor to Pastor ministry of Focus on the Family, H.B. hears from pastors and their wives all over the world — often about the very issues we discuss in this book. He counsels with them by telephone and through the mail, conducts pastoral training and evangelistic workshops, and has a media resource ministry. He holds revivals and travels worldwide in mission development.

NEIL B. WISEMAN also has a background in local ministry, having served as a pastor for twenty years. He is now pastoral development professor at Nazarene Bible College in Colorado Springs. In this role he not only teaches preaching and pastoring but is able to help ministry students — especially second-career people — prepare for a team approach to ministry with their spouse. He has served his denomination as continuing education director and as clergy educator for many years. He keeps his interest focused on pastors and local churches.

Neil is director of the Small Church Institute, and edits the quarterly journal *Grow,* a magazine dealing with church growth, evangelism, and discipleship. He has written and/or edited more than ten books, and is a resource person for several pastoral conferences each year.

H.B. and Neil previously coauthored *Pastors at Risk: Help for Pastors and Hope for the Church* and *The Heart of a Great Pastor.*

Pastors' wives, in this book we lead a salute to you. This book cherishes your uniqueness and honors your achievements. Though pastors' wives are as diverse in appearance and viewpoint as the colors of the rainbow, leaves on trees, and snowflakes in winter storms, you help make the church great and spiritually viable.

We believe you special ladies who spend so much of your lives in the religious limelight belong to a towering group of people described in Hebrews 11 as persons "of whom the world is not worthy" (Heb. 11:38).

We appreciate you for being imaginative, wise, resourceful, tender, competent, nurturing, innovative, spiritual, skillful, and so often given to tough love. We believe God entrusted you special ladies of faith with unprecedented opportunities to impact the soul of the nation, to renew the hearts of churches everywhere, and to lead your children and grandchildren to Christ. Ladies, you are a part of a great army of faith-nurturers whom the world could not get along without.

This book intends to acclaim, affirm, and admire pastors' wives on every page. It was written to help solve complex problems facing ministry couples and their families. But more than anything else, we want you pastors' wives to know how important you are to God, to the church, to your family, and to us.

Thanks for who you are. Our gratitude for what you are doing and appreciation for what you are becoming.

Great Women for Incredible Partnerships

1

"WHAT WOMEN THESE CHRISTIANS HAVE!"
Authentic Pastors' Wives Come in Many Sizes

◊◊◊◊◊

Father God, Designer and Sustainer of all ministry,
please give . . .
insight to fresh recruits,
grit to the disheartened,
anguish to the halfhearted,
healing to the hurting,
fervor to the lukewarm,
energy to the fatigued,
and vigor to the faithful. Amen.

◊◊◊◊◊

W HAT WOMEN THESE CHRISTIANS HAVE!" is the way Libanius, the Greek rhetorician and philosopher (A.D. 314–393) described women married to Christian workers in an early century of Christian history.[1] History shows Libanius to be more accurate than he knew, and even more on target now.

The strength and emotional mettle of women married to pastors is amazing and incredible wherever they appear in the halls of church history. In nearly every century, the minister's wife was expected never to stand in the pastor's way. But in many historic periods, she also partnered with him in ministry at whatever intensity she wished, or her energy allowed, or her husband desired or allowed.

"What women these Christians have!" applies to pastors' wives in every generation, whether they serve as supportive companions in their homes, selfless sacrificers who endure the encumbrances and privation of pastorates, or full-fledged, energetic helpmates who cheerfully add ministry roles to heavy loads of parenting and domestic responsibilities.

"WHAT WOMEN!"
IN CHRISTIAN HISTORY

As this book's central message was finely tuned, several startling statements like this were discovered:

> Long before feminists began speaking out against the imprisonment of wives in kitchens of dependency and for women's rights to manage financial affairs, assume business responsibilities, make important decisions and converse intelligently with their partners, ministers' wives had learned to embody these values and virtues.[2]

Apparently, tender sprouts of equality for women in the church pre-date the women's liberation movement by several centuries. For generations, in out of the way places and without much fanfare, women of God have shared ministry posts, social prominence, and phenomenal spiritual influence alongside their pastor/husbands.

The early church had capable women

Impressive and accurate historical evidence supports the idea that pastors' wives served as VIPs in church life well before the fourth century, when married men were regularly ordained. As might be expected, objective historic detail is hard to uncover because the church then did not have a professional clergy as it does now. It can be documented, however, that many Christian workers were married in those earlier periods. It seems useful for our purposes, then, to look for shared ministry patterns among Christian couples who did not make their livelihood at ministry.

In order to get a more accurate picture of the thought of the time, Paul's advice to remain unmarried must also be considered. His arguments for celibacy were apparently based on his view of the imminent return of Christ and the kingdom business remaining to be done. It appears that the apostle's reasoning had more to do with efficiency than with sin or sexual gratification.

From the historic record one thing is certain: Christian ministers, though not professional religious leaders as we have today, were married and in pastoral service for Christ to the people.

Later, when Pope Siricius (A.D. 384–398) banned sexual relationships for both unmarried and married clergy, he changed existing family practices and put into place what became a universal requirement of cleric celibacy. In the Reformation, however, Martin Luther challenged and changed that practice for Protestant clergy by taking Katherine as his wife.

Katherine Luther—a renegade nun

Luther's actions simply renewed from earlier centuries the practice of ministers marrying. One of the practical difficulties of the Reformation was the displacement and unemployment of priests and nuns who accepted Luther's teaching and left the Roman church. Thus, on June 13, 1525, at age forty-two Luther married a renegade nun, Katherine von Bora (still in her twenties). This relationship started when she was liberated from a convent on Easter eve in 1523, in a fishdealer's wagon. But the newly liberated nun had a serious problem. Like many former nuns, she had no place to go and no way to support herself economically. So Martin and Katherine's marriage started with a strong incentive to keep her from economic hardship after she left the convent. Thus, Luther's marriage validated his reform convictions as much as it met his personal needs for affection, intimacy, and the fathering of a family.

Katherine Luther mothered six children and transformed a bare cloister into an inviting home for her family. Charlotte Ross speaks of Katherine's ministry:

She was the director of a house that boarded university students. She was a nurse during the plague, at risk to her own health. And above all these she cared for and was supportive of her husband. In many ways, Katherine developed a role model for subsequent clergy wives that conveyed selflessness, skill, warmth, knowledge, and cooperation.[3]

Luther said of her in 1535, "My lord Kate drives a team, farms, pastures and sells cows . . . and between times reads the Bible."[4]

Roland Bainton underscores the bigger picture of the relationship between family and the Reformation when he concludes his impressive biography of Luther by saying,

> The influence of Luther on his people was deepest in the home. In fact, the home was the only sphere of life which the Reformation profoundly affected. Economics went the way of capitalism and politics the way of absolutism, but the home took on that quality of affection and godly patriarchalism which Luther had set as the pattern of his own household.[5]

Like so many clergy marriages since then, Martin and Katherine's union convinced the church and the world by example that biblical faith flourishes when it is homemade.

Susanna Wesley—outspoken mother of Methodism

Some students believe John Wesley actually gave the emancipation of women a quantum leap forward when he allowed them to take part in early Methodism's public services and its many new ministries to the masses.

Wesley's thoughts about these issues were apparently formed in his childhood as he experienced his mother's intense involvement in his father's pastorates. Some authorities consider Susanna Wesley the most influential woman of her century. As the mother of Methodism, she strongly advocated that girls be taught to read fluently before they were allowed to go to work.

What a Christian activist she was. She led worship services, counseled her husband's unruly parishioners, composed a catechism for her children, and wrote several unpublished theological treatises including commentaries on the Apostles' Creed, the Lord's Supper, and the Ten Commandments.[6] Without intending to do so, Mrs. Samuel Wesley, pastor's wife at Epworth and mother of John and Charles, personified the pagan Libanius' comment, "What women these Christians have!"

Lydia Finney—energetic evangelist's equal

After Wesley, the evangelist Finney took up the cause of women on the American side of the Atlantic. He allowed and even encouraged his wife, Lydia, and other women to fill highly visible roles in various phases of his ministry. Finney said of Lydia, "She participated in my labors and trials, my rejoicings and sorrows, through many of the most searching and powerful revivals of religion that I have ever seen, or of which I have read or heard."[7] Finney opened the door to useful service to many women who followed in Lydia's footsteps from then until now.

This practice apparently grew out of Finney's energetic belief in Christian usefulness, which Sweet explains: "The rationale that permitted Lydia to travel and toil alongside her husband was the energetic doctrine of Christian usefulness, or, to use a later term reclaimed from the Wesley brothers, 'practical Christianity,' the nineteenth-century expression of the Protestant work ethic."[8] And there is historic evidence to believe that Charles and Lydia Finney served as matchmakers for ministers and women seeking minister husbands so they could be "useful" servants of God. Often the criteria for mate selection was not love or physical attraction but a joint vision of useful service in pastorates, missionary service, or evangelistic campaigns.

Seeds of women's liberation

It is interesting to speculate whether or not women's liberation might actually be rooted in Christian history. After discussing the influential impact made by Susanna Wesley and Lydia Finney, Leonard I. Sweet observed, "With this distinguished lineage, it is little wonder that many evangelicals grew to like their women active, intelligent, independent, forceful, deeply spiritual and humble."[9]

Before leaving this brief historical focus, two charming quotes should be noted to help us understand the nature of their times near the turn of the last century. In 1898, an editorial in the *United Presbyterian* said some wives—by reporting on conditions in the parish, ministering to the pastor's moods, and helping control his tongue—made "their services more indispensable to the congregation than even the pastor's."[10] What an extraordinary trilogy: listen to the parish, be a faithful wife, and keep him quiet. That sounds a lot like what present pastors' wives do in many more modern settings.

Another reference showing the subtleties comes from Margaret E. Blackburn's 1898 manual for ministers' mates, entitled *Things a Pastor's Wife Can Do.* Blackburn advised, "Let us, as pastors' wives, make our home cages so large, so delightful, that the one we love will not feel the bars, but will always be more than glad to return."[11]

A relationship of trust

Throughout 2,000 years of Christian history, the role of the minister's mate has changed often, and it continues to change rapidly. Even in a single ten- or fifteen-year period, variations have often moved from caring companion to hearth keeper to resident sacrificer to spiritual sustainer to ministry partner to energetic helpmeet to institutional church leader to deputy pastor. But whatever direction the minister's wife's role tilts at any moment of human history, it always involves a position of trusted support for the work of ministry. And it is always an invaluable asset in the service of the kingdom.

All this historic evidence supports the idea that a woman's being one in ministry with her husband is not new to our time. Neither did feminism's influence on the church begin in this century. Or more correctly, the church's impact on feminism is not new.

"WHAT WOMEN!"
IN SCRIPTURE

Ministry couples, while facing the astounding demands contemporary ministry brings, can receive inspiration and strength from remembering women of God in Holy Scripture. Many of them were victorious in the middle of surprising problems and challenges. These first-century ministry models show us how to risk, how to prioritize our life, and how to serve Christ in a confused world that needs holy women of God so much.

Mary — commitment to God and children

As the earthly mother of Jesus, Mary didn't say to the angels or to her friends, "I'm too young and inexperienced to take on this assignment of the parenting of the Christ Child who will save the world." Rather, she obeyed even when she did not understand. As a result, God trusted her with the baby Jesus and used her youthful commitment to inspire believers across two millenniums. She helped put children at the center of Christianity with her prayer, "I am the Lord's servant. May it be to me as You have said" (Luke 1:38).

Lydia — businesswoman used by God

As a new convert and shopkeeper at Philippi, Lydia didn't say, "My house is too small for entertaining," or "My business keeps me too busy to help start a church here." God used her home, her business skills, and her network of contacts to advance the kingdom. She became a key spark plug in planting Paul's sweetheart church at Philippi with her commitment, "If you consider me a believer in the Lord, come and stay at my house" (Acts 16:15). She also used her home to cultivate soul friends, and as a site for the new church.

Anna — specialist in rigorous faith

The old prophetess Anna, who worshiped God with prayer and fasting day and night, never considered excusing herself by saying, "I'm too old for the new thing God is doing." From long experience, she knew the Lord's ways are often filled with exciting surprises. Her wholehearted devotion to God puts her in the middle of the spiritual action, and her example inspires us to enrich our souls with the spiritual disciplines (Luke 2:36-38).

The two Marys — trust or fear

The two Marys, with grief and fear, went to the tomb on Easter morning. As they felt an earthquake roll the stone away, they never considered saying, "This experience is too frightening for us. Since we don't understand all these events, we need to get out of the center of this action." No, they drew closer to God as the events became more unsettling. As a result, God used the trust of the two Marys. They were privileged to be the first to see the empty tomb, and the first to tell the good news about the Resurrection (Luke 24:1-12). What important women they are in Christian ministry.

Mary and Martha — housework or devotion

Lazarus' sisters, Mary and Martha, had two significant, life-changing encounters with Jesus. They were impacted by Jesus' resurrection power following their brother's death, but they are also remembered for their disagreement about housekeeping responsibilities. Mary didn't say, "The housework comes before the cause of Christ, so the kingdom will have to take second or third priority in our lives." As He always does, Jesus helped them sort through their priorities (Luke 10:38-42). (One commentator suggests that the sisters probably succeeded in getting Lazarus to help with housework after he was resurrected!)

Samaritan woman — curiosity for the Gospel

The Samaritan woman's curiosity kept her from dismissing Jesus with a surface comment like, "I have my own religion, and it's good enough for me." No, she wanted to hear more, and she was so impressed that she wanted to tell others what she had learned about God and herself. As a result, this woman became a soul-winning connection between Jesus and needy people of her nationality and community. He still uses curiosity, even in modern life.

Tryphena and Tryphosa — hard workers for a great cause

These women appear in an understated sentence at the end of the Book of Romans: "Greet Tryphena and Tryphosa, those women who work hard in the Lord" (Rom. 16:12). The New Testament scholar William Barclay develops an intriguing paragraph about these two women. After suggesting they were probably twins, Barclay says Paul uses the Greek word *kopian* for Christian work, meaning to toil to a stage of utter exhaustion. Barclay expands this delightful idea:

> That is what Paul said that Tryphena and Tryphosa were in the habit of doing; and the point of it all is that their names mean dainty and delicate, respectively; but they belie their names by working like Trojans for the sake of the Church and for Christ.[12]

Then Barclay says, "We can imagine a twinkle in Paul's eye and a smile passing across his face as he dictated that greeting."[13]

Priscilla — first pastor's wife

Her ministry started when she and her husband Aquila escaped the persecution of Christians under Claudius. Then at Corinth they met Paul and became his business partners in tent making and ministry partners in his efforts for the Gospel. From Corinth, Priscilla and Aquila moved with Paul to Ephesus where they risked their lives in the riots stirred up by worshipers of Diana. But, they were able to establish a church in Ephesus. In the new church, they discipled Apollos of Alexandria in the Christian faith. (See Acts 18.)

Apparently Priscilla was the first woman in Christian history to marry a man in a secular vocation who later became a pastor. It appears she was among the first in a long line of clergy wives who have made outstanding contributions to the work of the Gospel across 2,000 years. Maybe the partnership in ministry all started with Priscilla and her Gospel partnership with Aquila and Paul.

"WHAT WOMEN!"
IN CONTEMPORARY MINISTRY

These issues become more real and personal as we salute contemporary women who are married to pastors. Each of the women we are about to discuss is actually involved in the work of the church. Their names and settings have been camouflaged to preserve anonymity. Let's look behind the scenes to see what matters most to these courageous women who serve side by side with their husbands at the spiritual front lines of our society. Try to deliberately refocus your viewpoint so you see the church and world from their perspective. Try to cherish these unique women of devotion who are on a pilgrimage of ministry with their pastor/husbands every hour of every day. Their beauty is highlighted by the creative work of the Creator, who made no two exactly alike.

Mona — the dependable breadwinner

Mona, age twenty-eight, and Tim, who is thirty, are planting a church — his first assignment — in a suburb of Phoenix. When the church started three years ago after Tim graduated from a Bible college in their area, Mona secured a position as an administrative assistant to the manager of a community hospital. She believes in Tim's ability and call to ministry, and wants him to give all his efforts to establishing this baby church. Like many pastors' wives, she works in secular employment as an economic necessity. Mona and Tim have a son named Aaron, age four.

Tim helps Mona with household tasks and spends a full day each week with Aaron, who attends a Christian day-care center the other four days. Tim works hard to be a loving husband and good father, always keeping family high in his priorities. He views closeness to his family as a significant and enjoyable component of effective ministry. He sometimes feels guilty because Mona has to work to keep his ministry afloat economically, even though he knows she is willing to work to free him for full-time ministry.

Mona is seen by some members of their young church as a heroine who keeps Tim in the ministry. But women in two-paycheck families identify with her easily. Some days Mona fights self-pity when she feels as though the whole weight of family finances is on her shoulders. Other days she feels upbeat when she reminds herself that thousands of women work outside their home for reasons less important than keeping their husbands in the ministry. Like many other women, she wishes she worked outside the home because she wants to rather than because she has to.

Although Mona openly scorns the heroine accolades, she believes this breadwinner issue is an undiscussed and misunderstood fact of contemporary church life. She can make a convincing argument that many smaller churches can only be kept open by the valiant financial efforts of pastors' wives. And she is right. Hundreds of pastors' wives carry the financial problems of struggling churches on their backs. As they go off to work each morning, they cheer themselves with the assurance that God keeps good records. Though their secular work may not put actual new dollars in the offering plate, it relieves family and church economic pressures so their husbands can work for less—sometimes much less. Too often, these courageous acts are overlooked or ignored by laity and denominational leaders alike.

Mona tries to be a superwoman—a faithful wife and good mother—even as she keeps herself involved in church life. She is sensitive to the fact that many other women face the same outside work demands she does, but that does not keep her from being exhausted. At the same time, she knows she has physical and time limitations. Thus she narrows her church involvements to teaching a young couple's Sunday School class, and she does much of her studying for that assignment on her lunch hour at work. She sees her Sunday School class as a way to optimize her efforts at church, to keep spiritually alert, and to touch people her own age with the Gospel.

Linda—a modern woman who cannot be classified

Linda, twenty-seven, and Larry, twenty-eight, share ministry in an urban ghetto of one of America's largest megalopolises. She is a naturally gifted fourth-grade public school teacher. Linda, Larry, and their two-year-old son live in a "refurbished" apartment building that is reasonably secure. Their home is upscale by ghetto standards, but missionary status by middle-class America standards.

Like many young mother/professionals, Linda goes off to work every day. But her professional commitments have an important difference—she takes public transportation four miles to teach in an inner-city school where most teachers would not consider serving. When asked about this passion for her work, she replies,

"Someone has to make a difference in the lives of inner-city children. Why not me?" She sees teaching as a ministry to the urban poor of their city.

Without meaning to do so, she defies most traditional categories of what a pastor's wife should be. She loves the urban energy of the city, loves teaching, and loves making an impact on disadvantaged inner-city children.

When asked about problems, and when applauded for her commitment, she replies, "I'm doing what comes naturally for me as a Christian — trying to make a difference where I am, in the power of Jesus' name." When asked about the future, Linda and Larry simply say, "We are doing everything we can to bloom in the soil where God planted us."

Linda and Larry are living examples of a contemporary ministry couple who use their unique gifts continually in what they believe to be a divine assignment. No fancy worship space, no corporate-looking offices, no flashy cars, and no traditional way of dressing dominate their lives. No one has written books about how to do ministry where they serve, on the cutting edge of urban blight. Their ministry is simple and one-on-one to forgotten people in the inner city. To follow them around feels like a ministry style Jesus would likely use in such a setting.

Though Linda and Larry could easily move to a more pleasant setting, a safer community, and a stronger church, they have no interest in that kind of change. They feel called to love, care, and make a difference where they are, and they are doing that. They represent thousands of ministry couples who quietly and effectively go about life-changing kingdom work, who do not fit any category.

Meagan — the resident free spirit

Meagan tests limits and expectations wherever she goes. John, thirty-eight, and Meagan, twenty-nine, married nine years ago and have two sons — Mark, seven, and John Wayne, four. Meagan fights for women's rights, often with aggressive, confrontational behavior that is frequently misunderstood in the congregation and community.

John now serves in his third congregational assignment since their marriage, and Meagan has been grossly misunderstood in every church. Consequently, their family has been forced to move often, but John defends her right to be herself. It is a right she exercises and enjoys in every possible public setting.

In a pastors' wives meeting, Meagan once remarked, "No matter what I do, John defends me to the church. I couldn't act the way I do without his support." And she is right.

Calling herself a "free spirit," Meagan seems incredibly focused on "doing her own thing." She believes the church will be the last place to give women equal rights, so she fights for women's issues in their church and in denominational gatherings. She prides herself in creating controversy wherever she goes. She is a good person and speaks about the power of Christ at work in her life. Her best friends believe she is a conscientious disciple of Christ, though somewhat misguided and certainly misunderstood.

Their present church tolerates her "peculiar" behavior. She tested these limits almost to the breaking point recently when she applied for an opening as a policewoman and entered the Mrs. America Beauty Contest in their town. No one knows whether either opportunity will materialize, nor can anyone predict what the fallout will be from these actions. The thought of seeing their pastor's wife in a beauty contest dressed in a bathing suit has everyone in a state of shock.

When asked why she did not get more involved in church activities, she replied, "Lay leaders refuse to use my talents of teaching and singing because they never know what I will do next. I like shocking them. Sometimes they ask me to do things that do not interest me, so I refuse."

She continued, "Since they won't use me, I get involved in other things in the community. I never do anything dishonest or immoral, just controversial and unusual. I wonder why the church does not accept me the way I am."

Once the wife of a retired minister tried to help Meagan by suggesting, "Many conventional roles for pastors' wives still bring satisfaction, my dear, if you will just scrape the rust from the traditions and become a true servant to the people for God." Then Meagan made an embarrassing scene, and the woman apologized even though the breach was not her fault. But several in the group secretly agreed with the mature woman's statement.

Many in the congregation agree with Meagan that every person is unique and special and worthy of individual caring and nurturing. The difficulty, however, arises over how she goes about bringing attention to herself and these issues.

Kallie — a full ministry partner

Kallie, forty-five, is married to Jack. They live in a medium-sized Midwestern town, and she serves energetically at her husband's side. People sometimes joke at church, "If you want to know what Jack thinks, ask Kallie."

Jack enjoys having his wife involved in his work fully as much as she loves being involved. Most church members believe this husband-wife team effort helps their congregation flourish. Much of the time, Kallie is the more creative of the two and thinks up ideas which Jack happily carries out.

She is an unofficial assistant pastor, although she has no interest in being ordained. Their ministry is as fully shared as if she were credentialed. Trained as an RN, she resolved early in their marriage to give her energy to being Jack's comrade and coworker. And she is good at what she does.

Kallie brought up their three children without drawing clear lines between home and church. Until the children started public school, they attended the church-sponsored Kiddie Kollege whenever their mother was involved in ministry — and that was often. Two of their children are now in high school and one is a college freshman. Even though the kids sometimes grouse that their mother is more interested in the church than in them, she doubts the sincerity of their feelings because all three enjoy active participation in the congregation.

Kallie plays the organ for Sunday services, and works nearly full time in the church office as a volunteer. As official hostess, she entertains visiting resource people in her home and generally accompanies Jack when he takes church guests out for a meal. One of her most satisfying tasks is serving as church wedding coordinator; her joy for the task is based on the assumption that she relieves her husband from logistic wedding details. Some people believe she loves the high visibility the weddings bring, and they may be right. She also enjoys keeping in close touch with shut-ins.

This husband-wife partnership is so obvious that Jack calls her "the weaver of my ministry dreams." Local congregational leaders respond to her happily because they see this husband-wife relationship as a working style their pastor needs, enabling him to give optimum service to the church.

Kallie explains the relationship: "We have built-in needs to love others in Jesus' name, and we love doing it together."

Sarah — ministry is my husband's business

Sarah, age thirty-five, lives in a northwestern town of 125,000 located fifty miles from Seattle. Her children are Kevin, age two, and Kerry, age four. She teaches children's piano lessons in her living room three afternoons a week to earn enough to keep from working outside her home. She wants to resume her occupation as a social worker after the children start school.

Sarah and Tom have been married twelve years. They met and married while he was attending seminary in Boston and she was earning her master's degree in social work in an area college. Though a solid believer, she sees no point in sharing her home or energies as a full partner in ministry. She views ministry as Tom's profession, his fulfilling way of earning a living for his family. While she is not militant about these views of ministry, she does organize her life around them.

She reasons that if Tom were a physician, she would have no part in his medical practice. She would not know or be troubled by his patients' problems. Neither would she expect the patients' concerns to impact her life in any significant way. In the same trend of thought, she feels she should not tamper with his occupation as a minister. She often reminds herself, her friends, and church members, "I am a woman who just happens to be married to a pastor."

On the other hand, Sarah knows Tom needs her support at home. Since she wants Tom to be a strong, effective minister, she works at being a loving wife, a good mother, and a competent homemaker. On a scale of one to ten, she is a strong eight in all these family roles. Sarah sees her task as providing affirmation and affection for Tom and the children. Secretly and privately she is chronically lonely, and finds it difficult to develop close relationships with anyone outside her home.

In the work of the church, Sarah is no more or no less active than most laypersons. She teaches a class for six-year-olds and sings in the choir. She turns down requests to serve on committees with a humorous disclaimer, "I might be prejudiced in favor of Tom's ideas."

When Tom was interviewed for this pastorate — his second assignment since seminary graduation — he shared how much he needed Sarah to make their home a refuge of renewal, a place to recharge his emotions and renew his energies. He described Sarah's ministry to him as being fully as important as healthy food, regular exercise, and personal spiritual formation. In that same conversation, Tom said, "I can't function without a strong support system at home." The layleaders wholeheartedly accepted this explanation, although the idea was somewhat new to them.

In every way possible, Sarah tries to make Gale MacDonald's concept operational in their home and marriage: "I (the wife) can be a balancing agent for him (the pastor), calling him away from needless exhaustion and finding some creative way to get him to relax and absorb new strength."[14]

After years of making this relationship work well in their home, Tom sometimes compliments layleaders by saying, "Thanks for understanding that Sarah is a nurturer who keeps me going in ministry." Sarah believes her ministry to Tom also serves the church. She cheers him when he is discouraged, and she talks through issues with him when he is confused. She also serves as an emotional compass in the storms, tries to keep him focused on essentials, and loves him deeply.

Sonya — the career woman

Sonya, forty-two, and Bill, forty-six, are serving in their third pastorate in a settled, middle-class urban neighborhood in the greater Los Angeles area. Their fifty-year-old church is a settled congregation with an average worship attendance of 300. Their children are Bill, Jr., twenty, a college student; Gus, eighteen, a recent high school graduate who is working as a carpenter's laborer until he decides what he wants to do with his life; and Krista, fifteen, a high school junior. Bill enjoys his ministry, and the children think they have a good life.

Sonya is an urban planner for the city of Los Angeles. She has held her present job for eight years and wants to continue until retirement. She finds her professional work-world exhilarating, and is convinced that women have a promising future in her occupation. Although putting her children through college is one of her financial goals, she works because she enjoys her career. But she sometimes feels frustration when her job requires long hours, and she knows her hectic work schedule produces stress for their family.

Sonya believes people at church think of her as a traditional housewife who has allowed professional prestige to go to her head. She believes they think she should be home with her family, not the main staff person for the planning board of her city. She is unlike any pastor's wife they have ever had, and they are confused as to how they should respond to her. Even though keeping the logistics balanced at home is sometimes hectic, Bill encourages her to pursue her career goals because he believes her fulfillment is an important part of her life and their relationship.

However, her shifting priorities at work, home, and church are a constant source of frustrating distress. Sonya is conscientious and eager to have it all—at work, at home, and at church. She represents a new generation of professional women who want to develop a career although they are married to a pastor. Since career women being married to pastors is still a somewhat new idea, patterns have not been established; and this means Sonya sometimes feels like an modern pioneer.

Arlene—the friendly helper

Arlene, fifty-eight, has shared Sam's ministry as a friendly helper for thirty-four years. In their life together, they have served five churches in three southern states. She and Sam have four grown children who are active in churches in other locations.

She uses her ministry of helps to full measure, and loves to say, "Helping people brings more satisfaction than a million dollars can buy." She is a jewel of a person who always earns a never-to-be forgotten niche in people's affections.

Sam's church, located in a small Florida coastal town, has a worship attendance of 105. Half the church members are retired church transplants from Indiana, Michigan, and Illinois. Because of their geographic diversity, these people bring an amazing variety of viewpoints to church with them every Sunday. As a result, this congregation has a confusing collision of expectations of a pastor's wife, but it never bothers even-tempered Arlene.

Arlene overlooks their minor differences, smiles, and keeps amazingly active. She views herself as a friendly helper who conscientiously tries to follow the wise words of Scripture, "If you help, just help, don't take over" (Rom. 12:7, TM).

Her impressive list of compassionate activities changes every day. Most mornings she starts by calling six shut-ins to make sure they did not suffer emergencies during the night. On a recent, fairly typical day, she took an elderly neighbor to the doctor, invited a rebellious fifteen-year-old girl to lunch, delivered homemade cookies to a new family, and sat with an Alzheimer's patient so the patient's husband/caregiver could have a needed two-hour break. She once cared for a six-year-old boy who had chicken pox in her own home for two days while the child's mother, a small business owner, made an essential business trip to Chicago.

Arlene has a special ESP that tells her when someone needs her. While she never teaches a Sunday School class on a regular basis, nor has she ever led an adult Bible study, she has helped nearly everyone in their church in some way. Her ministry of helps is low-keyed, loving, and receives little publicity — the way she likes it.

Nearer the beginning of their ministry together, Sam urged her to accept more visible assignments in the church. She gently refused and remarked, "I could never fulfill my gift of helps if you push me to become a public person. God wants me to do in self-forgetful ways what nobody else wants to do. Why not let me please Him?" Sam wisely gave in, and both of them have received enormous satisfaction from her behind-the-scenes ministry.

WOMEN OF GOD!
YOU ARE ONE OF THEM

God made every woman original and unique and special and astounding and unpredictable. Yet in some ways, all women are also alike. This apparent contradiction keeps male pastors guessing much of the time. It is the main reason why marriage and ministry are such amazing adventures that change from day to day and minute to minute. Who knows what the next experience will be for a couple in ministry? And who knows what the response will be from either one of them?

Regardless, then, of the pastor's wife's style of establishing and maintaining association with the church, she must bring a spiritually sensitive, quality person to the relationship. Let's get the focus as clear as the morning sun. The task of shared ministry is a trust from God more than a demand from any congregation. Thus, such a whole person is needed because no known checklist will fit every person or every place or every marriage.

Let's shout it from the housetops. It's perfectly acceptable, maybe even desirable, for a pastor's wife to choose her own style for living her life. Or she might combine some components from the women discussed here. Or she might invent a completely new style. The secret is to fill the chosen style with a satisfying faith, a joyous outlook, and an attractive witness. People in the churches and the world are drawn to authentic faith and inner beauty based on the Word of the Lord:

> What matters is not your outer appearance — the styling of your hair, the jewelry you wear, the cut of your clothes — but your inner disposition. Cultivate inner beauty, the gentle, gracious kind that God delights in. The holy women of old were beautiful before God that way, and were good, loyal wives to their husbands (1 Pet. 3:3-5, TM).

Your Christ-exalting way of life — what Paul called "clothing yourself with the Lord Jesus" (Rom. 13:14) — initiates you into the hall of fame made up of all who serve Christ under the banner, "What women these Christians have!" And the second banner will proclaim, "What Christians these women are!"

CONTEMPORARY CHALLENGE
Ministry Lessons from Biblical Coaches

- Mary, the mother of Jesus, was obedient even when she did not understand.
- Anna refused to allow her advancing age to inhibit her active faith.
- Mary and Mary, first persons at the empty tomb, were forever impacted by the Resurrection.
- Mary and Martha, Lazarus' sisters, sought a balance between wholehearted devotion and household duties.
- Tryphena and Tryphosa gave incredible energy for a great cause.
- Priscilla shared ministry as a full partner with Aquila and Paul.

MARRIED TO A PLAIN PLAINS GIRL
FROM NEBRASKA
A Salute to Anna Hayford
by Pastor Jack Hayford

Her name is as plain and simple as her background and style. Anna was born on the plains of Nebraska in a straw-strewn corner of a dirt-floored hut to a pair of pioneer-spirited farmers named Elmer and Emma.

That their surname was Smith more or less summarizes the rather nondistinctive characteristics of that baby's beginnings and upbringing as the seventh of nine children. Her dad's recurrent heart problems relentlessly put the family at severe financial disadvantage, but the creativity of a close-knit family and the prayer-filled, faithful lifestyle of Christian parents bred a girl of unusually gracious temperament and tenacity to the purposes of God.

She was raised in church from birth, taught the Word of God from her earliest recollections of Sunday School, received Jesus Christ as her Savior before she was nine years old, and knew she was called to marry a pastor and be in the ministry by the time she was thirteen.

We met in college — L.I.F.E. Bible College — where we had both come to Los Angeles to enroll in pursuit of God's call on our lives. When I look back on our beginnings together, two foundational facts stand out — Anna's spiritual life and her social bearing. These are the reasons why my life as a minister has been blessed by this woman I call Lady Anna, but also intermittently address or refer to as Honey, Babe, Doll, or Mom — and, more frequently of late, Grandma.

Anna's supportive spiritual life

I met and married a woman who is totally committed to Jesus Christ. In assessing the fortitude Anna brought to my ministry, three strengths come instantly to mind.

Anna has never questioned that ministry is what our life is about. Through the toughest of times, whether as pastors of a struggling infant congregation in Indiana the first four years of our ministry, or under the heat and pressure of a rapidly growing, highly visible pastorate in an intensely urban setting, she has been strong at my side as a fellow shepherd as well as my wife. She has always been faithful to her call to the ministry and to mine. Her faithfulness has made it infinitely easier to be faithful to my call.

Anna is a happy-to-be-godly believer in holiness. She doesn't carry any excess baggage of religious prudery, but she definitely knows what it means to be Christ's completely, and she lives like it without any show of religious snobbery. I don't think people view her as a holy woman so much as a happy one. That's what makes the sheer fact of her holiness of life so desirable to those among whom we minister — and so joyous to live with for me.

Anna is a practical Christian with a simple, focused prayer life. I have no way to assess the strength I receive from her constant prayer. It may seem a paradox to some, or even impossible to others, but other than at church, I rarely see my wife on her knees. When we pray together, we're usually seated, and when she sustains most of her prayer life, she's usually in motion around the house.

I've heard her answer inquiring young pastoral wives who've asked about her prayer life; that's how I know she prays. But mostly, I have watched a woman grow into a stable, maturing life in God and pray with continued effectiveness and spiritual results that have blessed me and advanced our ministry; that's how I know that she prays.

Anna's good-sense simplicity

However, as strong as my wife's spiritual supportiveness has been, it is dramatically amplified by her social bearing — her style, if you please.

Anna, the plains girl, is absolutely genuine to the core. There is an even, unchangeable, dependable quality of "I-always-know-how-she's-going-to-be" that makes life immeasurably easier and happier for me. I certainly do not mean she's without flair, imagination, or creativity — "boring" would be the last term to describe her. But this girl, raised on the Nebraska plains where affectation or pretentiousness were immediately identified and either instantly spurned or laughed into social oblivion, is a no-nonsense kid. It's that particular quality about her that first captured my heart.

I met a cute girl with a clear head, good mind, and happy personality. But I married a solid woman with a majestic simplicity and forthright-but-gracious honesty . . . in everything.

Anna, the plains girl, is always there. All the years of our ministry, I've benefited by the fact that everyone believes in and likes my wife. It isn't because she swims through gatherings, slavishly pouring out social chatter or glitzy charm in an effort to captivate people or verify herself. Rather, the most impressive thing about her is how unimpressed she is with herself, and how she never labors to impress anyone. To the contrary, she simply shows up: she's there. And this quality of "you always know what you're going to get" — a happy, loving person you can trust — has won the hearts of those we've served over more than thirty-five years of ministry.

Oh, yes. Anna has taught Bible classes, led our women, served in every department from nursery to music, been active in denominational activities, and traveled with me in every continent. She's done all the "church-woman" things, and is always a joy to minister beside me wherever I go when her schedule allows her to travel with me. But the real reasons I've been mightily blessed by God with this woman are wrapped in those two points of assessment: spiritual life and social bearing.

Oh, yes, most people seem to like me; but they *love* Anna! They'll let me stay as long as she's with me, and most of them can't imagine being without her. Neither can I!

Pastor Jack W. Hayford
The Church On The Way
Van Nuys, California

2

STAND BY YOUR MINISTRY MAN

Helping Him Be All God Wants Him to Be

◇◇◇◇◇

Lord of ministry,
  Protect us from pride that turns people away from You.
    Save us from discouragement that causes us to lose hope.
  Resource our marriage so it is a sanctuary of tender affection.
    And make our ministry effective for the strengthening
  of Your people and the fulfillment of our call. Amen.

◇◇◇◇◇

COUNTRY SINGER TAMMY WYNETTE'S SONG "Stand By Your Man" has a true-to-life message for pastors' wives. The lyrics emphasize the need to keep loving him even when he is hard to understand. Standing by your ministry man helps him be all God wants him to be and you want him to be—a loving husband, a devoted parent, and a great pastor.

Husband, parent, and pastor—all those roles are enriched in a mysterious, marvelous way by the wife of a minister. More often than not, she is the emotional/spiritual spark plug that makes ministry fulfilling or depressing, effective or powerless for him.

Being "just a man" confuses and frustrates many pastors because the work of ministry demands so much more than mere human effort. Parishioners often refuse to accept the humanity of pastors. For whatever reason, nearly everyone wants their pastor to be bigger than life. But supermen do not exist in the church, only in the world of make-believe.

This fact causes confusion for the pastor and for everyone in his sphere of impact. So many inside and outside the church, for some puzzling reason, are unwilling to accept ministers as fellow human beings. Even many who live close to pastors—including wives, children, and layleaders—are part of this quiet, irrational conspiracy. Evidently they think they would lose a spiritual hero if their pastor were not stronger than the strongest, and more saintly than all the saints combined.

No matter how grand or noble or lofty an ordination ceremony may be, induction into ministry simply does not free a pastor from his weaknesses, temptations, or flaws. That truth is well known but seldom discussed by those of us who are ordained. Like every human being, pastors get tired, feel tempted, and consider giving up. To be authentic and well-adjusted, pastors and their wives must be aware of their own human frailties and the weaknesses of those about them. They seldom have to wait long to see these weaknesses appear in themselves or in their family, community, or church.

THE MEANING OF MINISTRY

To start correcting the mistaken idea that the pastor/husband is superhuman, a couple in ministry together must develop shared views of what valid ministry is. Whatever effort it takes for both of you to understand ministry will be worth it. Together you must become aware of the key assumptions the pastor/husband holds about ministry. To accomplish that, both of you must move beyond traditional views of ministry to determine what the work of God means to both of you and especially to him. This will require looking past long-held, old-time notions about ministry and considering how he personally views the essentials. In the process, the wife must guard herself from saying, "Ministers don't talk or think that way." Let him talk, long and creatively and even passionately, so you can understand and feel what his ministry is about.

What does ministry mean to both of you?

Learn all you can about how ministry works and what it is supposed to accomplish, but get your basic information from him. What is unique about his being set apart for a holy cause? How does he prepare for preaching, and what does he perceive to be his main message? How does he do pastoral care? How does he evaluate his competency as a pastor? And what is the most important part of ministry for him?

Remind your children and church members how privileged you feel to be married to your man, who is a pastor. Cherish his uniqueness. Remember, you did not marry the ministry — you fell in love with and married a man who is a minister. He has a name, a personality, and strong feelings about what ministry really is — but he is a one-of-a-kind human being and always will be.

Since you stand at the center of his world, remember that you play a large part in making his ministry joyful or sad. You help make it gratifying or insufferable. Together you stand heart to heart with goodness and Christ-centered, quality living. Few women ever experience such an opportunity for standing so close to potential greatness alongside their husbands.

However, if you are to maximize your impact on your husband and his work, you must understand him, his world, his commitment to ministry, and his beliefs about his calling.

As an example of how to do this, you might consider studying the meaning of ministry together, taking a class, or having in-depth conversations between yourselves. For example, raw recruits have their minds opened to the complexities of pastoral service in Neil's "Introduction to Ministry" course. As a result, students sometimes ask their wives to take the course the next year. Then, the couple starts seeing ministry together in a new light. Their new awareness increases dialogue, so they grow together in their views of ministry.

Most women do not feel ready to be a partner in ministry with their husbands. Nearly every pastors' wives' survey shows they do not feel prepared for their role nor do they understand their husband's concepts of ministry. Understandably, since they have no frame of reference, they wonder why he takes his work so seriously and why it takes so much energy and time.

The point, then, is for every couple to find effective ways to reach a happy agreement on what ministry is. They need to have a common understanding of the requirements of time, commitment, obedience, and spiritual ripening. Building such an awareness helps a couple see ministry for what it is—tough, rewarding, demanding, thrilling work. Let's admit it—pastoral effectiveness is determined largely by a couple's shared concepts of ministry. And everyone in ministry knows pastors who have had to struggle all their lives because their wives did not understand why they gave heart and soul to the ministry. In fact, the friends of one pastor I know jokingly observe, "His wife nagged him about ministry until he became a saint." If true, how sad for both of them; they missed the richness of giving complementary service for the cause of Christ.

Making ministry more than pious misery

Though your pastor/husband sometimes faces frustration and anguish, ministry is more than a lifetime of misery. Of course, ambiguities and perplexities sometimes scar his soul, loot his time, and crowd family and frustrate marriage commitments. And what he faces makes his earlier dreams of serving in some untroubled backwater church seem like an archeological age away. But ministry also has awe-inspiring satisfactions that cannot be found in other vocations.

As a starting point to enhance your husband/pastor's ministerial fulfillment, try dealing with these questions for yourself and with him. A forthright discussion about how both of you think about these matters will enrich your relationship and lower some of your frustrations.

- Do you know what ministry means to him?
- Do you realize ministry always involves people, and that quality relationships with them are a critical factor in his fulfillment? Nothing can be gained by a ministry couple depreciating those God has given them to serve.
- How can you help him be strong in the tough times but still keep him from wallowing in a thousand small crises?
- Can you help him blunt his fears about specific situations?
- How can you refocus his attention on the magnificent opportunities of the present moment?

45

In the light of these inquiries and ideals, consider the amazing combination of life-transforming opportunities and painful demands that are built into ministry.

● Ministry is twenty-five-year-old Sally begging for shelter after her husband's latest beating, only to have her return to him once her bruises start to heal. This couple's only hope is what your husband represents.

● It's fifty-one-year-old Tom, a cancer patient, praying to die and hoping to live, who raises puzzling questions about faith and eternity and healing. Helping people make peace with immortality is one of a pastor's specialties.

● It's Roger, a forty-five-year-old with a strange Greek fisherman's cap on his head and a brown briefcase over his left shoulder, who can't deal with his full-blown midlife crisis — a crisis which makes no sense to his wife, children, or boss. Where else could Roger turn for answers?

● It's Mary, age eighty, with her outspoken advice about commitment to everyone who will listen and some who do not want to listen. Her prayers and her energy for God strengthen your pastor/husband in ways he would never know if he were employed in a lesser occupation.

● It's Mark, the handsome youth pastor, denying his infatuation for a young divorcée, which his wife calls "emotional adultery." Helping a young minister stop this disastrous attraction could save his family and ministry.

All this accumulation of ministry piles up beside next Sunday's sermon. It must be added to five counseling appointments scheduled for tomorrow, two hospital calls on critically ill church members that have to be made today, and trying to make time for your son's Little League game on Thursday afternoon. All this affects the emotional energy your pastor/husband needs for Friday night's negotiations for the annual budget, finding funds for unexpected car repairs, and facing up to his frightening innerdryness.

But the greater the load, the more he needs a special someone in his life to remind him often that he is impacting lives in ways that really matter. He needs you to hold him in your arms and say, "You are a great man of God, and I'm grateful that God put us both on the same team. What you do really matters to me and to our church." Or you might try singing to him, "Has anybody told you that I love you today . . . put me on your list, let me be the first to say I love you today."

Making home a comfort zone

Almost without his realizing it, buildups of people's needs stalk a pastor like a nipping dog. Though the duties may not kill him, they nag him constantly. His heart and mind are continually filled with challenges. The pressures start when he wakes in the morning, crowd him all day, and sometimes torment his sleep at night.

For these reasons and more, a pastor needs refuge and nurturing at home. More than you know, he needs a place of calm and a home where his dream woman awaits him.

LIVING WITH A
FULFILLED MAN IS FUN

A pastor's marriage, family, ministry, and self-worth go better when he feels fulfilled and loved unconditionally by his spouse. Of course, marriage to a fulfilled person is more fun than trying to build a happy life with someone who lives on the edge of frustrating despair. Every pastor wants a joyous marriage. And every pastor's wife wants the same.

Consequently, a minister's wife does herself a magnificent kindness and gives her family a special gift when she does all she can to multiply her husband's fulfillment in ministry. More than the good she does for herself is the joy she brings to her husband and family. Although it is seldom stated, ministry, when done well, does everyone good, especially the minister who does it. Ministry, like love and service, always enriches the minister and makes him a more authentic human being, a more caring husband, and a more loving father. Ministry given often turns into blessings received.

Conversely, a woman set on stirring up an adversarial relationship with her husband's ministry complicates life for everyone at home and at church. Ministry can never be allowed to become the pastors' wife's rival or opponent. Many good pastors' wives

47

never really understand how their complaints hinder ministry and suffocate satisfaction out of their marriages.

Cherish the noble cause he loves

A pastor's satisfaction, more important than money, position, or power, is most often rooted in an awareness that he is God's instrument in a great cause, and giving oneself to that cause often makes others feel awe, curiosity, wonder, and confusion. However, the minister feels a surge of added strength in his soul when significant others in his life value the kingdom causes he cherishes and let him know it. Meaning multiplies even more for a minister when he feels he is fulfilling his calling from God, and his satisfaction escalates when he believes God is pleased with his efforts. At its essential essence, ministry is the all-powerful God, the senior partner in everything worthwhile that happens in the universe, inviting the pastor to be the junior partner. But he is a partner, nonetheless, in God's redemptive plans for the human family.

One pastor lovingly described his call to ministry by saying, "I can't help doing what has to be done when God takes me as His coworker and companion." An inspiring model for fulfillment in ministry can be seen in the Servant Jesus as He takes a towel and basin to use as a "show and tell" lesson for all who are serious about following Him.

Ministry's greatest fulfillment does not come from the little church filled with problem people on the corner of First and Main Streets, but from being used in the greatest cause known to the human family—the kingdom of God in its wonder and glory and impact. On the contrary, abandoning a call to kingdom ministry can create a hell of broken dreams. And women who live with "what might have been" men usually come to long for the time when he felt useful to God.

Watch your man's miraculous energy

Try to comprehend the reality that God responds with incredible empowerment when a person shows wholehearted devotion to kingdom priorities. The resulting enablement usually surprises those outside ministerial ranks. They seem unaware that ministers draw a supernatural energy from the Source at the time of their greatest demand. The Cause, with His awesome glory, is why pastors give radical self-sacrifice to the work of Christ without thought of increased compensation or trying to protect their health. Thus, what seems like genuine self-denial to those outside ministry is more often joyous privilege and blessing for a pastor.

A pastor's wife from a southeastern state understood her husband/pastor's need for fulfillment and how that interfaced with his faithfulness to a great cause. In a letter to H B she said, "Though our assignment seems inhumane, I can't imagine Bob without our struggles here. Though I often wonder how, he finds amazing meaning in the middle of the problems. He really believes God wants us to help bring about reconciliation and spiritual renewal in this place. So we toil on even when the going seems tough. Bob loves great causes, and I am always amazed at how much energy he has for the task."

Why be surprised? God always enables those who are willing to be used in great causes for Him.

Notice that Bob's wife intends, in spite of her frustrations, to be a part of the expected breakthrough. She believes their work is significant to God, even as it is important to them. Could it be that an equation for satisfaction in ministry might be C (commitment) + I (intentionality) + F (faith) = PF (pastoral fulfillment)?

Cultivate the art of contentment

A ministry couple were moving to their third charge since seminary graduation. They anticipated their new assignment would be better than former ministry settings, which they had found dull and empty. But they were forced to rethink their suppositions of happiness in a new location when a wise old pastor told them, "Your new place will be like all the other places because you take yourselves with you." In our heart of hearts, we all know the old gentleman is right.

Commit to the fact that contentment is a learnable skill, and that every problem holds some kind of gift in its hand. Paul thought so when he testified, "I have learned the secret of being content in every situation, whether well fed or hungry, whether living in plenty or in want" (Phil. 4:12). Then he adds these reassuring words, "I can do everything through Him who gives me strength" (v. 13). Evidently spiritual stamina and the mastery of contentment were closely connected in Paul's thought.

In learning contentment, face the reality that most situations contain people and circumstances that are both desirable and offensive. Your favorite blue carpet in the parsonage may create trauma for the next pastor's wife. Your new kitchen decorations with a theme from the '50s is fun for you, but the next parsonage family may think it is a visual disaster. Before you came to this church, someone thought the stained-glass windows were an ingenious work of art even though you may think they are grotesque. And the people you love the most may cause the next pastor's wife to have hives.

When contentment is learned, the lessons make life easier for everyone, especially for you and your husband. Look for positive things in your assignment. Dwell on reasons for satisfaction. Minimize problems. Boast about your assets. Then, as you emphasize the strengths of a situation, your husband and family will experience significantly increased fulfillment. Listen carefully to what you say to be sure it helps reinforce contentment.

Recognize your husband's uniqueness

Your ministry man is uniquely different from all others. He is unlike any other man who ever lived and, at the same time, he is frighteningly like every man who ever lived.

This means he does his ministry differently from everyone else, but that he also does it similarly to everyone else. He sees life and death differently than anyone else. Like an artist using oil paints, a minister uses paints, textures, canvas, brushes, and subjects like everyone else, but his picture is always somewhat unique. Yesterday, I saw an artist demonstrate oil painting on TV. I was shocked to observe his maverick technique, but I really liked his portrait. Every pastor has to paint on his own canvas with his own brushes. Everyone does well to recognize this uniqueness as a source of strength for the whole church. One church leader chuckled about this issue, remarking, "We can make young ministers into cookie-cutter pastors, but if we did, the church wouldn't want them. And besides, students won't stand for it."

STOP THE CIVIL WAR
BETWEEN THE SEXES

In the cultural war between the sexes, without intending for it to happen, we have allowed a Trojan horse of cynical mood and caustic talk into our homes and churches.

One beginning pastor's wife revealed a surprising discovery in a pastors' wives' support group: "I think I am overly sensitive about women's rights issues, and sometimes I bring a bad attitude concerning these notions home from the office and into my marriage."

Another wife added, "Me, too, and it always causes problems for Morris and me."

From noise to nourishment

This noisy conflict tends to make us think that men and women are pitted against each other and that it will always be that way. What misery often results in such a marriage! Sadly, in this often outlandish skirmish, women and men often form glaringly inaccurate pictures of each other. And bellowing stereotypes among both genders make conditions worse than they need to be.

For satisfying clergy marriages, such hostile situations have to change. The important issue is to develop a meaningful marriage at your house — not in the world, not in society, not in the culture in general, but at your house. Working to enrich each other's lives and to find selfless, meaningful expressions of affirmation are among the clergy couple's most important goals and most satisfying discoveries.

Instead of allowing these issues to undercut our marriages, we must nourish, uplift, and heal each other. We live in a different realm, you know — the kingdom realm on earth. Thus, since the love of God determines our pattern for ministry, tender relations between pastor and spouse can be a living laboratory of how to apply love to marriage.

For our own fulfillment, and to help heal marriage brokenness in our society, we must stop perpetuating the gender war and make a genuine truce. Author Charlotte Ross, herself a pastor's wife, helps us understand the primary issue:

51

A new woman is emerging who, perhaps for the first time, is a creation of female imagination. She encompasses a broad state of mind that asks new and serious questions about marriage, family life, jobs, power, and the nature of men and women themselves. The American woman who has married a clergyman shares the struggle for full equality. Such a new partnership calls for a careful balancing of obligation, privilege, and role fulfillment.[1]

All of this can be used to make things go better in clergy marriages, if we work at the task and recognize the possibilities.

But to complicate these matters even more, many modern-day men, including pastors, are thoroughly lost in the dark woods of women's liberation. The shouting and placards perplex them. They do not know how to respond or what to say. And neither men nor women seem to understand that there is a long lag between the changes women have already achieved and men's ability to change or accept the changes, even among men who want to do so. Primal, visceral ways of thinking and reacting change slowly, often very slowly. As one pastor summed it up, "I'm a man, but I do not know how to respond to the new women we find everywhere, including my wife."

Women, in the equality fight, tend to think men's careers and work provide them with a sense of wholeness, creativity, and self-worth. Such an assumption can be absolutely wrong. Work, for many men, is a lifelong ordeal of dashed hopes and a continuous violation of their spirits. Although society seems to require it, many men never wanted to be protectors or to die in war. Many men, because they were forced to become providers, feel they are locked out of their chance to explore their full range of potential and possibilities. And some of these feelings are present in clergymen.

Strategies for fulfillment

These confusions must be unraveled if your pastor/husband and you are to enjoy long-term fulfillment in ministry. When you stand by your man, try helping him find optimum meaning in his vocation as a minister. Here are some suggested strategies:

• *Start a "sending" ritual.* As often as you think about it, assure him of your prayers and interests as he faces a tough assignment. Even a brief prayer over the phone before he goes on a demanding call would help. One pastor's wife stops by her husband's study before a service begins to tell him again he is the best preacher she has ever heard. He always preaches better because of her encouragement.

- *Affirm his ministry.* Just like every other pastor who has ever lived, your pastor/husband makes mistakes in ministry. But tell him how well he did a certain phase of ministry: "The wedding was special." "The baby dedication was beautiful." "Your pastoral prayer today was anointed."

- *Resist atrophy of every kind.* Don't allow anything to shrivel your soul, destroy your dreams, or diminish your witness. Every event and circumstance that can dampen your devotion to the cause of Christ can also be used as a prod for growth and breakthrough.

- *Read old love letters to each other or write new ones.* The glow of your early romance will help you see how far your relationship has grown or stagnated. If it has grown, rejoice. If it has stagnated, work to renew it. The amazing thing about this process will be your recollection of how much love you had for each other at the start when you had so few material possessions. Refiring romance will be good for both of you.

- *Turn your problem into a game.* Ask each other, "If this were a problem-solving game like Clue or Monopoly, how would we resolve the issues?" Moving from questions like "Who did it?" and "Isn't this awful?" to "What can we do?" and "How can we grow in this difficulty?" will often turn a tough situation into a splendid victory.

- *Give your husband permission to be himself.* We have already discussed this issue, but it must be thoroughly considered: God made you and your husband unique because He wanted to use you in some special way. Cherish these uniquenesses as gifts from God. He has some special use for your distinctive characteristics.

One professor said of a ministerial student in his class, "He sure is different!" To which another faculty person replied, "Yes, and God has a special use for that difference."

- *Honor your husband's nurturing actions.* A great missing ingredient in much contemporary ministry is the willingness to nurture people—to believe in their potential, to trust their future in God's care, and to patiently wait for their spiritual blooming. Every pastor with even a hint of this dimension in his ministry needs to be encouraged to expand it.

• *Leave the day finished.* At the end of every day, try to finish the day's unfinished business. Talk with your pastor/husband about ways to lay down the burdens of a day. Several modern saints call it the art of relinquishment—simply saying to God and to each other, "We did the best we could with this problem or person today. Now we give this relationship or situation to You. Watch over these concerns as we sleep. Give us grace to trust You with everything that concerns us. And give us rest."

• *Make peace with what you cannot change.* Since few pastorates will be ideal, you can use up lots of energy wishing things were different. If you can make them different, do it. If you can't, ask God to help you accept them with grace.

• *Commit to holy wholeness.* In a dysfunctional society, it is very easy for us to accept difficulties from our past and our surroundings as inevitable hindrances that must be accepted rather than changed. While much of our circumstances cannot be changed, the good news of the Gospel is that we can allow the spirit of Jesus to change us. The Christ-saturated life, the best quality of life ever known to the human family, is available to all who earnestly seek holy wholeness. God will grace you with holiness and wholeness if you allow Him to shape you into what He really wants you to become.

• *Strive for family stability.* Too often the emotional and spiritual level of the pastor's family is determined by outside forces—the local congregation, the community, or something else. While it is true that outside circumstances influence a family, we can resist those influences and set our wills to follow the will of God. While your family may never be perfect, strive to improve it in every possible way. Do not wait a day longer, because opportunities with your children slip away as they grow and develop.

• *Refuse to be a peace breaker.* Nearly every church can be divided over some minor disagreement that is already in place. Talk about it, pick at it, and cluck about it, and you soon have a crisis that even a Solomon cannot solve. On the contrary, you can talk optimism, joy, and wholeness until people begin to practice it.

As a highly visible person in ministry, you have more influence on these matters than you could ever imagine. Remember: God never puts a pastor's wife in charge of getting everyone to be the way she wishes they were. But He can use someone like you in the church to spread love and affirmation and blessing. Try it—God blesses it every time.

CONTEMPORARY CHALLENGE
Do Yourself a Favor by Strengthening His Ministry

- Start a sending ritual.
- Affirm his ministry.
- Resist atrophy.
- Read old love letters or write new ones.
- Turn problems into a game.
- Honor his nurturing actions.
- Leave the day finished.
- Make peace with what you cannot change.
- Commit to holy wholeness.
- Strive for family stability.
- Refuse to be a peace breaker.

MARRIED TO A WOMAN WHO ALWAYS STANDS BY HER MAN

A Salute to Joyce Mehl
by Pastor Ron Mehl

J oyce and I are the real "Honeymooners," even through Ralph and Alice Kramden of TV fame are much more well known. Married twenty-seven years ago, we graduated from college on Friday, married on Saturday, and then left on Sunday for a cross-country public relations tour on behalf of L.I.F.E. Bible College in Los Angeles. We were zealous and wanted to win the world for Christ, but we also had delusions of grandeur about our work that summer — like staying in fancy hotels, driving late-model cars, enjoying expense accounts and speaking to crowds numbering in the hundreds or thousands.

Nothing could stop us — so we thought. But many things did stand in our way, and many surprises soon started coming our way.

Our "limo," as it turned out, was my 1968 dark-green VW bug. It was fast — downhill. I distinctly remember one occasion when Joyce and I were pretending to race a Dodge. I say "pretending" because the driver of the other car did not, in fact, know we were racing him. On the winding, mountainous roads of Colorado, we sped past him on a long downhill stretch, grinning madly as we let Sir Isaac Newton and the force of gravity augment our forty-two horsepower engine. Then, as we rounded the bend and headed up the next hill, the big black Dodge sped past, its driver enjoying air-conditioned, hi-fi, eight-track comfort and one-handed control, thanks to his car's power steering.

Our housing accommodations in the "Glory Days," as Joyce

and I affectionately refer to them, weren't much more wonderful than our transportation. We didn't get to stay at big name hotels; no Marriotts, Hiltons, nor even Motel 6s. No, instead we got church basements, parsonage attics, and high-rent digs like the Candlelight Inn. The Candlelight had that name for a reason — the power went off about 9 every night. I remember going to bed one evening, wildly excited to be "on the road for the Lord." We just lay there and dreamed of the throngs we were soon to preach to. I had been pondering for some time on what I would say about the college when I noticed Joyce hadn't fallen asleep yet. In fact, I could feel her wiggling about. Then, wiggling and scratching — lots of scratching. Serious itching is not a sensation you want to feel when you're lying in a strange bed in a cheap hotel or old attic.

"Turn on the light," Joyce whispered. I turned on the light and threw back the covers. And there they were. Bedbugs. I thought bedbugs were something made up by my grandmother to scare me into going to sleep at bedtime. I was worried about Joyce and her impressions of our start together in ministry. I prayed that Joyce wasn't thinking, "Why did I marry this Bozo?"

Grace under pressure

How would my wonderful new bride deal with these circumstances? How would she handle cross-country trips in a Volkswagen and sleeping on the floor in church basements? She handled it just the way you'd expect a woman of her stature to respond — with grace.

That's the way Joyce always responds — with grace, even under pressure. She never ceases to amaze me in the way she deals with all the things a pastor's wife is called to deal with. In fact, she's an incredibly difficult person to describe on paper because those who don't know her wouldn't believe she could be that nice. But I know she is. I've watched Joyce with awe and amazement for twenty-seven years as she has unselfishly demanded nothing and given everything — for me, our family, and the church.

High-maintenance pastor

Sometimes I feel like a "high maintenance" preacher, always needing help and encouragement, and Joyce has propped me up more times than I can remember. When you weigh only 100 pounds, that's quite a task. But she does it and enriches our lives in many different ways.

A gentle word and a soft touch. Proverbs 11:16 says, "A gracious woman retaineth honor," and I can tell you that the grace of Joyce's life has greatly affected our marriage. Whether we're flying down the hill of blessing or climbing slowly up the slope of struggle, Joyce is always the same: a gentle touch, a soft word, a strength in prayer.

Great mother. The touch of her life is always felt in our home. I can marvel at the stability and strength of our sons, Ron and Mark, but I know it's because of her. I agree with the Jewish rabbi who said, "God couldn't be everywhere, so He created mothers." Joyce really is God's representative to our sons and me.

And she is a great mother. When our boys were babies and toddlers, she would lie in bed, set them on a pillow next to her, and read books to them, everything from encyclopedias to books cataloging dinosaurs to the Word of God. No wonder our sons knew the difference between Titus and a T-Rex long before *Jurassic Park* ever hit the American scene.

Grace in ministry. Jesus went to the cross and sacrificed His life for us, and it cost Him everything; all that He was and all that He had, He gave up for you and me. If we love someone, and daily give our lives for them, it is always costly. Of course, Joyce is well aware of the costs of loving, but her priorities for family and ministry always remain the same.

The grace of Joyce's life has greatly impacted our ministry. When I first met her in college, she was either downtown at the Skid Row Mission in L.A. or visiting a rest home for the elderly. Her giving heart is not something new, nor is it forced, or a show.

She's a constant source of support to me in my work of ministry. When I'm in the pulpit, preaching my heart out yet feeling like I'm not saying much, I can always look out and see Joyce's smiling affirmation.

My special treasure

Joyce is a special treasure to me. I find myself wanting to guard and protect her like a piece of priceless china, because that's what she is to me . . . priceless. I remember learning one day in a new way just how much she meant to me. Joyce was unexpectedly stricken with diabetes; she wasted to seventy-eight pounds on her five-foot-three-inch frame. She was gravely ill and ended up in the hospital in intensive care.

I remember walking into her room and sitting gently on the bed next to her. She was weak and frail. As we talked, tears filled her eyes and I could tell something was bothering her.

She looked up at me and said, "I feel so bad. I know I'm going to be a burden to you. So many people need you and so many people love you. I just feel like I'm going to be a hindrance to you or the ministry. I don't want to be in your way."

The doctor had just finished telling her that she would have to eat specific foods at strictly regimented times of the day. She would also take insulin every day. And she was afraid she would be a burden to me.

By then, I was crying. I grabbed her little nightshirt and pulled her up close and said, "Don't ever say that again." I told her, "There's nothing more important to me than you. Nothing."

I just pray that after all the years of her loving me, living for me, caring for me, I have been able to learn how, in some small way, to love and care for her in return.

Joyce still goes everywhere I go, whether in a VW or a Ford.

She still sometimes eats liver and, on occasion, has slept on the floor.

Some things are the same and some things have changed so much in our years together. But one thing hasn't changed: her grace and love.

Back to the "Honeymooners" of TV fame for a closing word, as they say. No, Ralph Kramden, I don't want to be the king of our castle. Just the lover of the queen who lives there.

Pastor Ron Mehl
Foursquare Church
Beaverton, Oregon

3

BEAUTY SECRETS
FOR A WOMAN OF GOD
Keep Yourself Spiritually Fit

◇◇◇◇◇

God of grace and glory,
  allow the simple, magnificent beauty of a Christ-saturated life
    to radiate through me to
      my mate,
      my family,
      my congregation
      and my world. Amen.

◇◇◇◇◇

*M*Y PEOPLE-WATCHING HOBBY (Neil's) can be practiced and enjoyed almost anywhere, but it is especially entertaining in airports, shopping malls, and traffic jams. It's fun to watch crowds and speculate about people's background and how they are related to those they are with. And my mind really gets in a whirl when I think about how God can keep track of all of them.

I had a delightful experience recently, even though I was not thinking much about my hobby. It took place at a crowded lunch counter in Bloomingdale's in New York City. The customers and servers were outspoken, picturesque New Yorkers—the kind who speak their minds loud enough for everyone to hear.

I felt like a kid in a candy store as I counted six different conversations going on around me.

One nearby chat involved three well-to-do ladies in their seventies. They enjoyed discussing a mutual friend for whom they saved a seat. I had a before-and-after experience of hearing them talk about their friend and then later seeing her as she joined the group.

Woman One remarked: "She's a classic beauty. Like a splendid antique, she gets better with age."

Woman Two: "Why shouldn't she look good? She's always been pampered by her husband and sons. She has fine clothes, an expensive apartment . . . everything money can buy."

Woman Three: "I believe she has an inner beauty. We know others with nice clothes and a regal bearing, but they don't impact others the way she does. She could easily pass for fifty and she's ten months older than I."

Woman One: "Maybe you're right. But whatever it is, I wish I had known her beauty secrets years ago. Here she comes — look at how special she looks."

All four women greeted each other, commented positively about each other's dresses and negatively about the overcast weather. Soon all were caught up in small talk that no longer interested me.

Then my turn came to form an opinion about their friend. They were right — she possessed a striking presence. Her eyes sparkled. Her clothing was elegant and her figure petite. Her hairstyle beautifully framed her face. She really did have a difficult-to-describe classical attractiveness.

Her friends were right, but she had something more. She radiated inner beauty, especially evident when she bowed her head as her food was served. The others in her group did not do that. Even after the prayer, it seemed like she spoke for God to her friends, though she wasn't pompous or stuffy. Her beauty was an impressive fulfillment of Peter's admonition, "Be beautiful inside, in your hearts, with the lasting charm of a gentle and quiet spirit which is so precious to God" (1 Peter 3:4, TLB). Admittedly, not everyone could have this woman's outer attractiveness, but anyone who wants to can possess a spiritual beauty similar to hers if they want it.

LIVING A LIFE
OF HOLY BEAUTY

Exterior beauty secrets can be found in abundant supply in women's fashion magazines, at cosmetic counters, and on TV commercials. In fact, physical beauty aids are about as available as fast-food restaurants. A recent TV documentary even showed an Estee Lauder store just across the street from Red Square in Moscow.

But in spite of all these beauty aids promoted in ads and promised in products, exquisite exterior attractiveness seldom gets replicated in real people. Evidently manufacturers and marketing specialists are unable to make good on their promises to make everyone beautiful. Maybe their products are not properly used. Or perhaps all those creams, shampoos, hair colorings, and vitamins cost too much or take too long to use.

A preteen girl, about eleven going on nineteen, asked her mother at a cosmetics counter, "Why don't the girls and women I see in the store look like the pictures in the perfume commercials?" The same question could be asked about men. In our society, lots of false messages promise to make us eternally young, beautiful, and thin—a losing battle for most. So we identify instantly with the woman in the *New Yorker* cartoon who said, "I looked better before I tried to look my best."[1]

We all know that this desire for external beauty causes enormous frustrations. The problems are complicated when the many possible challenges are considered. Family features are seldom perfect. A funny nose, big ears, a double chin, or a protruding midsection are hard to hide or correct. Slowly but certainly, good looks erode over the years. And what seems attractive and chic today will make us laugh out loud when we look at pictures ten years from now.

HOLY BEAUTY
PROMISED IN SCRIPTURE

Inner beauty, on the contrary, is lasting, has no genetic limits, and is never determined by heredity. Spiritual qualities can be reshaped, improved, and renewed by the Spirit of God. Inner beauty can be cultivated by keeping close to the Savior. We can experience infinite inside restoration and renovation, which Peter described as the "unfading beauty of a gentle and quiet spirit, which is of great worth in God's sight" (1 Peter 3:4).

A recent cosmetics ad also offers useful advice for inner beauty: "Focus on individuality and avoid beauty stereotypes. No single makeup or technique can be recommended for all. Explore the new individualized beauty tips."[2]

Scripture is full of positive promises about an inner beauty that brings personal satisfaction to the God-seeker and attracts others to Christ through them. God's guarantee says, "Though outwardly we are wasting away, yet inwardly we are being renewed day by day" (2 Cor. 4:16).

And the Apostle Paul assured his Corinthian friends and us, "So we are being transfigured much like the Messiah, our lives are gradually becoming brighter and more beautiful as God enters our lives and we become like Him" (2 Cor. 3:18, TM).

Consider the inner beauty secrets which Peter calls precious in the sight of God. That sounds like beauty worth having. And though Peter's advice was directed to women believers married to heathen men, his spiritual principles enable anyone to grow a great soul.

Anyone can be beautiful, the way God counts beauty. Anyone can possess and radiate beautiful inner character traits that are both personally satisfying and bring glory to God.

Peter, easily the most imposing personality of the early church, with a well-known reputation for rankling abruptness, calls Christian wives to an attractive tenderness rooted in vibrant relationship to Christ. This charming soul beauty expresses itself as being loyal, responsive to her husband, and neither anxious nor intimidated by anything or anyone.

The Apostle Peter wants everyone to understand that this inner charm is more than elegant clothing, costly jewelry, or stylish hair. He suggests that this inner beauty in a holy woman of God delights her husband, even if he is completely indifferent to the Gospel. If such beauty charms and attracts unbelieving husbands, how much more pleasing will it be in a woman who is married to a minister of the Gospel. Here's how this beauty develops according to Scripture:

Be good wives to your husbands, responsive to their needs. There are husbands who, indifferent as they are to any words about God, will be captivated by your life of holy beauty. What matters is not your outer appearance — the styling of your hair, the jewelry you wear, the cut of your clothes — but your inner disposition.

Cultivate inner beauty, the gentle, gracious kind that God delights in. The holy women of old were beautiful before God that way, and were good, loyal wives to their husbands. Sarah, for instance, taking care of Abraham, would address him as "my dear husband." You'll be true daughters of Sarah if you do the same, unanxious and unintimidated (1 Peter 3:1-6, TM).

Let's look more closely at key phrases in this passage.

"There are husbands who, indifferent as they are to any words about God, will be captivated by your life of holy beauty" (1 Peter 3:1-2, TM). Peter's counsel — preach a nonverbal message with a holy, inner beauty. What a phrase — "holy beauty." Seldom is the word *holy* used to describe beauty. The NIV explains the powerful effectiveness of this silence, "so they may be won over without talk by the behavior of their wives."

And even though maintaining a happy husband/wife relationship should be easier in ministry marriages, the "silent but loud" principle applies to all human relationships. Peter believes that inner beauty is enhanced more by holy living and less preaching, arguing, or nagging. Such an impressive witness offers a fringe benefit that reaches into all human relationships. Even as it impacts one's mate, it is also spiritually convincing to one's children, members of the church, and neighbors in the community. Attitudes of love and actions of faith always make more impact than clever talk.

"When they see the purity and reverence of your lives" is the way the NIV translates the next invigorating phrase (v. 2). The idea is to set your own standards for attractive godliness that are pleasing to God. The world needs more attractive purity and appealing reverence — two captivating components of holy living.

Much too often when the words *purity* or *piety* are used to describe Christians, they create mental images of rigid self-righteousness or grating human relationships. Sadly, many people, inside and outside the church, expect a pious person to be a scold who displays a holier-than-thou attitude and behaves in obnoxious ways. Many have met ministry couples who live in a cocoon of professional pastoral piety like that.

But the impact can be so much stronger and so much more can happen. The masses and individuals closest to us need to see Christ in our daily actions, hear His kind of words in our speech, and observe His ways as the inner compass of our daily activities.

In reality, a genuinely holy life is a quality life that helps set standards in any group with its winsome ways, quality life, and clearheaded righteousness. Consider the positive influences true piety releases in the lives of others. Light dispels darkness, love overpowers hate, and forgiveness heals fractured relationships. A pastor's wife shapes the climate of her home, church, community, and nation by simply living a lovely, Christ-saturated life. God often uses a holy life as a powerful force for positive change in our world.

"They were submissive to their husbands" (1 Peter 3:1). The idea is to commit to voluntary selflessness. A New Testament scholar of another generation coined that captivating phrase "voluntary selflessness" as a synonym for submission as found in this verse. This kind of submission is not cowering compliance nor spineless conformity, but a willing surrender of selfishness, an intentional relinquishment of self-sovereignty, a deliberate abandonment of legitimate prerogatives, and a compelling desire for serving.

This kind of submission is among the most magnificent adventures one can imagine. It is a joyful way of life filled with fascinating associations, challenging circumstances, and amazing surprises. It helps bring new freshness to every day as we give ourselves away to God and His purposes. Then at the moment of our need, blazing new insights and divine energy come to us. And because of who is with us, the hardest places are turned into victorious battle grounds.

"Be beautiful inside, in your hearts, with the lasting charm of a gentle and quiet spirit which is precious to God" (1 Peter 3:4, TLB). This charm never fades, and it stays in style forever. An unknown eighteenth-century preacher described this inner quality as "soul clothing." He suggested that even more absurd than wearing expensive shoes with a cheap dress is the all-too-common practice of spending lots of money and effort to cloth a body that houses a shabby soul.

Think of the beauty of a soul clothed with a gentle and quiet spirit. This beautiful garb fits every gender, age-group, and generation. Clothing for the soul never goes out of season nor wears threadbare. And soul clothing gets more charming as it is worn.

Without dealing with intricate definitions for *gentle* and *quiet,* ask yourself, "Is my soul attired in a gentle and quiet spirit?" If yes, rejoice. Those dressed in gentleness and quietness are magnetically attractive to people God has called them to serve. Like honeybees drawn to spring flowers, saints and sinners feel drawn to gentle and quiet women of God. Those beauty traits are of "great worth in the sight of God."

"For this is the way the holy women of the past who put their hope in God used to make themselves beautiful" (1 Peter 3:5). Never give up hope. Writers of Holy Scripture tie hope into the way holy women of God functioned in the past. Hope always stands at the center of the Gospel and pursues us with charm on most pages of Scripture. But in spite of its appeal, many ministry couples have given up hope, and they just barely hold on to their kingdom efforts by a fine thread that could break at any minute.

Let's renew hope in our homes and churches. Hope is a lofty, encouraging, heartening, expectant word that reminds us how trustworthy God is for every day of our journey. This four-letter word summarizes all that is to be in the wonderful future God has planned for us.

Every pastor's wife needs hope. Every pastor needs hope. Every ministry family needs hope. Every church needs to multiply hope. And every layperson in every church needs hope. Simply stated, hope means you can count on God's promises, in spite of circumstances and limitations. He is always faithful, reliable, trustworthy, and honest. He fully guarantees His promises. Apply those words to your situation — faithful, reliable, honest, trustworthy, and guaranteeing. Try seeing your setting through God's perspective. Then, in a matter of seconds, obstacles and hindrances look so different. Keep hope alive, regardless of the obstacles.

"You are her [Sarah's] daughters if you do what is right" (1 Peter 3:6). The directive is to do right in human relationships. Of course, the pastor and his wife must give attention to being persons of substance on the inside before they can do much of anything for God on the outside. But far too many believers are frustrated simply because they are spiritually inactive.

While activity never buys God's grace, no one can be spiritually fit without purposeful activity. In the interest of trying to impact our times and renew the church, many do not give enough energy, creativity, and imagination to the cause.

Doing right always means doing the right thing at the right time for the right reason. Some ministry couples will never be abundantly blessed by God because they serve for wrong reasons. Wrongly motivated activities in the church are like first-grade busywork—they keep the person occupied but have almost nothing to do with the church's reason for being. Such activity should be understood to be activity for its own sake and should not be substituted for actual ministry.

"Do not give way to fear" (1 Peter 3:6). Relinquish your anxieties. Ministry fears and phobias create a crippling emotion that tends to feed on itself. If you are afraid to try some ministry, you probably can't do it very well. If you are afraid, you probably don't attempt much. If you are afraid, you will worry about nearly everything. If you are afraid, you will distrust people. If you are afraid, you will be bewildered. One translation of this passage reads, "Let nothing terrify you." That sounds like a direct command.

Isn't love God's answer to fear? Evidently the Apostle John thought so when he wrote, "There is no fear in love; but perfect love casts out fear, because fear involves torment. But he who fears has not been made perfect in love" (1 John 4:18). John's words are a promise and a challenge. Love is what motivates us to serve—and Jesus is our pattern. He wants us to serve without fear. But fear never leaves us just because we want it to go. Rather it starts to evaporate when we rely on God's enablement to help us accomplish great things for Him.

BEAUTY SECRETS
ANYONE CAN USE

Increasing interest in spirituality in our society has tended to broaden the meaning of the word. Now it has become popularized to describe everything from religion to pop-psychology, social concerns to sexual intimacy, child rearing to new-age notions and rigid legalism. And though every part of our life must be impacted by God, to make the meaning of this word so broad is to fog our thoughts about the adventuresome pilgrimage of the soul toward God.

To perfect this discussion, let's try using Henri Nouwen's definition that spirituality is an "at homeness with God." Consequently, by spirituality, we mean every influence, relationship, or resource that shapes you into the person whom God intends you to be or become. It is not something far away, super difficult to attain, or uncomfortable when you have it.

Every idea about spiritual beauty in this chapter relates to an inner loveliness that is part of a lifelong process that is individually unique for each Christian pilgrim. Spiritual "beauty secrets" are inward processes that produce a life of joy that radiates the magnetic beauty of Christ through us. Such a glorious adventure is a marvel to experience and a joy to behold.

Pray for an accurate perspective

When we view ourselves, our situation, and our opportunities from God's perspective, things always look different and better. An accurate view of our surroundings and potential enriches life. There is much unreality in the church—a kind of other-worldly fantasy. Thus, genuine prayer is needed to clarify our ministry.

For example, prayer helps us know that spiritual resistance among the masses may be as much ignorance as it is antagonism. Try to value prayer as an incredibly powerful resource for clarifying your vision.

Value prayer also as a way to listen to God. When we listen closely in prayer, we may become somewhat uncomfortable by what we hear, but it may also make us whole and well and fulfilled. Consider what happens to you, your spouse, your children, your extended family, and people in your congregation when you pray. You always see farther and clearer when you seek God's perspective on your knees.

S.D. Gordon, spiritual leader of another era, offers an important serendipity: "If a person has the right motives and puts the practice of prayer in its right place, then his serving and giving and speaking will be fairly fragrant with the presence of Christ."[3]

Resist spiritual flabbiness

Feed your life with intimacy with the Lord. Spiritual hunger is similar to physical hunger—we are not fed only once and not fed again. And, like physical conditioning, spiritual development cannot be stored up. It must be continuous. Spiritual stamina, strength, and endurance are built by a thousand efforts to develop spiritual fitness.

The Christian life produces a constant choice between settling in or growing up. One leadership specialist says everyone is as apathetic as they dare to be even though it is not fashionable to talk about it in our society or our churches. If he is correct, what does that say about those who lead the church?

The tell-tale signs of spiritual atrophy include relationships that are allowed to become superficial, activities that keep us from dealing with the main issues, and a noticeable loss of imagination, creativity, and interest in life. Could it be that author Scott Peck is correct when he says laziness is the single greatest impediment to spiritual growth?[4]

How strong do you want to be and when? And what are you doing about it? The quiet strength of spiritual maturity is magnificent to behold in others and an awesome delight to see in ourselves. If we can conquer spiritual flabbiness, we can overcome many other hurdles.

Give high priority to the sort of intimacy with God that is found in prayer, Scripture, and worship. Intimacy with the Father washes worldly soot from your soul. Closeness to God does for the soul what soap does for the body. An unpolluted soul in a dirty world gives us an inner beauty that is bound to get out on us.

Enjoy God. Like good music, you do not have to understand everything about God before you can enjoy Him. The nearer you get, the more you can see His harmony, holiness, and steadfast love.

Set your own standard of success

Far too many families and households, even those of some pastoral couples, confuse a quality life with a secular standard of living.

Secular society's treadmills always produce stress and create disappointment for those involved in ministry. Acquiring more things and money is not the golden pot at the end of the rainbow, nor is it even a happy highway to the rainbow.

Jesus replaced secular standards of success with something immeasurably better — significance, service, and long-term satisfaction. Why not replace chasing status symbols with cherishing grace symbols in yourself and the people you serve? Take delight in simple satisfactions along your journey of faith — the beauty of folks, the wonders of relationships, and the miracles of redemption. And avoid "awful-ing" about what you don't have, or about your situation.

Listen to nearby ordinary voices

For fresh insights about faith and the real meanings of life, listen to the wistful yearnings of your spouse and children. Eavesdrop on their concerns — those you know well and those you seldom hear. Listen carefully to those who live in a different world than yours.

What would happen if every ministry couple allowed themselves to be spiritually impacted by morally failed leaders and by their own grown, though sometimes spiritually alienated, children? Many folks who have gone spiritually AWOL have much to teach us.

Maximize your marriage

Far too many ministry couples have settled into a monotonous mediocrity in their marriages — no surprises, no meaningful conversations, no increased fulfillment, no exhilarating excitement, and no intentional efforts to make it better.

If marriage stands near the top of all meaningful relationships, it deserves more than many invest in it. Give more thought, time, and creativity to your marriage. Expect to give more and to get more from your marriage. Start with increased tenderness and touching. Try reading a book on marriage with your spouse every year. With a little effort, exhilaration and warmth can replace boredom and tedium. Try giving your partner preferential treatment above your time with your relatives, parents, coworkers, and even your children.

Act out your love by intentionally leaving the last piece of pizza, picking up the dry cleaning, or filling up the gas tank.

Become a contemporary saint

Regrettably, genuine piety seems to have an old-fogy reputation, a kind of antique relic from another generation. Meanwhile, all around us, contemporary challenges cry out for spiritual solutions that only the spiritually mature can apply. For these times, a beautiful life can be fed by a faith that is taken into the details of living.

Four questions help unlock this beauty secret: (1) How does your faith sustain you in your struggles and who knows it? (2) How does faith make living more fun today and how do you express it? (3) How does faith make you better able to understand your times and minister to contemporary people? (4) And what does your faith enable you to say to the new generation about the up-to-date meaning of godliness?

Delight in God's creation

Get close to nature regularly so you can celebrate God's goodness, dependability, creativity, and originality. A rejuvenating and exhilarating something takes place inside us when we get close to nature. Try getting to know the seashore, the mountains, the woods, and God's people. Then you will more fully understand the English philosopher John Locke's summary: "The visible marks of extraordinary wisdom and power appear so plainly in all the works of creation that a rational creature who will but seriously reflect on them cannot miss the discovery of a deity."[5]

Stop all manipulation

Manipulating and exploiting others is a subtle, cunning practice that strangles too many marriages, ministries, and relationships. But controlling others to make them do what you want makes you miserable and almost always angers them. The starting point toward non-manipulation is to give up being in control of another's life or of your church. Like envy and gossip, manipulation is deadly even though it is often endured in human relationships.

Sadly, in too many churches, manipulation is a socially acceptable way to steal advantages, gain favors, and ruin reputations. Isn't author Marilyn Norquist Gustin right?

> When we flatter another or threaten another, when we relate to another expecting a certain return, we are really stealing emotionally. That is, we are trying to grab certain responses like approval or particular efforts or favors. It is possible to manipulate some people so as to evoke the response we want, but the favor is not freely given.[6]

Those words produce a scary self-awareness that we too often pass off as the way things are. All of us know church people who spend their lives trying to get and keep control of others — people who don't need to be controlled by anyone. Sometimes pastors and their spouses are more guilty of manipulation than anyone else. Our disturbing dilemma is that we enjoy manipulating but hate being manipulated.

Think how the process destroys inner beauty and ages the soul. Every manipulative encounter with friend, family, church member, or stranger results in an inner tenseness at our spiritual center that warns us we are not behaving like Christ. This self-induced flaw squanders spiritual vigor and hardens our sensitivities. However, as one stops manipulating others, he/she discovers an inner assurance of being pleasing to God and at peace with others. God is in control of all things, and that means I don't need to fret about the outcomes.

Expect the unexpected

God has many surprises for you, your family, and your congregation. Too often, we feel and talk about being blindsided by pain, negligence, or obstructions when things do not seem to move along normally. But how easy to forget the wonderful surprises that come as we receive God's unforeseen bounty all the days of our lives.

An evangelist for the World Methodist Council, Eddie Fox, tells about visiting Germany soon after the Berlin Wall fell and asking Christian leaders, "Did you expect the wall to fall in your lifetime?" They answered negatively. Then he said, "Did anyone expect the wall to fall in our lifetime?" They answered, "Yes, there were some crazy dreamers who thought it might be possible." Evangelist Fox requested, "Take me to meet those crazy dreamers."[7] We should keep close to dreamers too.

In literally thousands of places, churches need crazy dreamers who expect God to give a flood tide of revival and renewal. As a beauty secret for your soul, dare to expect the unexpected.

Resist boredom

Why be bored when you can be happy and fulfilled? You have a choice. Boredom is really ludicrous in any ministry assignment. Think of the possibilities when you live as close to the action as you do. Learning to enjoy God is a lifelong pursuit, but it is a fascinating, adventuresome journey. Like climbing a mountain summit, each successive height achieved enables you to see another incredible peak to climb. And you always have a Friend with you for the climb.

Think of the variety, excitement, and potential all around you. Someone always needs you. Another person always stands ready to open his heart to you. There is always another person for whom you represent his only hope. And an entire congregation needs you and holds you close in its affection and acceptance.

No need to choose monotony or tedium when God intends for you to be His redemptive agent who brings faith, hope, and love to those whose lives you touch. One woman writes, "I have come to see that my boredom is my lack of connectedness to God more than it is the limitations of this ministry setting."

Realize that inner beauty is never automatic

Spiritual development always requires purposeful effort. Jesus taught, "Seek first His kingdom and His righteousness, and all these things will be given to you as well" (Matt. 6:33), and "Blessed are those who hunger and thirst for righteousness, for they will be filled" (5:6). Seeking, hungering, and thirsting are active efforts that require a committed will and a desire to know God better at any cost.

Give yourself to inner beauty. One must pray in order to enjoy prayer. One must fast to learn the meaning of self-denial. One must know the Bible before applying its teachings to life. One must trust God in the sunshine to have triumphant faith in the valleys. And one must practice the spiritual disciplines to grow in grace. All this action, however energetic or well intended, never earns the favor of God, but it opens our inner world to His direction and teaches us dependence on His enablement.

To be Christlike, we must purposefully choose love over hate, peace over confusion, compassion over hostility, and faith over cynicism. But every positive choice draws us closer to Him.

When we aspire to enrich God's people and to get to know Him better, He gives us incredible help—more assistance, enablement, and affirmation than we ever dreamed of receiving. God's enabling grace for His children in ministry is abundantly sufficient, so we are often startled by resources we would never know without Him—fullness of joy, surprising insights, abounding love, supernatural energies, and a continuous awareness of divine protection.

Recondition your will

Try enjoying the bliss of following God's will fully. The old-time evangelists made a vital point when they insisted that our emotions and our will are different from and independent of each other. We can will to do God's will even when we do not feel very much like it or even when our emotions resist. We can will forgiveness when we do not feel like forgiving. We can will integrity even when it would be easier to manipulate. We can will to positive thinking even when we are about to slip into negative assumptions. Our will needs to be reconditioned so we do what is right even when we do not feel like it. The process is like the gossip columnist's advice to the woman who thought she had fallen out of love with her husband, "Choose to do acts of love for your husband, and warm, fuzzy feelings will return."

In a life of inner beauty, the firmly set will finally impact the emotions. One devotional writer says the will becomes our Rorschach test, telling us more about ourselves than about our circumstances.

Reacquaint yourself with Scripture

Good people often do not know or use Scripture because they think it is hard to understand, or they have been taught that Scripture reading was a demanding obligation—something like required textbook reading in a high school class or college course. The Bible, however, is a series of letters from old pilgrims who know every twist and turn in the spiritual journey before us. They stand ready to advise us anywhere, anytime.

For enhancing and magnifying your spiritual beauty, read those parts of the Bible that fascinate you. Mine gold on whatever page you find it. Beginning and continuing are more important than where you read. In uncounted ways the Bible most often speaks to the reader within a few verses or a chapter or two. Scripture is God's smorgasbord of inspiration and instruction filled with the daily minimum requirements for living a beautiful life.

Expect fruit from faithfulness

Too often we waste needless energy thinking about negative, past actions which cannot be changed. Or we worry about what might have been or regret some useless detour we traveled. Why not surrender that rubbish and look to the positive impacts of your life? Learn from the lessons and move on.

Too often we completely forget a different reality. True faithfulness always bears some positive fruit. Think about it. Almost everyone can tell about someone who influenced them greatly, even though they never had an opportunity to tell them about it. Faithfulness may take years to grow fruit, but it will finally produce.

Recall the women of God from your past who believed in you and mentored you. Think of pastors' wives who prayed for you and encouraged you. Remember neighbors or public school teachers who impacted you in unforgettable ways. Though you may not realize it, you already have a similar influence on others, maybe someone you do not even know or someone you haven't heard from in years.

This beauty secret draws strength and encouragement for three awesomely energizing roots. First, you are privileged to touch others' lives. Second, every faithful act produces some positive fruit. And third, God can be trusted with the results of what you do for Him—no service done in His name is wasted.

An eighty-five-year-old pastor's wife in the Midwest said to me, "How do I handle my life as old age closes in on me? I keep involved. I am faithful to the instructions of Jesus about helping others, and it makes me spiritually rich."

Refuse to underrate yourself

You are OK to God and significant to His cause. Be grateful to the Father that He created you like you are. You are original and special—He will never make someone exactly like you again. He needs you and loves you and cherishes you. Refuse to denigrate yourself, loathe yourself, or put yourself down. An African-American church on the west coast closes each Sunday's worship service with a cheer, "Rejoice! You are somebody!"

Because of who God made you to be, let yourself grow and develop. Change your perspective for the better. See yourself as having significant worth in building the kingdom. Be glad you are you. You are really something special to God and His church. That fact requires you to grow, to apply every beauty secret you know, and to refuse to neglect your own spiritual growth and emotional balance.

To stimulate your sense of spiritual self-worth, use your church directory or mailing list as a personal achievement encourager. As you view the list of names, ask yourself how many people you have impacted for Christ in this setting. After you have been in a place for a while, you will be astounded at how many people God has allowed you to serve in significant ways.

Too often we do not view our ministry landscape over a long enough time frame. Most pastors' wives can vastly improve their own self-worth by viewing a list of names that triggers a memory of how much they have impacted people. How heartwarming it is to look back on what God has helped you accomplish. He always gives meaning to our existence when we serve others.

Welcome the future

Today's joys and tomorrow's adventures are often lost while we spend emotional and spiritual energy regretting the passing of the past. Yesterday is gone forever. For good or bad, it cannot be repeated or changed. And tomorrow is not here yet.

Get ready for the next phase. Welcome it as a friend. Don't allow the future to threaten you or to merely happen. What is your next stage of life? Is it a new assignment? Is it a unique task? Is it a new baby or an empty nest? Is it a divorced child coming home? Is it retirement years?

Salute tomorrow like a new friend. Get prepared. Be ready to accept what it brings and integrate each new happening into your life. Use the adjustments tomorrow will require as an opportunity for growth. Adjusting to the seasons of life helps us remember that in an amazing sense who we are determines what we become.

Keep a journal

Your journaling system need not be complicated nor the entries overly detailed. But a journal can become a way to be accountable to God and to provide an encouragement for your growth.

In a letter, a pastor's wife gives several impressive ways her journal-keeping contributes to her inner beauty:

1. It provides a realistic plan for assessing the past.
2. It monitors personal spiritual growth.
3. It helps me see mistakes I can avoid in the future.
4. It catalogues answers to prayer.
5. It shows me changes I have made in my outlook on ministry—an improvement that changed my life.

Appreciate what you have

All of us will one day lose most of what we have—possessions, relationships, and stamina. Ministry assignments also change over time. Life consists of a constant flux. A ministry couple moves to a new location, their children go off to college, they buy a new home, their aging parents need more care, key players in a church move away, a fire or a storm destroys cherished possessions, an illness limits levels of involvement, or one partner dies. All this brings a feeling of loss. But some of our most painful griefs are actually rooted in not enjoying what we have while we have it.

The American way teaches everyone to want more, to move

up, and to dream of a better life in the future. Most of us know how to do those things quite well, but it is cherishing what we have that often makes life and ministry beautiful this day. Cherish your opportunities, your influence, your faith, your children, your parents, and your mate.

Take parenting as an example. While the children are at home, every day is a special time to celebrate their development, health, and imagination. Every day with a child, from birth until the day he leaves home, is a day for gratitude. But too many families endure today and long for some future time, thus missing the meaning of what they have now.

Today, the first day of the rest of our lives, is a good day if we know what to do with it.

MORE THAN DRESSES, JEWELRY, AND HAIRSTYLES

A truly beautiful life for God, as Peter likes to remind us, is more than stylish clothes, extravagant jewelry, or fancy hairstyles. Though Scripture does not forbid these external beauty enhancers, something much more lasting, satisfying, and attractive — a holy beauty — is offered.

But how is it found?

Try singing,

> Let the beauty of Jesus be seen in me,
> All His wonderful passion and purity!
> O Thou Spirit divine, All my nature refine,
> Til the beauty of Jesus be seen in me.

Such a life of holy beauty is a real-life answer to Paul's prayer for the faithful in the church at Colosse, and for us:

> That you may live a life worthy of the Lord,
> Please Him in every way,
> Bear fruit in every good work,
> Grow in the knowledge of God,

Be strengthened with His power so that you may have
great endurance and patience,
And joyfully give thanks to the Father (Col. 1:10-12).

CONTEMPORARY CHALLENGE
Beauty Secrets for a Life of Holy Beauty

- Pray for perspective.
- Resist spiritual flabbiness.
- Set your own success standards.
- Listen to ordinary voices.
- Maximize your marriage.
- Become a contemporary saint.
- Delight in God's creation.
- Stop all manipulation.
- Expect the unexpected.
- Recondition your will.
- Reacquaint yourself with Scripture.
- Expect fruit from faithfulness.
- Refuse to underrate yourself.
- Welcome the future.
- Keep a journal.
- Appreciate what you have.

MARRIED TO A BEAUTIFUL WOMAN OF FAITH

A Salute to Anna Pearl Reid
by Pastor Benjamin Reid

My wife's greatest asset has been her call to mission. She married me believing that her mission was to be a total support to my ministry. She believed that God had given her to me to assist me in every way possible to "make full proof" of the pastoral ministry to which God had called me.

Shortly after we married, we went to pastor a storefront church of four members. Salary was $25 per month plus $40 per month from our state convention. Without a murmur of complaint, she prayed with me, played the piano, taught Sunday School, cheered me on in times of desperation and despair, brought forth our first child, and believed God in spite of all the adversities.

For more than thirty-five years this gracious woman has laughed, cried, prayed, and rejoiced with me in struggles and victories, in adversity and success, in poverty and plenty. At the same time she has successfully pursued higher education; developed in her chosen career as a Christian school executive; accepted and matured in an excellent speaking ministry; mothered three children and helped to raise three "adopted" children; maintained a warm, hospitable "open house" for hundreds of members, ministers, and guests; and yet has found time, energy, and skill to make her husband feel like the world's greatest husband, father, and pastor.

For more than thirty-five years, Pearl has been my closest friend and confidante, my wisest and most effective critic, my counselor and adviser, my playmate and prayer partner. She is secure in her calling, her motherhood, her profession, and her ministry. She speaks her piece, knows her own mind, asserts her own personality — yet totally undergirds and supports my ministry.

Well, how did this all come about? First, she was raised in a pastor's family. She saw closeup the problems, privileges, pressures, and blessings of ministerial life. Second, she made a total commitment of her life to Christ as a teenager and set about trying to grow in that commitment as she matured in age. Third, when she became engaged to a minister, there were long and fruitful discussions between us concerning the costs of ministry, the rewards of serving God, the reality of the "fish bowl" existence, the stress of raising children in a parsonage, the time pressures of ministry, and so on. She entered into marriage with realistic expectations and wholehearted commitment.

As first lady of a congregation of more than 5,000 constituents, she is admired, loved, and respected. She leads a growing women's ministry in our church and is in increasing demand as a speaker and seminar leader. She teaches a weekly class on "male-female relations" that is packed with young adults.

A number of women in the church were asked to give anonymous evaluations of their pastor's wife. Responses included: "She is so supportive." "She is so easy to talk to." "She is a real role model for effective wives." "She is a true professional." "She is supportive and gentle, a very effective leader." "She is the best thing that ever happened to our Pastor!"

And to all of the above, this preacher says AMEN!

Pastor Benjamin F. Reid
First Church of God
Inglewood, California

Facing Realities Together

4

WHO CREATED
THIS CHAOS?

*What Pastors' Wives Believe
about Contemporary Ministry*

◇◇◇◇◇

Holy Enabler,
Who promised to empower us for resourceful kingdom effectiveness,
  help us see beyond the confusion and chaos of our times
    into Your mission for the assignment where You have
      providentially placed us.
  Use my abilities for Your purpose, my energy for Your people,
  and my speech for Your glory. Amen.

◇◇◇◇◇

*A*T LEAST TWENTY-SIX ROLES for pastors have been identified in recent articles, magazines, and textbooks. This long list zigzags from evangelist to prophet, from administrator to preacher, from counselor to soul friend, ad infinitum. The fact that no one can possibly live up to all of them is why ministers feel like they are being pulled on some torturous stretching rack between ministry and marriage, and pastoring and parenting. And the fallout from these frustrations negatively affects wives and children.

Added to this sorting-through-the-chaos dilemma is the difficulty of discussing with any amount of precision a modern minister's wife's role. Such an assortment. Pastors' wives' roles are lived out in so many different ways in such a variety of settings — urban, rural, small town, denominational churches, independent fellowships, traditional churches, and contemporary congregations, to name a few. And beyond all these prominent similarities, each woman's individuality and the contemporary influence of the feminist movement must also be considered. No single description can possibly portray such diversity.

But some commonalities are obvious in spite of these variations. For example, every pastor's wife is an original creation — she is not exactly like anyone else. And everyone in the family and church should expect and encourage her to bring her own special skills, talents, commitments, and personality to her situation. Since she is so unlike every other pastor's wife in the world, this chapter discusses many different perspectives about the challenges faced by women married to pastors. Listening to other sisters of the faith with diverse viewpoints often lessens feelings of isolation, and liberates pastors' wives to make full use of their uniqueness. Human beings of every gender are always strengthened when they know others experience what they do.

There is another pivotal point to consider. The way each pastor responds or refuses to respond to the demands of ministry must be factored into unraveling priority problems for his spouse. Since pastors are unique also, their way of dealing with priorities range from putting the church first, to blending family and ministry, or to a flat public pronouncement that family comes first.

Questions about priorities and uniqueness create more potential conflict between clergy marriage partners than any other problem. These all-too-common contentions cause chronic hurt and displaced anger.

MELINDA'S TRUE-TO-LIFE FRUSTRATIONS

Here's how Melinda expressed her thinly veiled anger and disappointments:

Being married to a preacher, for me, is like being the wife of a man who is having an affair. For me the church is "the other woman." I'm like the wife who knows her husband is being unfaithful but doesn't do anything about it. I know my husband loves me, but the "other woman" will also be there. Though I know what's going on, I love him too much to let him go. I'm afraid to make him choose between us because in my heart I know he will choose "her," the church. "She" is the one that he works late with. "She" gets his energy and enthusiasm.[1]

Melinda continues the agonizing allegory:

I give him respectability. I am the constant in his life. I represent the American Dream—home, wife and kids. But she provides his excitement and is the joy of his life. After he has tended "her" needs, I get what is left over. Though I complain—oh how I nag—he sees no reason to give "her" up, and can you blame him? "She" brings him social prestige and occasions compliments from many people.[2]

PIVOTAL QUESTIONS FOR UNDERSTANDING MINISTRY

To form a more comprehensive understanding of the causes and cures for pastoral chaos, the following questions should be considered.

1. Is a problem a ministry issue or a common problem anyone might face? Many ministry problems are exaggerated human problems that any couple employed in any other occupational field might experience. On the other hand, common problems are often intensified because the partners are in ministry.

2. Can I accurately compare my circumstances in ministry to another person's circumstances outside ministry? It is doubtful that we fully know how other persons feel or what they experience in their circumstances. As the old saying goes, the grass always looks greener on the other side of the fence. For instance, a pastor's wife might think a layman's wife's life is much easier than it really is, or a laywoman might think living in a clergy marriage is more rosy than it actually is. Both perspectives could be erroneous.

3. Do fulfilling pastorates exist anywhere anymore? The

answer is Yes! Not all ministers and mates are in a state of disillusionment or hopelessness. Many are happily convinced this is the best time in all of human history for doing ministry. One fulfilled pastor's wife said, "It is getting harder because we make it harder!" Steps for making every setting better are given in our earlier books, *Pastors at Risk* and *The Heart of a Great Pastor.*[3]

4. What if a wife has no sense of calling to be a pastor's wife? Ministry mate Charlotte Ross offers an insightful paragraph that connects ministry and marriage together in insightful, almost poetic language:

> It was an act of love that called forth the giving of herself in marriage. It is an act of love that calls forth the giving of herself in ministry. The clergy wife is one who, for the love of a man — her husband — is a partner in love with THE GOD/MAN — her Lord Jesus. The giving of herself in ministry is a cherished gift to be held in honor, and it will be used by the Lord Jesus.[4]

As Melinda's letter shows, not all ministers' wives share this sentiment. Yet, while her letter seems overly severe, every issue she discussed comes up in nearly every ministry conference, in much of the literature, and in phone calls and letters H.B. London receives at Focus on the Family. Let's listen to pastors' wives as they open their hearts and speak their minds.

WHAT PASTORS' WIVES SAY ABOUT THEIR MARRIAGES

In the National Association of Evangelical (NAE) Family Task Force Ministers' Wives Survey, representing a cross-section of fifty-four denominational groups, the respondents appraised their marriages as follows.[5]

Happy marriage				
85.0% have a healthy, compatible marriage				
under 30	*ages 30–39*	*40–49*	*50–59*	*60 and older*
91.3%	84.1%	85.1%	80.6%	87.9%

Sexual relationships
22.1% felt need for current help in having
better sexual relationships with their husbands

under 30	30–39	40–49	50–59	60 and older
34.8%	27.1%	20.8%	19.0%	12.3%

Competition
20.4% felt they compete with congregational demands on husband

under 30	30–39	40–49	50–59	60 and older
40.0%	27.1%	18.1%	12.2%	7.0%

Emotional needs
20.3% felt emotional needs were not being met by husbands

under 30	30–39	40–49	50–59	60 and older
28.0%	22.3%	11.6%	15.6%	11.3%

Communication difficulties
19.5% felt lack of communication with husband

under 30	30–39	40–49	50–59	60 and older
28.0%	19.6%	21.7%	18.1%	8.8%

• **Observations** — Apparently some clergy marriage difficulties improve with age, or perhaps younger women are more willing and accustomed to admitting such needs. The survey shows several specific problems are more real for women under fifty. When the three age-groups under fifty were placed together, nearly 5 women out of 100 (4.7%) have had thoughts of having an extramarital relationship, and slightly more than 5 out of 100 (about 5.1%) feel disqualified for ministry because of marital problems.

In all age categories, 80.8% of the pastors' wives surveyed had confidence in pastor/husband's fidelity; only 3.4% would consider divorce if it were not for the embarrassment; 26.5% would like to have help in improving their marriages; and 51% love being a pastor's wife.

Now we turn to real live personal responses from phone calls, mail, pastors' wives conference surveys, and Riley's listening line. The listening line is a service of Called Together Ministries — a resource and referral service for pastors' wives directed by Linda Riley.[6]

• **Best friends with husband** — "I have the most loving, gentle, kind man in the whole world who is also my best friend." — from Neil's conference survey.

• **Emotional adultery** — "My husband has had a four-week, intense friendship with a woman member in her late twenties who is married to an unbeliever. I have pleaded with him and spoken to the other woman to cease this relationship. They say they understand my fears but will not modify their behavior. My husband wants a promise that all this will be kept secret. Will this relationship cool off if I become more loving at home? I am disturbed by Linda's advice to take intervention action, immediately." — from Riley's listening line.

• **I'm jealous** — "My greatest sin is jealousy of my husband's ministry. I am jealous of his involvement in the church, and I often ask God to help me with these feelings." — from letter to H.B.

• **Sexual attraction** — "I am attracted to a male coworker at my secular job. I am afraid of my feelings. My marriage is stagnant. Should I tell my husband?" — from Riley's listening line.

WHAT PASTORS' WIVES SAY ABOUT LONELINESS

In the NAE survey, pastors' wives reported the following about their feelings of isolation and loneliness.

Support
29.6% have no personal friends for support

under 30	30–39	40–49	50–59	60 and older
26.1%	33.1%	24.5%	30.5%	28.1%

Husband's friends
26.8% say husband has no friends for support

under 30	30–39	40–49	50–59	60 and older
22.7%	33.3%	21.3%	30.9%	20.0%

Friends
44.4% need a trusted friend

under 30	39–39	40–49	50–59	60 and older
51.4%	46.2%	38.0%	37.5%	17.1%

Support group
41.2% need a support group

under 30	30–39	40–49	50–59	60 and older
48.0%	51.3%	40.5%	31.3%	21.8%

Loneliness
40.6% describe their role as being lonely

under 30	30–39	40–49	50–59	60 and older
40.6%	49.0%	39.0%	38.0%	22.0%

Now we turn to personal and sometimes painful responses from phone calls, mail, pastors' wives conference surveys, and Riley's listening line.

• **Loneliness undercuts effectiveness**—"I struggle a great deal with loneliness. Trying to handle these feelings often distracts me from the actual work of ministry. But it is also true that these difficulties are agents of blessing and growth as I learn more and more to turn to the Lord and His Word for every need I have."—from letter to H.B.

• **Potential friends move**—"Loneliness is my biggest frustration. For twelve and one-half years I really have not had a friend that I could talk to or do things with. Just about the time I think I have one, she leaves either the church or the area. Our kids have similar problems. It seems people are afraid of the pastor's family. Ministry is not some contagious disease."—from letter to H.B.

• **Loneliness related in expectations**—"I feel lonely when I cannot live up to the demands: time, money, energy, family, church, and witnessing. I feel that our children and I do not have enough time with my husband. I feel lonely in a crowd."—letter from Ohio.

• **Emotional distance from pastor/husband**—"Loneliness is my problem. There are times when I feel really lonely and distant from my husband because he is not able to share with me what is going on at church and the secrets of people's lives. And there is the age-old question of a pastor's wife's friendships — I have established one close friendship which I desperately need. However, I feel I have to 'hide this friendship' so as not to offend anyone else at church. How frustrating!" — from H.B.'s conference survey.

• **Professional jealousy** — "My husband is a good Bible teacher, and this has been appreciated by the congregation. However, we needed encouragement from our ministerial peers during this past year, but it has not been forthcoming from our Presbytery level. In fact, it would seem there is jealousy and rivalry because so many of the university students have loved our Sunday evening service. Over here we might call it a 'tall poppy syndrome.' " — letter from a United Kingdom country.

• **Criticism causes loneliness** — "I deal often with loneliness, which for me means trying to keep a good attitude when you get so much negative feedback from so many in the congregation." — from letter to H.B.

• **Thankful for ministry sisters** — "I sure would like to have a woman friend in the church to confide in. But since it is a no-no, I thank God daily for my friends who are pastor's wives." — from Neil's conference survey.

WHAT PASTORS' WIVES
SAY ABOUT FINANCES

In the NAE survey, pastors' wives had this to say about money:

Personal finances

28.5% indicated they needed help handling personal finances

under 30	30–39	40–49	50–59	60 and older
30.0%	34.0%	27.0%	28.0%	9.0%

Retirement funds

46.0% needed help preparing for retirement

under 30	30–39	40–49	50–59	60 and older
34.0%	30.0%	48.0%	66.0%	56.0%

Now we turn to responses about money from phone calls, mail, pastors' wives conference surveys, and Riley's listening line.

• **Money keeps them from having a baby**—"As a PW, I am tired of being poor. We have two small children and would like to have another baby but cannot afford it. I try not to blame financial problems on the church."—from Riley's listening line.

• **Poverty always stares us in the face**—"My greatest challenges are lack of time [with] my husband [and] family due to the fact that I have to work to support our family at a reasonable standard of living. I worry about his health [and] our financial security. Poverty stares us in the face constantly, while members' priorities are on things rather than Christ."—from H.B.'s mail.

• **Church wonders why we spend money**—"Financial strain is with us every day. And when we get a little ahead, we feel pressured to explain why we spent money for something that was not an absolute necessity. Why do we feel we have to explain how we acquired something?"—from letter from Oregon.

• **Laypersons don't understand**—"I wish laymen knew how tight money is for most pastors, including us. Our people feel that God will provide for us, but the laymen are free to do things to better themselves like get a better paying job or work a second job when things get tight. We have money problems but have almost no way to work out of them."—from Neil's conference survey.

• **Can't keep up economically**—"The parsonage family cannot afford to do for their families what lay families can do. Why are we always expected to get by on less?"—from a letter to H.B.

WHAT PASTORS' WIVES SAY
ABOUT THEIR PERSONAL MINISTRY

In the NAE survey, pastors' wives discussed their skills and involvement in ministry.

Training				
Only 51.7% feel adequately trained for their role				
under 30	30–39	40–49	50–59	60 and older
50.0%	44.6%	52.7%	66.0%	61.8%

Leadership skills
44.0% need help in developing leadership skills

under 30	30–39	40–49	50–59	60 and older
69.5%	49.0%	45.7%	33.4%	30.9%

Counseling skills
57.3% need help in developing counseling skills

under 30	30–39	40–49	50–59	60 and older
76.2%	61.3%	58.3%	51.6%	45.5%

Disciple women's groups
56.6% need help learning to disciple other women

under 30	30–39	40–49	50–59	60 and older
83.3%	65.6%	50.0%	45.3%	53.9%

Bible knowledge
22.4% don't know the Bible as well as people assume they do

under 30	30–39	40–49	50–59	60 and older
25.0%	23.4%	17.7%	22.4%	15.1%

Responses about involvement in ministry from phone calls, mail, pastors' wives conference surveys, and Riley's listening line include the following:

● **Too small results** — "I am frustrated by seeing my husband put heart and soul into ministry, often with such little results. It seems that some of the most concentrated efforts are those that reap nothing." — from Neil's conference survey.

● **Open opportunities** — "My greatest joy as a pastor's wife is finding that the door always seems open to me to minister to people. Some people even seek my counsel, and they seem to receive it more readily than they did before we were in ministry." — from H.B.'s mail.

● **Pastoral calling** — "I just devoured your book *Pastors at Risk,* and I feel compelled to write. Even though it is my husband who is the pastor, in reading your book I have realized that I, too, have a pastoral calling on my life, which God intends for me to live out as a pastor's wife. Even though my job description is unofficial, its authenticity is not, and I look forward to learning to let God make the principles in your book a part of my personal, family, and ministry life." — from Guam.

• **Influence of leadership** — "I see leadership as serving people and leading them by providing vision, example, love, and commitment. As a leader, I have influence, and that means having a positive attitude toward my family, my position of leadership, and my ministry." — letter from a pastor's wife in the Northwest.

• **Spiritual growth through serving** — "Yes, I've been expected to do many things and have been stretched far beyond my ability, but we must be willing to allow God to work through us if our accepting a responsibility will help our husbands or their ministry. Pastors need their wives beside them with full support to encourage them, not at a safe distance, making excuses to stay out. When we married, we became one flesh. God has led me at times to say 'no,' but more often reluctantly to say 'yes.' Then He has rewarded me and our whole family as I grew spiritually through the assignment. Perhaps my situation is different from most. My pastor/husband is extremely kind and helpful and gives of himself 100 percent to his work. His dedication and devotion make me want to work with him." — from H.B.'s mail.

• **Outside employment frustration** — "I feel a strong commitment to my family, and I struggle with having to work to meet financial demands while caring for my family and being what the church people think I should be within the church and community. Doesn't my outside employment to keep my husband in the ministry count as some kind of Christian service?" — from H.B.'s conference survey.

• **Someone's stealing my ministry** — "After three years in a small rural church, new people seem to be pushing me out of my ministry. My husband wants me to drop responsibilities when men are available to do them. But I want ministry more than position. I feel even that is being taken away. My husband thought I would be happy with less responsibility." — from Riley's listening line.

WHAT PASTORS' WIVES SAY ABOUT FAMILY AND PARENTING

In the NAE survey, pastors' wives had this to say about their families and children.

Time
42.2% have problem with time for family and ministry

under 30	30–39	40–49	50–59	60 and older
40.0%	48.0%	45.0%	36.8%	27.0%

Children
64.0% think children like being ministers' children

under 30	30–39	40–49	50–59	60 and older
80.0	66.7%	60.2%	62.8%	69.0%

Problem children
15.1% say their children are causing them real concern

under 30	30–39	40–49	50–59	60 and older
00.0%	9.3%	19.7%	16.3%	28.3%

What about responses regarding parenting from phone calls, mail, pastors' wives conference surveys, and Riley's listening line?

• **Family time** — "My husband attends seminary, serves as an assistant pastor, and works a second job. My biggest challenge is finding even a few hours to reserve as family time. We have three children, and they're growing fast." — from a seminary student's wife.

• **Children's father is too busy** — "My husband is a bi-vocational pastor, so we have little time for family. For example, our sons, seven and eleven, played basketball games last Saturday. My husband had to attend an out-of-town Church Growth Conference.

"He got back for the second game but missed the first one. Missing family events happens so often the boys seldom ask their father to come to anything. They assume he will be too busy." — from Neil's conference survey.

• **Mother and wife first** — "The people in our church understand that I am a wife and mother first, and I am my husband's helper in ministry second. I like that. Most churches don't feel that way about the pastor's family." — from H.B.'s mail.

• **Church loves teens** — "We had five children, and when they were all teenagers at the same time, the church loved them to Christ, and I will always be grateful for that." — from Neil's conference survey.

WHAT PASTORS' WIVES SAY ABOUT ACCEPTANCE AND CRITICISM

In the NAE survey, pastors' wives expressed their feelings about acceptance and criticism. These issues are especially difficult because most pastors' wives do not feel free to defend their husbands and/or share information that would question the credibility of the criticism. Few pastors and their wives understand the reality that those in public life naturally cause curiosity. Thus non-public people are more likely to express opinions about a leader's life or family. More often pastors' wives see the criticism issue as petty and intentionally destructive even when it may be rooted in mere inquisitiveness.

Appreciation
70.2% think their pastor/husband's ministry is appreciated

under 30	30–39	40–49	50–59	60 and older
74.0%	71.0%	67.0%	70.0%	73.0%

Misunderstood
20.3% think the church people do not understand them

under 30	30–39	40–49	50–59	60 and older
26.3%	21.8%	21.4%	18.1%	9.1%

Anger
26.1% struggle with feelings of anger

under 30	30–39	40–49	50–59	60 and older
21.0%	33.3%	26.9%	23.7%	14.9%

Now we turn to responses about parenting from phone calls, mail, pastors' wives conference surveys, and Riley's listening line.

- **Disillusioned and deceived** — "We live in a fishbowl, and everyone not only knows what you do, but no one seems to approve. It definitely affects our family life. I think lately I have been very disillusioned about the church and Christian people. I almost feel deceived." — from H.B.'s conference survey.
- **Lies are hard to take** — "I never knew 'Christians' could be such a nasty bunch of people. It hurts me to be lied and

gossiped about, but even more, some of the awful things the church board have said about my husband have made it difficult for me to even want to be around them, let alone to minister to them. All this has definitely made worshiping at church difficult." — from a fax sent to H.B.

• **Forced to resign** — "My husband has been asked to resign. They gave him a choice of resigning or they would read a letter to the congregation that we feel would split the church. I have prayed for the Lord to forgive those who have treated us so badly. I have told the Lord to remove all bitterness, but the hurt is so overwhelming when I see board members who have been dishonest. How do I come to terms with my inner turmoil? I do not have anyone I can talk with." — letter to H.B. from Canada.

• **Who put them in charge?** — "My greatest challenge is that people are always looking at us and expressing their opinions about things that do not matter. They expect one standard of conduct from our family and live by another one for themselves." — from H.B.'s mail.

• **Breakfast for barracudas** — "After being forced to resign our last church, my husband has managed to land a part-time assignment pastoring a church that has just finished eating up their fifth pastor, so we are waiting to see if he will be the dessert. The salary of $1,000 per month is not enough to support our family of eight, but we are trusting the Lord for His help to make it stretch." — from letter from a Washington pastor's wife.

• **Hard to love** — "I pray every day that the Lord will help me to love critical people as He does, but, boy, is it a challenge. I fight against bitterness constantly, and I fear I'm not doing a good job of it. And this is our first pastorate. Does it get better?" — letter to H.B.

• **Less judgment, please** — "If I could tell lay people about ministry, I would implore them to be more loving and caring and less critical. Too often, the church seems to claim rights to every part of our lives and to pass judgment upon them even though they are not fully informed of the situation." — letter to H.B.

• **Resentments** — "I deal often with the frustration over a few people's attitude toward my husband. I realize not everyone is in agreement; therefore, I want to not hold resentment or bitterness toward these people. But it is hard for us to work, sacrifice, and have a poverty standard of living and then have people criticize our best efforts." — H.B.'s conference survey.

• **Others control us** — "Our lives — probably more subtly than overtly — are controlled by other people, the denomination, the opinions of board members, and the wishes of people who have very little understanding of what ministry is supposed to be." — Neil's conference survey.

WHAT PASTORS' WIVES SAY ABOUT THEIR SPIRITUAL HEALTH

In the NAE survey, pastors' wives had this to say about their personal faith and spiritual development.

Relationship with God
55.0% need help in developing deeper relationships with God

under 30	30–39	40–49	50–59	60 and older
77.3%	62.6%	51.5%	44.2%	35.8%

Spiritual gifts
30.9% need help in discovering and using spiritual gifts

under 30	30–39	40–49	50–59	60 and older
65.2%	30.7%	29.5%	24.0%	25.0%

Bible knowledge
51.7% need help in increasing Bible knowledge

under 30	30–39	40–49	50–59	60 and older
68.0%	55.1%	50.8%	45.9%	40.7%

Now we turn to responses about personal spiritual development from phone calls, mail, pastors' wives conference surveys, and Riley's listening line.

• **First priority** — "My greatest challenge is keeping a love relationship with God as my number one priority." — H.B.'s conference survey.

• **Growth in grace** — "My biggest need is staying in God's hands and in a state of growth in grace so that the things I do can be blessed by God and really help people." — Neil's conference survey.

• **Personal prayer needed** — "I work hard at finding prayer time to pray for myself. I need it." — letter to H.B.

• **Wants to pray with husband** — "I lack a consistent daily devotional life. I also yearn for sweet fellowship with my pastor/husband — devotions and prayer time together. But it all so often gets crowded out by time pressures." — letter to H.B.

• **Hungry for meaningful worship** — "I struggled as my husband made changes from traditional to contemporary worship styles. The adjustment seemed more intense because I had no choice — I couldn't change churches like others do." — Neil's conference survey.

• **Prayer and fasting suggested** — "I believe that if more pastoral couples prayed and fasted together, we would have less problems in the ministry." — H.B.'s conference survey.

• **How to change commitments** — "I feel stretched in too many directions at once — children, teaching in Sunday School, directing the choir, and visitation. It's too much, but I do not know how to change these commitments." — letter to H.B.

• **Hard to worship** — "My husband and I find it hard to worship when we both perform each week in every service." — from Neil's conference survey.

• **Real me** — "My frustration is trying to keep a balance in being mom, wife of the pastor, and also ministering with my husband. Sometimes I feel lost. I would like to be real, but people won't let me." — letter from Ohio.

• **Resign from human race** — "All my life I have had a compulsion to fix whatever is broken, and I always think the people expect me to be on top of every program in our small church — choir, missions, and Sunday School. Sometimes I want to resign from the human race." — from H.B.'s conference survey.

PASTORS' WIVES SHARE UNIQUE VIEWS OF MINISTRY

Several intriguing, positive ways of viewing ministry surfaced in the conference surveys done by Neil and H.B. in different settings.

- **Every occupation has frustrations** — "I found new joy in ministry when I realized there are some frustrations for every wife in any occupation her husband would choose. My mother was a farmer's wife, and that was no easy task with pressures of deadlines and finances. Frustrations are a part of living in any occupation."

- **Spiritually strong self-esteem helps** — "If pastors' wives felt secure in themselves because of Jesus Christ in their lives, there would be fewer negative issues to deal with. God is leading me to pray for sister pastors' wives who are struggling; sadly, there seems to be many."

- **Greater opportunities for serving Christ** — "My greatest joy in being married to a pastor is the privilege of serving in capacities that many women never have. People are open to me because of my husband's ministry."

- **God's original creation** — "I wish every pastor's wife could begin ministry with the knowledge that God can use her just as she is. Then I wish every troubled pastor's wife would reach out for help from another pastor's wife."

- **A nobody becomes queen** — "My greatest joy in being a pastor's wife is being treated as a queen when I'm just an ordinary nobody."

Thanks, ladies, for opening your heart so others can share your yearning for spiritual wellness and ministry effectiveness. Thanks for new insights. Thanks for rekindling hope for churches, ministries, and individuals. You are making an incredible impact on our troubled world.

Your responses show there does not need be any contradiction between partnering with your husband's ministry, doing good for others, and giving yourself spiritual self-care. Though ministry usually requires sacrifice and self-denial, it is a thousand times more satisfying than living an empty life. Your service to your Lord makes the world better and the church more productive in its mission.

Since most clergy couples cannot change their settings and circumstances, why not revolutionize the circumstances you already have? Even as land on a farm can be built up, seeded, cultivated, and prodded into productivity, why not build up congregations, cultivate happy relationships with church people, and make your life productive for the kingdom of God? This is a labor of love for Christ, and in the process, you are developing people for eternity.

CONTEMPORARY CHALLENGE
What Are the Most Pressing Issues in Pastoral Ministry?

- What problems are unique to the ministry?
- Can a ministry couple accurately compare their situation to a family not in ministry?
- Are fulfilling pastoral assignments discovered or made?
- Can a ministry couple function happily if the wife senses no call to ministry?
- Can a marriage and ministry flourish or even survive if the two relationships are in competition in the minds of the couple?
- Are loneliness and expectations related in the work of ministry?
- How many expectations do we create for ourselves?
- Can lay leaders actually steal ministry from a pastor's wife?
- How can a pastor and wife deal with criticism?
- What are the unique privileges of being married to a pastor?

MARRIED TO A STAR
OF MY MINISTRY
A Salute to Marja Barnett
by Pastor Tommy Barnett

I was thirteen years old. I belonged to a church where everyone was excited about sports figures, and I will never forget when a handsome athlete came to the front of the church and announced he was entering the ministry. You should have heard the uproar of the congregation. Like God was gaining something special. And He did!

On a subsequent Sunday, a ballplayer announced his profession as a Christian. The people were ecstatic. Surely the kingdom would grow with these kinds of special people.

But the atmosphere and response were quite different in the service that changed my life. It was a Sunday when a sixty-nine-pound kid walked the same aisle as the athletes did earlier and made the announcement he was called to the ministry. No one got too excited. Maybe someone dared think the angels folded their wings and wept.

But I'll never forget my earnest prayer of dedication. I was painfully aware I didn't bring the athletic prowess of the former athletes. I wasn't tall and handsome as they were, but I told God I could give Him something no one else could. I gave Him all sixty-nine pounds of Tommy Barnett.

In reverence I had tiptoed up to the front of the church to deposit my life into the treasury of the Lord. It was my best gift. I made God a vow that would not be broken. My life henceforth would be His to command.

Marja was God's surprise to me

Little did I perceive when I made that commitment the wonder and extraordinary blessings that were on the horizon. I started preaching at sixteen and was soon holding revivals around the country and the world. A few years into the ministry, one of those ultimate blessings arrived in a magnificent package at a meeting in Palo Alto, California.

Let me tell you about her. Marja Kaarina Holmstrong was born in Helsinki, Finland. Her father was killed in the war. She was sickly and malnourished. Her grandmother was an alcoholic, and her mother worked the streets. Codependent before she walked, Marja ate from garbage cans and was passed from orphanage to orphanage, wandering in a whirlpool of the unknown.

Subsequently, at six years of age, she was shipped to Sweden to be adopted by caring parents. Neither parent knew the Lord, but one of her treasures was a tiny crucifix — the child's early touchstone with prayer.

The little girl grew in stature and beauty to become a fashion model and runner-up for Miss Sweden. She had a deep desire to come to the United States and become a "star." With work visa in hand, she and a friend journeyed to the "land of opportunity" where she settled into a disappointing position as a maid.

Marja came to Christ under my ministry

One day she was intrigued by a Swedish friend who invited her to visit an American church and hear a young evangelist. She agreed. I was the evangelist, and when I first noticed her in the audience, I was struck by her beauty and presence.

She returned the second night, after questioning her friend about why this preacher got so red in the face. Was he mad at people? Because she knew little English, the Christian friend explained the message as best she could. The gracious hand of God had brought her back to a second service, and the Holy Spirit drew her to the altar to learn more about Christ.

There are those who say "I ran to the altar" that night to help her find Jesus. At times I am teased as to whether my zeal was human or spiritual. It was both. Later I drove her home, and until 4 A.M., across a major language barrier, explained who Jesus was and what He wanted to be for her. She opened her Scandinavian heart to Him that night, and to this day she will say it was the most beautiful night of her life.

That was August. We were married in December. In the interim, she spent three months with my mother and dad. Dad was my hero, and Mother modeled a great pastor's wife. My parents had prayed for my future since I was an infant. Now they were ready to meet, enrich, and encourage "the most beautiful girl in the world" who had entered my life. Both were discerning of her potential, her fervor to help, and her uninhibited attempts
at the English language. She clipped words and fragmented sentences, only to further endear herself to those she'd
meet.

Marja shared my ministry from the start

Our honeymoon took us on an evangelistic crusade that spanned Hawaii, the Philippines, Thailand, India, Sweden, and England. It was anything but storybook. We lived in mission homes and tents. We ate foreign food, and there were more language chal-lenges. Difficult? Very, but Marja's heart of compassion was spawned in those early days — compassion for people, missions, and ministry.

The years have passed. Years display well on this magnificent lady. Even yet, I often look for her in our congregation when I am on the platform; when I discover her, my heart still skips a beat.

Marja is tender and kind

She is gentle with her suggestions, and I have learned to listen to her wisdom. She is a strong force in my life. Through the years, no matter how many people compliment my sermon, I am never satisfied until I hear what she thinks. Then I feel warmly affirmed by a godly woman.

Marja loves people

She is fun-loving. She enjoys games and has an infectious laugh. When I walk into a room full of people and she is not there, it feels empty. I can walk into an empty room, and when she appears the room seems full.

My children love this pastor's wife I married. They forever wanted to bring their friends home when they were growing up — and still do now that they are mature. The same is true with our grandchildren.

Marja gives me strength

People often ask me the source of my strength and help. It will be no surprise that it comes from the Lord, but it is enhanced by Marja. Being visible and such a focus of attention in a congregation as large as ours could create problems. Not for Marja. She knows her God-given role. The people love her. She is a gracious participant in many activities, yet she never has neglected being a wife and mother. I always feel proud when I hear her say, "Tommy Barnett is my husband and my pastor."

Marja is my special star

Marja came to America to become a "star." She is, and her brightness fills my life. I am humbled when I realize that in many ways she accepted the challenge of Ruth in the Bible by choosing to journey with me.

> Whither thou goest, I will go;
>   and where thou lodgest, I will lodge:
> thy people shall be my people,
>   and thy God my God (Ruth 1:16).

I am married to a pastor's wife. Her price is above rubies, and my heart is safely entrusted to her. We have learned that when two fond hearts under God unite, the yoke is easy and the burden light!

Pastor Tommy Barnett
First Assembly of God
Phoenix, Arizona

5

UNDERSTANDING A PASTOR'S INNER LANDSCAPE

What Goes on Inside Him?

◇◇◇◇◇

O Lord, the ministry is too much for me.
I need You to make me strong
 to understand my mate,
  to accept people's demands,
 to offer Your strength,
  to be patient with spiritual immaturity in myself and others,
 to believe in Your church even when it is human,
  to seek Your face in my midnights,
 and to see Your glory in every person we serve in this place. Amen.

◇◇◇◇◇

*J*ESUS TAUGHT THAT AUTHENTIC FAITH starts in the inner life.
All the way through the Gospels, Christianity insists that actions and attitudes flow out from what is inside a person. This is the reason a pastor's inner life needs constant renewal and self-evaluation.

We all know that ministry at its deepest levels stretches the minister's inner resources at the center of his being, the place where reason, conscience, will, and integrity meet. But often wives of ministers have no clue about what's happening inside their man.

Sometimes wives face a stone wall of silence, mostly because our culture discourages men from discussing deep feelings. Given these realities, it seems useful for two male writers—H.B. and Neil—to pull back the curtain on several inner issues ministers grapple with. Though space limitations force us to narrow our list of subjects, we invite you to consider some elements of your man's inner world.

THREE ROCK-OF-GIBRALTAR STRENGTHS

It is a gracious reality of ministerial life: pastors (1) who are secure in their relationship to God, (2) who center their ministry around an authentic, divine call to service and (3) who enjoy a satisfying family life possess inner strengths which no tough circumstances, troubling persons, or frightening catastrophes can take from them. You can help nourish all three strengths in your husband. Pastors who have it "together" are close to God, enjoy a nonnegotiable call, and cherish a meaningful marriage. They possess the essential inner ingredients of ministry wholeness.

However, from observing an alarming number of tragedies in ministry couples, we know many pastors suffer spiritual struggles, emotional exhaustion, or moral failures. When left unattended, even the first hint of these trials of the soul undermine a pastor's effectiveness, create chronic psychic pain, and sometimes make him quit altogether. But prevention and renewal are available.

PAUL'S HUMBLING CLAY POT REMINDER

Though it is humbling, Paul does pastors an extraordinary kindness when he reminds us who we really are. Remember? He said we "carry this precious Message around in the unadorned clay pots of our ordinary lives" (2 Cor. 4:7, TM). Ministers too often tend to forget they are mere mortals whom God enables to do extraordinary things. In our heart of hearts, we know very little that matters ever gets done without divine enablement. Like the long-distance runner, self-care, healthy food, ample rest, and regular exercise must be a pastor's daily commitments if ministry is to flourish and thrive.

The Apostle Paul continues with his warning and wisdom:

> We've been surrounded and battered by troubles, but we're not demoralized; we're not sure what to do, but we know that God knows what to do; we've been spiritually terrorized, but God hasn't left our side; we've been thrown down, but we haven't broken. What they did to Jesus, they do to us (2 Cor. 4:8-10, TM).

Then he adds the affirming declaration of realism, "While we're going through the worst, we're getting in on the best!" (TM) What encouragement and inspiration—the worst and the best—as we live at the frontiers of the Gospel.

In pastoral work, suffering and satisfaction go together. To borrow Henri Nouwen's idea, effective ministry is usually done best by those who are being healed from their own wounds. Pain cured by grace provides an impeccable credential for ministry. However, the weight of our discussion between wounds and healing must come down on the side of healing.

Thus, to keep from overdosing on pastoral pathological problems, we must concentrate on how to develop our spiritual wellness in place of fearing the emotional perils we all so frequently face. To nourish wholeness, we must identify and understand the hazards of ministry and transform them into giant steps toward wholeness and wellness.

BUILD APPROPRIATE
SUPPORT SYSTEMS

Building an emotional support system is significantly different from adequate financial compensation, though that is also vitally important. Most ministers simply do not have adequate support systems to provide feedback for their preaching, teaching, counseling, and leading. The implications for creating dysfunctional ministries are frightening. Too often pastors start thinking they are minute messiahs when they are only lone rangers. They are lonely in a crowd of the very people they serve; they view their people as something like clients, communicants, or customers, but seldom as soul friends or fellow strugglers in the Way. Too few seek and pay the price to build strong accountability relationships.

To make matters worse, people in the parish tend to lock ministers into roles of super piety. This tends to create barriers against friendly interpersonal relationships. As a result, when ministers try to take themselves out of traditional roles, church members put them back in their place.

Human wellness requires that every human being needs someone to provide social support and accountability. For the man of God, this should be someone who loves him for his work in the Gospel. This can sometimes be achieved for a pastor through accountability groups, Bible study groups, peer groups, or family, but it has to be done. To hobble through ministry without relationships is a serious and needless mistake. To live in an environment of empty, shallow relationships is like exposing oneself to a deadly germ or virus—you may survive, but the risk is not worth it.

Think of what healthy relationships provide a pastor:

• A problem looks significantly different when shared with a trusted confidant.

• An accepting friend's viewpoint nearly always provides a new slant on an old problem.

• Others often possess relevant information about an issue we would not discover without discussing it with them.

• Difficulties change their shape and lose their strength when they are shared.

An Olympic swimmer appears to win a swim meet alone, but the fact is that he has coaches, nutritional advisers, trainers, sponsors, family, and fans in the stands. Likewise, every pastor who apparently stands in his pulpit alone has mentors, trainers, ecclesiastical superiors, lay leaders, peer advisers, family, and fellow strugglers cheering him on.

Pastors also need people who lovingly hold them accountable. No pastor can function well for long without several somebodies to help him achieve effective ministry and hold him accountable for keeping his own soul healthy. One effective mentor to many ministers suggested:

Improving a minister's personal functioning involves proactively and strategically finding places in his social support network for sharing private feelings and getting realistic feedback. . . . Finding other sources of friendships like other ministers in the community, support groups, clubs and reinvesting in old friends is often part of this process.[1]

DEPRESSION IS MORE THAN A YUCKY DAY

Fuller Seminary professor and psychologist Archibald Hart opens windows of insight when he introduces the idea of adrenaline over demand and depletion. He makes a convincing case for ministry being a high adrenaline-demanding profession because of Sunday work demands, unexpected emergencies at inconvenient times, constant public visibility, dealing with dysfunctional people, and tension-causing committee work. Hart estimated that 40 percent of all pastors feel significantly depressed on Monday due to their high adrenaline demands on Sunday. Just an awareness of this problem frees a pastor when he understands he is not the only pastor who feels emotionally exhausted on Monday, and that a day of rest usually provides full recovery.

Depression is also thought to have many other causes. In addition to the adrenaline expenditure, anger, loss, and false criteria for success are some of the other entangling causes for pastoral depression. Though the issues may be complicated and complex, it is important that a ministry couple recognize the potential problems of depression and do what they can to prevent them. Just because we may not understand the technical psychological dimensions does not mean we cannot build preventions and put some correctives in place.

What can you do together? Several possible remedies for your husband/pastor's proneness to depression are:

● You can help him become aware of adrenaline loss depression.

● You can help him adopt realistic success criteria for his ministry. Standards that are too low will be as damaging as those that are too high. Many pastors are chronically discouraged because they do not see potential in their assignment.

• You can help him initiate strategies for dealing with problem people, vocational opportunities, aging, and organizational authority.

• You can help him seek professional help if depression becomes chronic.

• You can help him develop outside interests and friendships with nonparishioners.

• You can help him find a balance between personal and pastoral roles.

• You can be realistic in your expectations of his involvement in marriage and family. Some pastors are much too isolated from family, while others overly indulge these relationships.

UNDERSTAND AND IDENTIFY SYMPTOMS OF STRESS

Several studies indicate pastors feel overstressed because they think they are inadequate to perform one or more functions of ministry. How confusing this can be in a vocation with such a variety of functions. Consequently, a pastor finds it easy to fasten his feeling of inadequacy on a performance area where he feels unsuited or inexperienced. Realistically, because no pastor can be equally competent in all areas of pastoral ministry, he should seek to be as competent as possible but not expect himself to be able to perform every facet of ministry equally well.

Burnout, as distinguished from day-by-day occupational stress, usually comes from emotional overload. Its primary manifestations are emotional exhaustion, feeling emotionally drained, or a sense of depersonalization. Burnout is often accompanied by a feeling of hopelessness, a reduced sense of accomplishment, and of being disconnected from people. When these symptoms appear, it is a warning to a pastor that he is giving too much of himself to others while giving too little to himself and his family. Some corrections must be made immediately.

Following are some ways pastors' wives can help their husbands prevent and recover from stress, burnout, and depression:

• Help him commit to a self-care schedule, including emotional, physical, and spiritual balance and exercise.

• Encourage him to stop feeling guilty for unfinished work. At the end of every day of ministry there will always be more responsibilities waiting to be done.

• Help him sharpen his coping skills with additional learning and training in conflict resolution, time management, support networks, and avoiding overloads of responsibilities.

• Discuss ways he could work smarter rather than harder.

• Encourage him to develop a satisfying family life. Helping him enjoy being at home is much more effective then merely whimpering about his schedule.

GET REALISTIC
ABOUT SEXUALITY

A veteran minister's wife who knew a lot about life told her young preacher son who was about to be married, "Son, for happier marriages, pastors ought to spend more money dating their wives, taking them to nice places, buying flowers and sexy negligees, and a lot less on new cars."

Though sexuality is somewhat related to earlier discussions about relationships, much more needs to be written, discussed, reasoned, and understood about a clergy couple's sexuality. Several immediate concerns become crystal clear to anyone who thinks seriously about these issues for even a short period of time.

As a starting point, let's hear the Bible say it again: "Honor marriage, and guard the sacredness of sexual intimacy between husband and wife" (Heb. 13:4, TM). Let's admit that sexual wholeness and/or sexual dysfunction among pastors and spouses receives little attention in the literature, in ministerial preparation programs, in pastors' continuing education events, and at informational/inspirational seminars.

A great many intimacy problems are predictable human problems, not necessarily ministry issues, that begin as flaws in childhood or teenage development, long before the individual was in ministry. But those human problems, when left uncorrected, can affect ministry in catastrophic ways.

Thus, what goes on behind a pastoral couple's bedroom doors needs to be informed and inspired by Scripture, by wholesome findings of social science, by the experiences and advice of well-adjusted persons in the pastoral profession, and by the individual needs of the partners in this particular marriage.

Paying an alarming price

Inappropriate and sinful sexual behavior among ministers is alarmingly common and destructive these days. Recently, a moral failure hurricane snapped the relationships of a pastor we know. He made good on his flirtations with his secretary and lost the meaning of twenty-five years with his wife, the respect of his college-age children, his livelihood, his faith, his friends at church, and his self-respect. The price of sexual unfaithfulness is incredibly high.

But let's bring it even closer to our own marriages. Several scientific studies support the findings that more than 35 percent of pastors surveyed acknowledge they have engaged in what they consider "inappropriate sexual behavior for a minister." And 12 percent acknowledge having sexual intercourse with a member of their congregation other than their wife. Those numbers sound like a lot more attention and prevention need to be done to build solid marriages, to increase commitment to marital intimacy, and to establish strategies to prevent breakdown.

Marital intimacy for a ministry couple must have high priority and can generally be improved. The basic elements are a willingness to discuss sexual matters with one's spouse, a lifelong commitment to each other, and a realization that sexual intimacy affects nearly every other area of life. We must joyfully affirm that satisfying sex is as significant to a clergy marriage as it is to all other marriages.

Far too many ministry couples seem bogged down in some rut that hinders their emotional, spiritual, and physical intimacy. Such a situation must be changed. As needed, dialogue between partners, study of factual resources, and even professional help should be sought to make sexual fulfillment as noble and joyous as God intended when He created male and female. It is time to say it loud and clear: a healthy marriage, including satisfying sex, is a strong defense against immorality among ministers.

Too many couples drift apart emotionally, almost without realizing it. A little while ago, a pastor's wife complained to a friend, "My husband never touches me except when he wants to have sex." The friend asked, "Why not start touching him the way you want to be touched?" She did and he responded. A little tenderness is often more effective than blame, complaint, or pouting.

Building protective walls

Any attempt to short-circuit lofty standards of moral purity must be avoided with eternal vigilance. Couples in ministry must love and value their marriages enough to build high walls to protect them. Even the appearance of moral compromise must be avoided, off-color jokes shunned, and questionable conduct rejected. Helps for building protective hedges around marriages are discussed in the earlier books, *Pastors at Risk* and *The Heart of a Great Pastor.*

An effective prevention strategy starts when a ministry couple commits to openly discuss these issues with each other.

Then, too, every pastor must pay close attention and exercise serious caution when his wife expresses suspicions of another woman's sexual attraction and intentions toward him. Such premonitions are often uncannily accurate, and many pastors have lost their way morally by not listening to their wives.

Ministers can also develop useful prevention insights by learning, understanding, and applying the concept of transference and countertransference in counseling relationships. This information is readily available in counseling textbooks and in college courses at most educational institutions.

Then, too, a pastor should schedule counseling sessions with persons of the opposite sex only when his wife, secretary, or some mature person is nearby—preferably in the next room. Maintaining this practice sends a beneficial message to the counselee, builds credibility with the whole church, and helps a pastor keep his counseling practices pure and professional.

Some pastors, to heighten moral credibility and increase efficiency, have implemented dual counseling with their wives serving as cocounselors. Then the counseling session becomes a kind of family perspective that provides insights and wisdom for the counselee's concerns from more than one person.

Additionally, other pastors have installed large windows in areas where counseling is done. Why not install big glass windows and doors leading into your study or office?

Another safeguard currently is taking place as more and more pastors refer parishioners to the growing network of Christian counselors who are increasingly available in so many places.

Above all else, keeping the home fires burning brightly is the most effective and satisfying prevention strategy against sexual temptation for both husband and wife. Such effort goes a long way to make their own marital relationship happy, and helps them live above reproach. At the same time, it models good marriages for people in the church and community—everybody wins.

ADVICE-ABOUT-
THE AUTHORITY TRAP

A short time ago, I shared ministry responsibilities for a week with an old friend. Let's call him David.

Cynthia, his wife, believes ministers are no longer respected or cherished by their congregations. No one can fault her conclusions because they sound so right and her evidence seems so trustworthy. She wants something done about it. And she wants her husband to lead the band. She was quick to say her husband allows lay church leaders to "run everything—including our family." He smiled as she talked and offered no reply.

Later in the day, she continued, "If David would just stand up for his rights, things would get better around here. He is called of God, ordained by the church, and has the confidence of the congregation. But he will not assert himself. If he would stand up, speak his mind, and take charge, most of the problems in this church would be solved. Why be a doormat when you can be king? He has paid his dues across twenty years of ministry."

Cynthia has obvious trouble with her husband's lack of assertiveness. She is convinced that more aggressive assertiveness is needed in their church, and that this is the key to many other things. But a word of caution may be helpful here. Criticism of another's lack of assertiveness, more often than not, is a lot like children volunteering to hold the coats of those they want to lead the fight. It's a far different proposition to advise others to fight than to get into the thick of a battle yourself or to clean up the blood after a battle. Holding coats is a lot less painful than black eyes.

The "A" words

In contemporary ministry, six "A" words—ability, assertiveness, anger, aggression, authority, and assuredness—frequently bang together and cause problems. We sometimes even have trouble completely understanding the meaning of those words.

Let's look at their potential problems. Ability, especially when we talk about our own talents, takes us uncomfortably near pride and arrogance. Assertiveness sounds like unnecessary domination and unwelcomed control. Anger is thought to be out of character for a pastor. Aggression sounds dictatorial. Authority reminds us too much of secularized corporate or governmental red tape and gridlock. And assuredness almost sounds conceited or even egotistical. In ourselves and in others, we want some of what these words represent, but not too much.

Consider how this dilemma plays out in individual ministries. No pastor wants either to be too aggressive or considered a passive pushover. Likely, every pastor wants to be a strong leader, but not dictatorial. No church member enjoys following an overly assertive minister, but few would not, on the other hand, voluntarily choose to follow a docile pastor. And ministerial students are surprisingly resistant in classes and seminars whenever assertiveness or aggression is taught.

This problem multiplies even more as Hart and Blackmon report: "Clinical experience shows that underassertive and excessively overassertive ministers are much more likely to suffer from depression, burnout, helplessness, and especially problems with anger and resentment."[2]

Who would have thought to classify the underassertive and excessively overassertive together in this way? And who would have thought these "A" words would contribute to emotional crises in a pastor's inner world? But they do.

Strategy and prevention for dealing with too much assertiveness starts with the servanthood model found in Scripture. It requires that the pastor view his task as being the resident representative of Christ, who leads by integrity and love rather than by authority and dominance. Though our Lord had the full power of God, He led with love. He showed us how love always wins, while insisting on our rights usually loses.

The balance we seek

Sometimes a pastor's love must be tough — the kind of love that cares enough to refuse to allow people to harm themselves with their actions or attitudes. It is also true that every minister must at times learn to be more gentle. I like the balance William Barclay recommends:

> The hardest temptation of all is the temptation which comes from protecting love. There are times when fond love seeks to deflect us from the perils of the path of God; but real love (tough love) is not the love which holds the knight at home when he should be in the battle, but the love which sends him out to obey the commandment of chivalry which is given, not to make life easy, but to make life great.[3]

This is holy work because we are helping people be more like Jesus rather than controlling them through just another human organization called the church.

Knowing how to love, doing loving acts, and knowing in what degree to love is the confusing difficulty we so often face. Spiritual formation specialist Richard J. Foster's prayer helps us discover the needed balance:

> Dear God,
> I stand against the fear that makes me want to
>   manage and control others.
> Grant me the gift of faith, O Lord, to overcome my fear.
> I stand against the greed that makes me use others
>   for my own selfish purposes.
> Grant me a spirit of generosity, O Lord, to temper my greed.
> I stand against the pride that drives me to seek inordinate attention.
> Grant me the grace of service, O Lord, to conquer my pride.
> May faith, hope, and love have increasing sway over every
>   thought and action. Amen.[4]

Help your pastor/husband give this work of loving people in Christ's stead his best shot. Someone may take advantage of his kindness and think he is too soft or too pious or too weak. But others will cheer and believe and rejoice that they see love at work in a world that specializes in toughness and assertiveness and being in control.

Back to David and Cynthia and their efforts to use and understand authority and power: the loving pattern of Jesus is the main test that must be applied to their work together in the kingdom of Christ and to ours. The powerfully awesome Lord of glory chose to become the tender, saving, and serving Jesus. He is our dependable guide and our role model. His rule of love always attracts people to follow Him. Can we do less? And dare we try to do more? Our time is now. There is much improvement to be made.

CONTEMPORARY CHALLENGE
Pastor Preservation — Essential Principles

- Pastors need three steadfast strengths:
  (1) A vital relationship with Christ.
  (2) A conclusive call to the ministry.
  (3) A satisfying marriage.
- Wounded healers often make the most effective pastors.
- Lone rangers can easily believe themselves to be minute messiahs.
- High adrenaline drains can cause temporary depression.
- No pastor can be equally competent in all areas of ministry.
- Long-term emotional overload creates burnout.
- A healthy marriage, including satisfying sexual relationships, is a strong defense against moral failure.
- A pastor is seldom helped by criticism about how he uses his pastoral authority.
- Our pattern for ministry is the awesome Lord of glory who chose to become the tender, serving, and saving Jesus.

MARRIED TO A WOMAN WHO UNDERSTANDS MY INNER WORLD

A Salute to Lois Evans
by Pastor Tony Evans

When the wise old sage, Solomon, penned the words "her worth is above rubies," he unknowingly had my wife Lois in mind. As a Christian leader in our various expressions of ministry, I'm glad that I don't have to pay my wife according to her worth, for then I wouldn't only need rubies, but diamonds and pearls as well, to give her what is truly her due. Lois' contribution to my life and ministry is invaluable. Over the past twenty-four years she has been the single greatest cause for the effectiveness, growth, and impact of my ministry. She, like none other, has influenced the direction of my life and the lives of our children.

Early in our dating relationship, I knew I had a gem when she told me she found her joy in sharing my joy. Since my greatest joy in life is serving Christ, my joy has been made that much more complete by the infusion of her joy into my own. It has also led to the credibility, quality, and expansion of our ministry together.

As a mother and wife, Lois committed herself to raising a godly family by foregoing her career in business administration to raising our four children and serving as my typist, study partner, and emotional release valve as I went through four years of seminary for my master's degree and an additional four years for a doctorate of theology degree. When I was burdened down with the pressures of tests and papers, she would encourage me with a cup of hot coffee and the warm motivation to go on another day. When there was the thought to drop out of school due to the pressures of finances and studies, it was her tender reminder that God hadn't brought us this far to leave us that kept me fighting the good fight. She possessed the marvelous ability to turn hot dogs and baked beans — the traditional diet of seminary students — into a five-star cuisine fit for a king.

Each Thursday night, she would go to the seminary wives' fellowship to receive the spiritual encouragement and fellowship she needed. There she would get the strength to carry on her often thankless role. It was during this time that she continued, as time allowed, working on her degree in business administration. Little did either of us know how crucial these skills would be for our future ministry together.

Lois' greatness shone all the more as a pastor's wife. Our church, Oak Cliff Bible Fellowship, began in our home with ten people. Week after week, she prepared our home for worship and Bible study, often serving as the sole baby-sitter, Sunday School teacher, hospitality coordinator, church pianist, soloist, church secretary, and janitor — sometimes being all of these in one day. Then, after the house services were over, she would prepare our kids for bed while I continued ministering to the church members on a more personal basis.

In addition, Lois helped to initiate and develop many other areas of church life that are flourishing today due to the strong foundation she laid. Lois used her God-given gifts in music to begin our church choir. Then she began our women's fellowship. Her hard work provides a significant jump-start for those who would follow her in Christian service. Our growth from 10 people to over 3,000 can easily be traced in large measure to the influence and skills of the wife of my youth. Each Sunday morning she would rise with me and attend both morning services to be my support and encouragement. Her constructive criticism has made me a better preacher of God's Word.

As a trained businesswoman, Lois brought an important dimension to our national ministry, The Urban Alternative. TUA is an organization designed to bring spiritual renewal to urban America through the church. Because we were both novices in the development of a parachurch ministry, and since there was no money to hire others to develop it for us, Lois again became my Mrs. Everything. She learned by studying other effective parachurch ministries like Focus on the Family and Insight for Living, carefully analyzing and adopting their commitments to technical excellence and spiritual integrity to our new ministry. She first developed the tape ministry which led to the development of the TUA radio broadcast. Lois then organized all the administrative processes for the organization, overseeing setting up our computer system, phone system, data entry, and fulfillments departments, and did whatever else was necessary to move the ministry forward. As a result of her commitment to her Lord and her husband, TUA has grown to be one of the largest minority-led ministries in the country. As executive vice president, she continues to move the administrative aspects of the ministry in a way that causes others in much larger ministries to marvel. They ask, "How can you accomplish so much with so little?"

I answer, "The way she turned our leftovers at home into a dinner fit for a king."

What was so amazing to me was that in the midst of all these responsibilities at church, none of her priorities at home went lacking. She would rise at 5:30 A.M. and cook the meals for the day. Our children's care remained her highest priority, and there was always a meal for guests who came by and a listening ear for ladies who were struggling in their own lives. Without any fanfare, Lois uniquely balances home, church, and career with such feminine strength that she epitomizes the meaning of woman for me.

I guess my son said it best when he declared that he wanted to marry a woman just like Mom. I guess there is no better compliment than that; or maybe there is, for if I had it to do all over again, I would gladly say "I do" again and again for this woman of excellence, a woman about whom Solomon wrote in Proverbs 31—women like Lois Evans whose works speak for themselves, leaving behind them a trail of blessing and glory for all who have come across her path. "Her works truly do praise her."

Lois Evans is indeed "A Woman for All Seasons," and only eternity will reveal the worth that is uniquely hers.

Pastor Tony Evans
Oak Cliff Bible Fellowship
Dallas, Texas

6

I HATE THE "E" WORD
Can She Play the Piano or Shoot a Pistol?

◇◇◇◇◇

Giver of every good and perfect gift,
Give us love for You and others which will
grudge no expectation,
refuse no obedience,
resent no trial.
Give us true goodness which
is holy and lovely,
is pure but loves the sinner,
reflects the charm of the life of Jesus. Amen.[1]

◇◇◇◇◇

N OW THAT OUR KIDS ARE GROWN, my wife is realizing her lifelong dream to study New Testament Greek," a minister remarked in passing in a speech. "It's handy too, because she's helping me with my research for preaching."

After the meeting, other wives teased the speaker with a half-serious note, "Thanks a lot. We already cook their meals and wash their clothes and listen day and night to their problems. Now you want us to do research too. NO WAY!" Nervous laughter followed, but everyone was overly weary of unrealistic expectations—

the dreaded "E" word, which we have already met a few times earlier in this book.

Outlandish expectations for ministers' mates is nothing new. Strange as it seems, however, many expectations start in our heads. Expectations have been around for a long time, at least for a hundred years. For example, an old book published near the turn of the last century advised that a pastor's wife should be 50 percent tidy, 50 percent timid, and 100 percent covered up. A "closet women's libber," after reading that sentence, remarked, "See, more than 100 percent was expected even then! And even in these enlightened times, pastors' wives are more valued for what they can do for a congregation than for who they are. It's absurdly ridiculous."

Unrealistic or unmet expectations often lead to disappointments or outright hostility for a pastor or his spouse. A typical though nonexhaustive list of expectations taken from surveys and letters highlight the contradictions—and some outright impossibilities:

"Pressure to live up to others' ideals of family or life style."

"Feeling there is no room for mistakes."

"We are expected to keep up a middle-class appearance on a poverty salary."

"People regularly invade our privacy."

"I'm confused—church members want me to be a regular Jane, down-to-earth person but they also want me to be classy and dignified and well dressed."

"Does God know my children are supposed to be perfect?"

In dealing with the "E" word, the point is not to resist, reject, or blindly follow someone else's agenda. Rather, the way to find balance is to establish God-shaped principles and practices of ministry which are built on your abilities and strengths, and the needs you find in a given situation.

PEDESTALS AND FISHBOWLS— PRESSURES TO CONFORM

One insightful member of a pastoral search committee, weary of silly questions being asked of a potential candidate, remarked cynically, "Can your wife play the piano while sitting on a pedestal, shooting a .22, and living in a fishbowl?" When unrealism and tradition are all stripped away, many expectations would be comical if they were not so unreasonable and intimidating.

Like a mysterious plague, real, assumed, self-imposed, and misunderstood expectations create debilitating difficulties for many ministry couples. No human being can live up to all of them. Malaise, despondency, pessimism, bewilderment, resentment, and even outright defeat are incapacitating symptoms of this uncalled-for epidemic.

In a 1993 survey, 53 percent of ministers' wives believed unrealistic expectations to be the biggest problem they face in the ministry they share with their pastor/husbands.[2] Other surveys report a similar conclusion — expectations are a gigantic problem for ministers' mates. Horror stories abound about wives with too much to do, too many people to please, and too many burdens to bear. A civil war of the spirit seems to be waged concerning the rights and responsibilities of women married to ministers. Something has to be done to relieve these pressures.

Some suggest these loads become easier for those who passively comply with what is expected. Others argue that a compliant pastor's wife is likely to feel a passive inner rage that gets displaced into her marriage, parenting, relationships at church, or at her secular work place.

While many writers, seminar speakers, and ecclesiastical leaders believe that stereotypes of ministers' wives are changing in contemporary churches, apparently some congregations are blissfully unaware of such changes. Greenbacker and Taylor in *Private Lives of Ministers' Wives* believe confusing and sometimes paradoxical clergy placements make this problem worse:

> Women who want the traditional role of the minister's wife seem rarely to match up with congregations willing to let them assume all the duties and leadership they want. And wives who want freedom to choose how much, or how little, they'll do in the church seem rarely to match up with the congregations willing to leave them alone to do their own thing.[3]

If this evaluation is accurate, the pastor's wife should be given more consideration as to where her pastor/husband serves.

Four things seem obvious, then:
(1) unreasonable expectations are real;
(2) demanded animosity by the wife, however well stated or loudly debated, does little to change them;
(3) expectations change slowly in most places; and
(4) the problem could probably be lessened with more intentional placement of clergy couples.

EVERYONE FACES EXPECTATIONS EVERY DAY

Everyone in every line of work deals with perplexing expectations every day because they are built into the fabric of human life. Expectations and demands are with us always, like death and taxes. And the list seems to keep growing longer all the time. Married couples expect a lot of each other. Expectations are a part of every human relationship, including children and parents, employees and bosses, students and teachers, patients and doctors, and clients and lawyers. Citizens expect much of statesmen, and the newspapers often discuss how much more the public wants from politicians. Clergy expect a lot from churches, and congregations expect more from their pastor and his spouse than they could ever humanly provide.

The expectation complication

Living in any human relational connection like marriage, family, church, neighborhood, or workplace means that expectations frequently complicate our lives. Everyone has them. Even a lonely recluse, though he may not be pressured by other's expectations, has expectations for himself when nobody else is around.

Even when they are not aware of it, everyone continually deals with a two-way interplay of expectations: (1) what others expect of them and (2) what they expect of others. No one can totally avoid or abolish the impact expectations have on the details of living.

A surprising paradox that we do not often consider is at work in our formation of expectations. For some reason, every human being at some time in their life resents expectations others seem to impose on them. So it is common to think our boss, mother-in-law, neighbor, or spouse expects too much of us. But at the same time, without realizing it, we freely increase our expectations of others, usually without considering their feelings in the matter. What an astonishing inconsistency—we resist expectations for ourselves, while we freely impose them on others.

"E" word peevishness

These days, the church is experiencing incredible problems with expectations. In many congregations and church agencies, people have become ill-tempered and cantankerous over expectations. Laypeople think pastors shirk their duties. Pastors suspect laymen are apathetic and undermotivated. The issue has grown so peevish that the "E" word dominates conversation wherever pastors or spouses get together. Laypersons feel frustrated by the same issue. It seems as if everyone inside and outside the church, including secularists on Wall Street, stylish folks at the upscale mall, and mountaineers in the Rockies, has an opinion of what a pastor is supposed to be and do.

Regrettably, for many ministers and their mates, even a hint at conflicting opinions about how ministry should be done causes fear, conflict, and/or emotional nausea. Even to mention the word *expectation* causes trauma for so many couples in ministry—a fact that can easily sidetrack a pastor and his wife from making their best contribution for Christ in their present assignment.

Like a child who could not see the sun because he held a penny so close to his eye, the expectation problem has been discussed so often that ministry for some has been mesmerized by unrealistic expectations.

WHO CAUSED THE EXPECTATION DILEMMA?

Often the sources of unrealistic expectations are confusing and contradictory, even ludicrous. Some church members expect their minister and wife to fit predetermined molds even when those expectations are totally unreasonable or seventy-five years out of date. But let's face the solemn music. Some expectations come from pastors themselves whose assumptions about their wives' roles in the church and community clash with views held by their spouse and/or church.

The question of irrational response to expectations by the pastor or spouse must also be considered. Jesse Benson, a pastor's wife in the Northwest, described her reactions, "I sometimes exaggerate expectations—my own and the expectations others have of me." When asked to explain this surprising practice, she replied, "I am confused about why. Maybe it's a sly way to get people to feel sorry for me." Obviously Jesse's expectations are in her head and of her own making.

Admittedly, however, many expectations are real and frustrating—so real a pastor's wife can feel browbeaten or bewildered by confusing or contradictory expectations. One wife explains that other people's notions about her life feel like an emotional noose choking spiritual life out of her as she tries to live up to church members' notions, community customs, and the biblical directive to "seek first the kingdom of God." Those three often conflict. Regrettably, these frustrations often increase even more when a pastor/husband has a messiah-like commitment to keep himself and his family in a frenzy of responding to everyone's beck and call. The accumulation easily adds up to spirit-breaking fed-up-ness.

One woman of God from the Midwest recently suggested in a pastors/wives' meeting, "I think it's time to give the word 'expectations' a needed rest. We are drowning in rhetoric about this issue and don't have energy for anything else." Though she may be right about too much discussion and not enough action, to suspend the talk does not eliminate the mounting pressure that easily accelerates into explosive proportions.

HELPS FOR UNRAVELING THE CONFUSION

How can we unravel this complex problem? As a starting point, try answering these four questions: Who does a pastor's wife listen to? Who can she talk to? What is she to do? And where does God fit into this picture of a hundred different voices telling her what to do? There must be a better way than being pulled through a life in ministry kicking and resisting.

The first collision of expectations frequently begins when a pastor is invited to consider a new church. He agrees to participate in an interview or preach a trial sermon. Often his wife is invited into the interview process so the group can get a good look at her. Then, if things go well, congregational leaders start believing they have found a happy match. Like starry-eyed adolescents on their first date, pastor and people start considering a long-term relationship. All parties think their fantasies about an ideal church have come true. A pastor's wife can easily get caught as an emotional hostage between her husband and the congregation in the middle of this unrealistic view of the new relationship.

Before long, church and pastor commit to each other and an ecclesiastical honeymoon begins. No one thinks to remind either party that neither new pastor nor congregation is perfect, or even close to it. Everyone hopes they have an ideal marriage even though all parties bring unspoken, unrealistic standards to the relationship that the other party is simply not able to meet.

Then reality sets in. The pastor does not preach as well as the decision group thought he would. Lay leaders do not give as much energy or financial support as the pastor thought they promised. The pastor's wife expects new carpeting, and her life style shocks someone. The pastor's children are disappointed by their new schools. Shut-ins expect the pastor to call more than he seems able to do. Youth leaders need more supervision than the pastor can give them. Choice lay leaders move, taking their skills and their generous giving with them. Soon a thousand tiny, unmet brush fires erupt into a ten-alarm conflagration.

Then it is easy to give up and say, "Things just did not work out in our assignment." The pastor quits and some key members leave. Broken relationships follow, which causes a decline in church attendance and giving. The pastor's wife feels caught again, forced into angry silence about the way her husband has been treated and about the adjustments she and her children are forced to make because things did not work out. And often, the pastor gets heartsick over the defeat of his dream for the place.

Such a dilemma is like that faced by a couple in a marriage that is overly charged with unrealistic expectations. Dr. Dennis

Karpowitz, University of Kansas psychologist, explains how this happens to a married couple: "A person has an ideal image of their partner that is very different from who that person really is. The danger is that when they see that person cannot meet their needs, they throw away the good part of the relationship along with the weaker part of it."[4] That happens in pastoral relationships too, so a pastor mentally checks out or leaves without fully considering the strong points of the church. Disillusionments increase when the good part of the relationship is not recognized and cherished. Without a meeting of meanings, trouble usually follows. As a result, the pastor moves to a new set of unrealistic demands in a new church in a new setting. And another pastor moves into this assignment to be nibbled nearly to death by unrealistic standards. Within two months, the vicious cycle continues in both places.

EXPECTATIONS COME FROM MANY TANGLED ROOTS

The negative and far-reaching impact of expectations multiplies when we consider their diverse roots. Goals, aspirations, priorities, and demands in pastoral work bang together like an emotional earthquake inside many pastors and their spouses. The resulting storm creates noisy sounds and massive injuries that ripple from the epicenter to every direction of church life. To prevent such ecclesiastical disasters, it may be useful to identify the original causes and try to find ways to test the reliability of every notion or idea.

Where do expectations begin? Are they always bad? What is their seedbed and how do they grow? Who speaks for an entire congregation? And why are these unrealistic demands so uppermost in the minds of Christian workers?

Expectations rooted in congregational life

Expectations are frequently intimated by someone in the congregation. Sometimes they are an old tradition that someone started years ago. Seldom, if ever, does a decision-making group or a congregation thoroughly discuss the issues, probably because it would be almost impossible to reach a consensus. More often, expectations are supposed or implied in veiled or disguised language. All this adds up to the fact that some expectations are phantom notions perpetuated across decades without any test of validity or rationality.

Group memories. "We'd love it if your wife would lead our children's ministry like Mrs. Pastor Smith did years ago."

Before you respond, try to think through what may be taking place in the speaker's mind. This statement might mean a whole generation of our children enjoyed ministry from a former pastor's wife, and we wish those happy experiences could be repeated. It could be a mere sentimental memory of something that didn't actually happen. Then again, it may only be a gracious statement about a former pastor's wife. Or the person speaking may be expressing regret that they know it cannot happen again, something like the ol' swimming hole you enjoyed when you were ten.

Such comments should be viewed by the pastor and his wife as a pleasant memory of effective ministry rather than a confrontational mandate for them to repeat the past. Resist allowing yourself to develop an adversarial attitude over comments about past ministry. What people intend to say and what you hear may be quite different.

False assumptions. "We need your wife to teach our largest adult class." Laypersons, without considering the possible fallout, sometimes assume a minister's vocational commitments determine his wife's involvements in congregational life. Such archaic ideas can best be circumvented by a pastor's wife's taking the lead about her involvement in Christian service. Instead of waiting to be asked to take a particular assignment, she can volunteer for satisfying service where she is comfortable, gifted, and motivated.

Another possible solution is frequently overlooked in dealing with congregational assumptions. Try simple negotiations. Many lay leaders have had experience with negotiations on similar matters when they changed previous pastors. Therefore, such a situation may not be as difficult to resolve as it first seems. Try discussing their expectations and yours in an unemotional, rational way. Such a nonjudgmental discussion goes a long way to resolving these issues for fair-minded people.

Remember, too, that one lay leader's blustery overstatement does not speak for a whole decision group or an entire congregation. You can often sort through what appears to be an unacceptable congregational impasse by simply asking a decision group, "Does everyone agree?" Much of the time they don't.

Desperate congregational needs. "We hope your wife has musical ability. It would be so nice to hear the organ again. The organ has not been played since Mary Alice moved to Dallas three years ago."

Quite often a congregation really needs a church musician or a women's group leader. In those situations, such statements should not be thought of as a demand, but a dream or a wish or a regret. And though you may suspect a church of wanting to secure two people for one salary, they may simply be expressing a pressing problem they want their prospective leader to know about. They may be verbalizing a hope that their new minister will be able to solve a long-time defect or scarcity.

Limited perspective by laypersons. "We hope you take part in community events as a way to attract new people."

Without intending to cause an unfavorable response, the message may be, "We need community visibility and we would like the community to know you better." Likely, the statement could mean we hope you and your wife are friendly individuals whom the whole community will enjoy knowing. They may be saying, "We want to be proud of you in the community so people will think well of our church."

Try seeing it from their limited perspective. Even active lay leaders often do not understand what a pastor and spouse do in the church. Therefore, they may try to communicate a desire to have a full range of ministry but don't say it well.

Sadly, I know a minister's widow in her eighties who grumbled all her life because people tried to include her in church life. Since she imagined they wanted to invade her privacy, she missed the congregation's desire to include her in its life and ministry. Even in her sunset years, she does not understand that her friends at church are trying to help her circumvent her sense of isolation.

Outspoken malcontents. "My dear, I know you're new here, so you didn't know that there are times you'll find casual dress to be, well, *too* casual." In many congregations, one or two habitual malcontents who, by faultfinding and antagonism, can communicate to the pastor and/or his wife an impression that is entirely inaccurate. Ruth Levi, a rabbi's wife, vividly describes the same problem in their synagogue:

141

If she is brilliant or militant or persuaded of her ability to be a leader, she is likely to be considered forward, aggressive; if she is timid, hesitant, or just convinced that it is wiser that only her husband's voice should be raised in the house of worship, she will be called stupid or lacking in initiative. If she is lovely to look upon, she will be said to be vain and frivolous; if she considers extreme stylishness trivial and unworthy of the time it requires, her critics will pronounce her dowdy, "old timey," obsolete.[5]

Grumblers need to be loved, even though they create problems in the church. They should be accepted but not taken seriously when they vent opinions and promote distortions.

Your own personal and family expectations

Ministry has many traditions that get passed from generation to generation in the pastor's extended family. There is also the problem that pastoral couples from dysfunctional families sometimes have trouble functioning happily in the family of God. Expectations for others, such as their personal standards of ministry and their individual ideas of what they want from their marriages and/or from their ministry, are rooted in their soil of the soul. And some pastors raised in a layman's home, without thinking through the source, take their parents' view of ministry into a pastorate.

Among the most dangerous of all these land mines is the fact that many ministers and their wives have greater expectations of themselves than their congregations have. Lowering your inner tensions about expectations most often begins within yourself. Few if anyone in any congregation expects you to be flawless, to be all things to everyone, or to perform all aspects of ministry perfectly at all times. Try to climb off such self-imposed treadmills.

Massive changes in the culture are obvious. But a more elusive, though infrequently discussed, change is taking place—it is the increasing inner commitment of ministers for what they are prepared to give to ministry and for what they expect to receive from ministry. In earlier generations, ministers expected only minimal support with a possibility of serving a group of people in the name of the Lord God. If salary, status, and satisfaction resulted, so much the better. But faithfulness to their task, fidelity to a doctrine, and loyalty to a denomination were what they expected to give all their lives, and they were surprised if they received much in return.

But that has changed, at least for some. Recently, I heard about a pastor who turned down an invitation to a new church because the master bedroom in the parsonage was not large enough to accommodate his waterbed. Another prospective pastor said in his interview with a church, "I could never go to a place where they do not have a shower." Though their parsonage had three showers, the church did not call this prospective pastor because they thought his demands were superfluous. These are real-life examples that show that all problems with expectations do not come just from the laity.

In this confusion, our challenge is to determine what values govern our lives. Will we choose the prosperity-oriented, achievement-driven, and secular kind of living or the mysterious, God-centered life that is governed and nourished by love, forgiveness, and understanding.

Childhood memories. "I wish my pastor-husband and I could spiritually impact people like my childhood pastor did for me."

Pastors and spouses often have warm, fuzzy memories of ministers from their childhood or youth. In fact, those memories may be the strongest influence on their answering a call into ministry. Deep down they want to duplicate the life-impacting relationships they experienced in their youth.

It is easy in those instances, however, to impose unrealistic demands. Better to admit that some things are gone forever, and then try to accomplish a similar contemporary impact, rather than trying to duplicate the actual happenings from out of the past.

Our own idealism. "A pastor's wife is supposed to be both a charming hostess and a spiritual leader."

A pastor's wife near Toronto reported her frustration about not being able to be the kind of pastor's wife she thought others wanted her to be. She suffered for years under the delusion that she was not fulfilling what the congregation expected of her. She felt bound by an internal standard of operations that originated in her own mind and had little root in reality.

The congregation, though they never said much about it, thought she was a nearly ideal pastor's wife. They wanted her to be herself, and they felt she did that well. Meanwhile, she kept trying to live up to an ideal of her role, an impossible dream no one else shared. Without realizing it, she had created her own emotional ball and chain. Try not to live by preprogrammed messages about ministry because your notions may be pure fantasy. The issue is to be your best self under the direction of God.

Marriage expectations by pastor and spouse. Regardless of the career commitments of marriage partners, growing a solid relationship takes an intentional investment of time and effort. Consequently, because of such close ties between family and kingdom interests, it is easy to blame ministry for unrealistic expectations in a clergy marriage. Wives can easily get out of focus concerning the realities of ministry. Or a pastor can be grossly unrealistic about his wife's involvement in the church and about her being the most important factor in his emotional support system.

A fairly typical example shows in Martha Moore's rationalized passive withdrawal from her marriage and her husband's ministry:

> My pastor husband expects me to listen to him, day or night, to entertain for him, to always "be there" when he needs reassuring, to be the most active layperson in the church, to shoulder eighty percent of the care of the house and children in order to leave him completely free for his work. . . . It may be true that he would expect this of me no matter what his work might be, but because he is around home so much, I notice it a lot. And I can't be everything he wants me to be.[6]

Since ministry tends to fog and complicate husband/wife relationships, the need for more realism, more flexibility, and better communication is evident. But care should be taken to see that ministry is not blamed for personal problems or marriage issues a couple bring with them into ministry. A woman, married to a pastor for twenty-five years, remarked with insight in a focus group: "I married a workaholic, and I can't change him. I doubt that he can change. I do not blame my husband's work habits on the church, the denomination, or God because he would be work-addicted in any occupation."

This woman learned a liberating secret that even though her husband, the Rev. John Doe, is an ordained pastor, he is still John

Doe, with all his strengths and weaknesses. And most of those strengths and weaknesses should not be blamed or credited to the fact he is a minister. Though this separation of marriage and ministry issues is difficult, it needs to be done in every clergy marriage.

The inability or unwillingness to separate work and marriage is a common difficulty for executives and professional persons. But because ministry takes such a total immersion of time and energy, it is even more difficult for pastors and their spouses. A pastor's wife who felt completely frustrated by this problem wrote:

> The other night after a particularly warm and intimate time together, I was lying on his shoulder. At that moment, there was nothing in the world on my mind but him, and I was feeling completely loved and happy. Then he said something like, "I think I'll suggest to the nominating committee that they elect Samuel Jones as lay leader."[7]

This minister's wife rightfully resented this intrusion into their intimacy. But it happens easily, usually in less obvious ways, when ministry and marriage are too closely related in the mind of the pastor. In this situation, the pastor/husband tries to mollify her resentment by saying, "But it also works the other way. I always think of you in the most important moments of ministry." Though she was not especially convinced, their conversation helped them discuss possible solutions for the abrasions that come up between home and church.

Without a couple's commitment to work through issues where marriage and ministry sandpaper each other, a woman is likely to feel frighteningly isolated in the midst of busy church activity. On the other hand, a pastor does not have a clue about how to work through these issues unless he understands his spouse's outlook, maintains open communication with her, and commits to the reality that marriage and ministry always impact each other, either helpfully or harmfully.

Personal problems. A clear illustration of this point appears in what one woman wrote in a survey of pastors' wives:

> The roots of my problem reached far beyond the years of my life as a minister's wife; however, my whole attitude toward this

life of ministry was colored and often contorted by this warp of personality, and certainly the tremendous pressures of the ministry were what finally broke my set of defenses and made psychiatric help imperative.[8]

William Douglas, in his well-researched book *Ministers' Wives,* offers this insightful summary: "When pastors' wives are unhappy it tends to be as women, wives and mothers and not as ministers' wives," and he finds many problems rooted in long-term, unresolved issues.[9] Without such awareness, many chronic personal problems are never discussed or unraveled. It becomes something like thinking a lung infection is making you limp when you walk. The problems are never solved and ministry gets blamed.

Impressing heroes. "I want to do ministry so well that it will please people who believe in me, like my old Sunday School teacher and my college professors."

This expectation is rooted in our "imagined audience" made up of persons who shaped our ministerial development, such as a former pastor, a classmate, a parent, a childhood Sunday School teacher, or a mentor. Others we want to please might include a favorite author, beloved professor, or a super-church pastor we met at a conference. But such expectations may not be realistic in light of your setting, time, gifts, and resources. High standards of excellence might be better motivated by more lofty objectives.

Our Lord's remarkably fair expectation

All ministry expectations that truly matter are rooted and nourished by prayer and Scripture. How freeing it is to be assured that the Father's expectations of us are reasonable, doable, and productive. He expects our best, and He knows exactly what that is.

Pleasing God is fun. Keep reminding yourself: "Pleasing God matters more than anything else." He is not a tyrannical taskmaster, but a loving Father with our best interest in mind.

A pastor and his spouse's hope for finding equilibrium in all the expectations rests in their personal relationship with God. His expectations are worth doing. The Apostle Paul put this issue in clear as day perspective when he wrote, "Cheerfully pleasing God is the main thing, and that's what we aim to do regardless of our

146

conditions" (2 Cor. 5:9, TM). What powerful concepts he offers for sorting through our expectations—(1) cheerfully please God, (2) regardless of our conditions.

Joyfully serving God is its own reward. Pearl Buck, the American novelist from a previous generation, said it well: "To serve is beautiful, but only if it is done with joy, a whole heart and a free mind."[10] The Lord wants our service for Him to be intentional, voluntary, competent, and joyful. In fulfilling His expectations, we rest in Him and give up our feverish fretting about what others think. When God is pleased, most other people will be satisfied too.

Seeing issues God's way. Say to yourself, "I want to view every expectation from God's perspective."

That clarifies a lot of things. All expectations, regardless of their source, should be tested by what God wants done—and Scripture is our main guide. Then the focus changes from what others think or say about our kingdom efforts to seeking God's approval.

But another facet of this truth must also be considered. No one can become spiritually strong and stable by their relationship to another person regardless of how mature the other person is. Thus, a pastor's wife's spiritual development never comes automatically because of her marriage to a minister. The pastor's wife must be an authentic Christian like everyone else. Like all serious believers, she must nourish her own soul and strengthen her own faith.

Using God's help. Keep reminding yourself, "Ministry is impossible without God's enablement. But it is satisfying and productive with His help."

The devotional writer Henri Nouwen clears away much of our confusing underbrush when he asks: "Am I a prisoner of people's expectations or liberated by divine promises?"[11] That is a pivotal question of ministry. An individual's answer goes a long way to clarify the expectations issue.

We serve a God who offers divine resourcing that makes the fulfillment of His will for us possible. This provision of divine empowerment is the important difference between human and divine expectations. God always energizes us to do what He wants done if we allow Him to do it. Like a human father knows his children's abilities, God knows us so well He can accurately determine just what we can do. The bottom line: He always provides empowerment to meet His demands.

Debate with yourself about your expectations

Try interrogating your assumptions before allowing them to anger, frustrate, or paralyze you. Ask hard questions. Perhaps you may even want to distrust your own reactions to them. Ask yourself, Why do I respond this way? Remind yourself that in themselves expectations are neither good nor bad. Expectations are useful or destructive depending on how we think about them and how we allow them to affect our life, our relationships, and our ministry. To get over these negative reactions, learn to debate your negative thoughts about them.

Expectations, when properly understood and used, sometimes lead us to highly productive ministry. Conversely, when they are inappropriately viewed, used, or exploited, they generate frustrations, make us cynical, or mesmerize us into passive melancholy.

"Expectations are the lifeblood of ministry. What others expect of us and what we expect of ourselves determine what we will become."[12] This is how Pastor Richard P. Hansen of Palos Park, Illinois explains the positive notion that we sometimes resist or completely overlook. When properly accepted and applied, they go a long way to helping us live up to what Christ wants us to do for His kingdom. Expectations can beneficially shape our ministry. Try using these questions to examine how expectations can positively mold your efforts for Christ.

- Is my attitude and behavior Christ centered?
- What tasks do I do well, and enjoy doing?
- Do people know I genuinely want to serve God?
- Do I give myself to authentic acts of servanthood, or just merely talk about doing it?
- Do I use my gifts and graces for the kingdom?
- Do I expect more of others than of myself?
- Do I realize that conduct creates consequences?
- Do I grouse about duties I actually enjoy?

HOW TO REFOCUS
FEELINGS ABOUT EXPECTATIONS

As we have seen, the toughest, most bizarre ideas about the demands of ministry are frequently rooted in our erroneous assumptions or inaccurate feelings. Often churches and systems do not have the expectations we charge them with having. The fertile soil for such ideas may be our own need to be people pleasers. If these possibilities are even partially accurate, relief from these shackling notions starts with refocusing our feelings and continues with some reality check about what we believe about ourselves and our work for the kingdom.

Living by this standard takes us to satisfying spiritual reality much more effectively than all our attempts to please others, to fit into ecclesiastical systems, or to live up to our own expectations.

Contemporary Challenge
Realistic Ways to Cope with What Others Think

- Realize that all occupations have unique demands.
- View some expectations as useful.
- Understand that ministry presuppositions come from many sources.
- Admit that many ministry demands are homemade.
- Look inside to see if you exaggerate expectations to gain sympathy or attention.
- Discuss expectations fully with a church before accepting their call to become pastor.
- Remember that one complainer does not determine what an entire congregation believes about ministry.
- Face the fact that some ministry couples have unrealistic expectations of their churches and church members.
- Commit to please Christ, and that will be enough.
- Test all demands on ministry by what God wants done.

MARRIED TO A WOMAN WHO
LIVES BEYOND THE EXPECTATIONS
A Salute to Margaret Maxwell
by Pastor John Maxwell

A picture of me is on a table close to my wife Margaret's side of the bed. When I gave it to her a few years ago, I wrote on the bottom of it, "My greatest accomplishment was marrying you."

That wonderful event occurred on June 14, 1969. But the story really begins a couple of years earlier when we became engaged. I have kept the note Margaret wrote her parents the following day after she consented to be my wife. It read . . .

> Mom and Dad—John and I are getting married but don't get excited, not until he's out of school.
>
> We have talked about it for awhile, but last night he asked me officially. I was going to get a ring, but he is using the money to pay for the car damage . . . so, I get to wait 'til he's rich again. I know you're not surprised, and John said you could tell anyone.

Her note says it all about Margaret and me. I'm goal-oriented, and she has always been patient. I have good intentions, and she has been forgiving when I couldn't "pull them off." I've wanted to give her everything, but she has been satisfied with having me.

Ours has been a shared ministry all the way.

I graduated from college on June 1, 1969, and we were married two weeks later. On July 1 of the same year, we started our first pastorate in Hillham, Indiana. We both rolled up our sleeves and began to minister. In that small church, Margaret led the youth group, missions department, and women's organization.

Margaret took a job to support my ministry

The church leaders in the first church could only afford to pay me $80 per week. So they sat down with us and gave me permission to work outside the church. Before I could respond, Margaret stood up and said, "God has called John to be a full-time pastor, and he's going to be a great man of God. Therefore, I will work and make the extra money we need." And work she did. Margaret taught school, cleaned houses, and clerked in a jewelry store on the weekends.

Each Friday night we would take a different couple from our church out to eat. These times became special to our church family as we bonded relationally to them. Margaret would slip $20 of her own money into my hand so we could pay for the meal.

Because of her willingness to sacrifice for me and share with me, we have always been full partners in the ministry. Her commitment reminds me of one of my favorite quotes: "There is no success without sacrifice. If you sacrifice and fail to succeed, someone who follows you will have success. If you succeed without sacrifice, it is because someone who came before you paid the price." Today my ministry is a result of God's blessing and lots of sacrifice from Margaret.

Margaret lets me know she believes in me

One of the many things I appreciate about Margaret is her belief in me. At the age of seven, she asked God to give her a Christian husband. She was with me the night I publicly answered the call to preach. Immediately she bought me a beautiful book to keep a record of my messages, weddings, and funerals. The Christmas before our marriage, she had an artist draw a picture of the Good Shepherd. These gifts are precious possessions, and represent her initial support of my calling.

If Margaret is in the congregation when I speak, I try to find her immediately. When our eyes meet, she gives me "that smile" or "that nod" that says, "John, I love you." And when I am finished speaking,

Margaret's words have more weight than those of a thousand others. As I write this, I am holding a three-by-five card that contains my schedule for the day. On the bottom of the card, Margaret has written, "You are a great man of God. I love you. M.M." Those expressions of her support sustain me in these more mature years of my ministry.

Margaret has a serious commitment to our family

Her willingness to give of herself for our family has been a blessing to me and our children. Margaret is a teacher by profession. When our daughter Elizabeth was a baby, Margaret gave up a career to provide the care she felt was needed in the home. She has truly lived for us and loved us across the years.

Margaret gave me away to ministry

Her willingness to share me with the people has added great value to my ministry. Very few wives would be willing to allow their husbands the freedom to minister and travel as she has given to me. When I am gone, we spend about thirty minutes each evening talking on the phone about the events of our day. Some of the events that have occurred while I was gone include both children breaking their arms, the bad news of a staff member being diagnosed with a brain tumor, the kitchen ceiling falling because of a leak in our water pipes, and many, many more. In spite of all of this, Margaret has remained steady and released me to do ministry.

Margaret keeps growing

The area that I most respect in Margaret is her desire and ability to keep growing. I believe that when one spouse develops and grows while the other spouse stays the same, the marriage will eventually be in trouble. But Margaret has never allowed me to outgrow her.

Early in our marriage, we decided that I would not experience something exciting without her. That means that if I travel anywhere that is interesting to her, she goes with me if it is at all possible. If I attend any conference that will bring growth to me, she often attends. This commitment to each other has at times cost us financially, but it

152

has always paid off relationally. Perhaps I have outgrown some of my fellow ministers, but not my wife.

Both of us are avid readers. Several years ago, Margaret started reading my books and magazines before I read them. She marks interesting thoughts which allows me to read the material very quickly. At times she will make comments on a page such as "Talk to me about this" or "Amen." Reading the same material and experiencing the same events allows us to have common issues to discuss, and we do.

Margaret has always influenced me. I hold her opinions higher than all others. I seek her advice before I go to anyone else. I always share good news with her. Why shouldn't I? After all, Margaret is my best friend.

Pastor John C. Maxwell
Skyline Wesleyan Church
Lemon Grove, California

SEVEN KEYS FOR MAKING MINISTRY ENJOYABLE

How to Transform Pressure Points into Growth Opportunities

◇◇◇◇◇

O God, our Father,
unless You help us,
   we can see the ideal,
     but we cannot reach it;
   we can know the right,
     but we cannot do it;
   we can recognize our duty,
     but we cannot perform it;
   we can see the truth,
     but we can never wholly live by it.
O God, our Father, this day we rest our weaknesses in Your
completeness. Amen. [1]

◇◇◇◇◇

A BEGINNING PASTOR remarked to fellow students on the night of his seminary graduation, "I plan to consider every idea anyone presents as a possible priority. Then, as I sift through expectations, I'll be more alert to opportunities. This will be my way to encourage ideas from everyone in the congregation."

He is right up to a point. Four key words must be underscored, however, in his comment: "consider," "possible priority," and "sift." Viable ministry can often be strengthened by fresh perspective, spiritual creativity, and shared information from others, especially from religious nonprofessionals. Thus, a pastor and spouse may profit greatly by allowing others to inform ministry. But they must guard their responsibility to set their personal agenda for ministry and service. It is a fine line, but it can be done.

One pastoral couple in the Midwest thanked their first congregation just before they moved to their second assignment: "You people lovingly taught us about pastoring. And we are grateful. Thanks for sharing suggestions and ideas but not expecting us to be like anyone else. Thanks too for allowing our children to be children"

Another minister's wife, who lives near Lansing, Michigan told a women's group: "Your acceptance helped me tame and reinvent God's pattern for me so I could see expectations as positive forces in my life. I used to think of expectations as bars over the windows of my soul and as a ball and chain around my heart."

And a retiring clergy couple closing their ministry in the Dakotas observed: "Our last church taught us how to survive while serving. For years, the messiah trap we lived in created a spiritual distortion that we held of ourselves and God. We have learned our needs are as important to God as anyone else's."

EMPOWERING EXPECTATIONS—EVEN TOUGH ONES

To keep assumptions accurate, try formulating strategies to determine whether your expectations for ministry come from inside or from without. Many expectations are homemade and come from our own inner world. Often we are the only one in the congregation who holds them. But as long as expectations control us, our feelings of helplessness, powerlessness, and servitude will increase.

Expectations are a part of life we cannot avoid. Nor should we try. It is more useful to find ways to transform, confront, change, use, and even embrace them. Then we may even learn to welcome the reasonable expectations of others.

How inspiring, then, to understand that by choosing our responses, we powerfully shape our future ministry. At the same time, our bondage of reactionary resistance gets broken down and we are able to free ourselves from the prison of self-pity.

A giant step to growing past chafing expectations usually takes place when the focus of ministry is turned outward — outward from your feelings about things and outward to needs of people around you. Perhaps there is a lesson about ministry to be learned from an unknown psychologist's statement about married love, "Married love does not consist in gazing at each other, but in looking outward together in the same direction." Ministry enjoys increased fulfillment when we look outside ourselves in the same direction God wants His church to move.

Mother Teresa explains this idea in a poetic and prophetic way: "We wait impatiently for the paradise where God is, but we have it in our power to be in paradise with Him now; being happy with Him means:

> To love as He loves,
> To help as He helps,
> To give as He gives,
> And to serve as He serves.[2]

Why not take the initiative to reverse your negative feelings about what others think about your ministry? Then, instead of viewing these issues as intrusions on privacy or impositions on freedom, think of them as first drafts of revolutionary blueprints God is helping you design for effective ministry where you now serve.

The following strategies will help you empower the ways you choose to do ministry. These ministry exercises will contribute to your overall spiritual growth and increase the productivity of your service to Christ and His church.

Key one: become proactive

Being proactive means that you thoroughly understand your circumstances and intentionally improve situations and relationships. In applying a proactive perspective to the church, it is necessary to differentiate between what needs to be done, what others think needs to be done, and what cannot be done. Our first commitment, then, is to take initiative to do what needs to be done now.

More than diagnosis. Many people see things to be done in a church and tell someone about the need. They operate like a middle manager who thinks they improve their company by calling attention to a problem in a memo to the chief executive officer. Communicating a need and accomplishing something great for God is as different as daylight and dark.

Translated into ministry, proactivity takes the initiative to achieve some significant ministry rather than merely talking about it.

Establish priority. The capability to see new vistas of service coupled with an ability to prioritize existing expressions of ministry are two ministry skills a couple can use in the work of the church. And nearly anyone, with a little effort, can develop these talents.

Regrettably, in the haze of conflicting opinions about ministry, priorities are too often shaped by the loudest voice or the most pressing traditions.

See possibilities. An important caution, however, should be sounded about a common hindrance. Far too many ministry couples come to believe too quickly that they are at the mercy of their situation. Thus, they come to see themselves as so locked in by their limitations and other's expectations that they can do nothing effective. Their passive acceptance of despair shows in snatches of conversations: "I can't." "I must not." "If only." "They won't like it." "There is nothing I can do." "They would fire my husband if. . . ." Frustrating, nonproductive inactivity follows.

But for proactive Christian workers who view themselves as being in partnership with the Living Christ nothing is ever as hopeless as it seems at first. They know something that has eternal significance can be done in every place.

See solutions. Becoming proactive creates an intentionally optimistic confidence that dares to believe that most problems have solutions. This outlook provides a great way to be sure your ministry and your church do not become stale, boring, and dull. An example of being proactive is the new pastor's wife who, before being asked, volunteers to launch a women's ministry. This is especially helpful in a new assignment. Such a proactive stance impacts the situation with creativity, allows her gifts to be used, and adds zest to church life before subtle forces impose stereotypes on her.

Change yourself from the inside. The key idea here is that a proactive person takes initiative to make things happen.

Then their passion for Christ is stronger than outside limitations. Best-selling author Stephen R. Covey offers useful insights that apply to the pastor and his wife: "Proactive people aren't pushy. They're smart, they're value driven, they read reality, and they know what's needed." Covey continues with a challenge that can help Christian workers revolutionize their existing conditions: "The proactive approach is to change from the inside out: to be different, and by being different, to effect positive change in what's out there. I can be more resourceful, I can be more diligent, I can be more creative, I can be more cooperative."[3] Such thinking shows us how to avoid being victims of unfavorable circumstances, and provides a corrective lens for viewing ministry positively and zealously.

Take initiative. A much more proactive focus on parish ministry is needed in so much of contemporary ministry. God does not intend for your ministry to cause you frustration or outright despair. Rather, He wants you to use your creative, Christ-centered initiative to do something vital in every circumstance. God needs you to do that. He challenges you to find an important place and fill it. Stop fretting about darkness—punch holes in it. Take the initiative. Refuse to be an adversary or cynic. Find solutions rather than being locked into difficulties.

Key two: emphasize benefits and advantages

Ministry receives an unfair rap when only difficulties are discussed. Let's get our perspective straight—many ministry couples enjoy wonderful privileges and golden kingdom opportunities. Ministry always provides more meaning when viewed as an adventure instead of seeing it as a life of victimization.

Consider several satisfying advantages. More people love you than you think. More people care about you than you think. More people pray for you than you think.

List your advantages. Your list of advantages is long. In *Private Lives of Ministers' Wives,* Liz Greenbacker and Sherry Taylor publish advantages gleaned from a survey of pastors' wives (the percentage shows how pastors' wives ranked each advantage):

Ready-made friends in the church family (51 percent).
Seeing people helped by husband's ministry (25 percent).
Sharing in joys and sorrows of laity (19 percent).
Pride in husband's work (12 percent).
Members' generosity (12 percent).
Opportunity to serve with my husband (11 percent).
Meeting all kinds of people (9 percent).[4]

Satisfaction in ministry often increases when we live out the songwriter's advice, "Count your many blessings . . . and it will surprise you what the Lord has done." Maybe the words could be revised to, "Count your blessings and it will surprise you what the Lord *is doing right now.*"

A Texas pastor's wife dropped all resistance to ministry when she started considering her advantages. She rejoices that her family shares involvement in her husband's work, so that ministry has actually become a family affair. She knows her pastor/husband, though maintaining a packed calendar, has flextime so he can arrange to be present for many of the children's athletic events and parent/teacher conferences. She is grateful that he is able to build weekly times into his Day-Timer for each child. She knows their family enjoys a caring congregation of accepting friends like a large extended family. This woman said in an interview, "Even highly placed business executives or military officers when transferred to a new place do not have an edge like ours." She concluded that it helps to rejoice in what you have rather than to fret about what you think you want.

Give thanks for affirmation and support. To see beyond your problems, consider the phenomenal support so many pastors receive from so many in their congregations. Consider the affirmations and advantages Pastor David Lewis received after a Sunday morning service in his small church in North Carolina. On a particular Sunday, four believers assured him of their intercessory prayers. He was given a casserole by a new convert, received a hug from a six-year-old, was handed a note of appreciation from a Sunday School teacher, and received thanks from eight individuals for the sermon. The crowning affirmation came from an eight-year-old girl who slipped him a note which read, "I think you are special."

Express your gratitude. Though their income is likely to be much higher, no doctor, lawyer, or teacher ever fared better than pastors in fringe benefits that really count. Such satisfying support is expressed in hundreds of ways and in differing intensity in every church. But personal gratitude to God and to the people for their unique support helps keep our views of ministry in balance.

Enjoy service options. Many pastors and their families have additional advantages. In many settings, the pastor's spouse and family are free to make choices at the smorgasbord of service. Often they can choose and implement an area of ministry they enjoy most— an advantage not open to all laypersons. As a result, a pastor's wife's service can become a golden opportunity for happy, fulfilling involvement.

And there are more privileges. When a minister moves to a new place, his family finds people waiting to become instant friends.

The opportunity to represent Christ in a parishioner's life during times of joy and pain also provides a wide range of satisfactions. Such a redemptive connection produces a satisfying bond between pastor and parishioner not available to those who work in any other occupation.

Another important satisfaction suggested by a pastor's wife in Indiana is "the right to kiss the preacher anytime I want to."

Lessons from Chris. A minister's wife named Chris, who lives in the Midwest, recently worked through advantages which she had taken for granted. Her eleven-year-old son died five months ago of leukemia. Trying to make sense of his painful death, she sometimes fantasized that the boy would have had a better life if her husband had not been a pastor. Sometimes she even imagined the boy would not have been sick if his father had been in another occupation. Her questions about life and death and meaning persist, though she knows no profession could have provided a cure.

Still, she keeps asking herself, What field of work would have given my husband more time with his son? What occupation would have given us a more loving network than we experienced from the congregation? At the end of her questioning, she realized in a wonderful new way that ministry offered many advantages that other people seldom experience in their times of loss. Finally she concluded that it was a positive providence that allowed them to be in their particular setting at such a trying time in their lives.

Key three: check your perspective

Plant yourself in another's perspective so you may see the world through their eyes. Face the reality that expectations are like a double-edged sword. The more you expect, the more others expect of you. On the contrary, fanning faith in others often creates a live-and-let-live style that is attractive and satisfying.

After years of frustration, one New England pastor's wife wrote: "I try not to expect too much of others. I am even working on not expecting too much from myself. Then I am surprised by how much they do and how much I accomplish. This new way is a thousand times better than the old way."

Stop locking others in. Did you catch the freedom the New England pastor's wife allows herself and others? Any fair-minded person can see that expectations work two ways. This pastor's wife has learned that planting seeds of faith in oneself and others and watching the plant grow on God's timetable is fun and gratifying.

Conversely, unrealistic commitments, deadlines, and demands for self or others can be disappointing or even damaging to the cause of Christ.

Try a reality check. Try the following experiment to clarify your expectations quotient. Make a list of what you expect from others. Next, make another list of everything you expect people of the congregation to provide for you and your family. And finally, make a third list of everything you expect to do for individuals in the congregation. Do you find balance between the lists?

Now do a reality check. What percentage of entries on your list is possible? Does anyone in any other profession receive what you expect to receive? An even more sobering question must be considered — can you possibly do what you expect of yourself? Could you really live by the standards you set for others? Could it be that some expectations are self-imposed monsters?

One problem is that what we expect is simply not realistic or possible or doable. Too often expectations are sheer fantasy that do not happen in real life. Many expectations on all three lists are not possible for self or others when levels of spiritual intensity, life-experiences, lack of training, available funds, and adequate time are factored in. To expect the impossible is to sandpaper relationships and multiply our own stress.

Key four: let God empower you for change

For some unexplainable reason, many Christian leaders fear change without seeing its possibilities. Perhaps this happens because rapid change causes inner conflict when we do not know how to assimilate it. But every pastor and wife must deal with change because it is a constant, inside and outside the church. No one escapes it. Everything seems to be in flux, or perhaps revolution would be a more accurate word. But those who focus ministry on unrealistic expectations—theirs or others'—tend to lock their thinking into yesterday's way of doing things. This leads them to question whether God has any new answers for new problems. Meanwhile, much to our surprise, God is often already doing a new thing among us.

Change is here to stay. Failing to respond to change may be a way of fooling ourselves into believing it will go away. It won't. It's here to stay. The only realistic response is to learn to use change and see how God works through it. For this reason and others, ministry requires us to creatively use change, something much different from passive reluctant or even hostile resistance.

Draw on old resources. Reinventing ministry for these times requires us to draw on God's unlimited resource. We know, don't we, that God wants the Gospel's revolutionary power taken to the front lines of modern life? And we know that He will go with us. His resources become more obvious and available when we intentionally trust a higher wisdom and draw strength from His supernatural empowerment.

Devotional writer John Powell reminds us that "the power of God is ready to enlighten our darkness, mend our brokenness, fill our emptiness, brace our courage, strengthen our twistedness, and create in us hearts of love." He continues, "The connection to all this power is prayer."[5] The psalmist assures us: "The Lord is near to all who call upon Him" (Ps. 145:18).

God never intended for His work to be done with our energy, spirit, and insight alone. Rather, we are able to accomplish the incredible achievement God wants by looking up and taking His strength: "I lift up my eyes to the hills—where does my help come from? My help comes from the Lord, the Maker of heaven and earth" (Ps. 121:1-2).

God enables us to use change creatively at the precise point where we have given our best efforts. This is good news. We no longer have to meet every need we encounter with our limited resources because we have His power.

God uses change agents. Intriguingly, a pastor or pastor's wife who responds to nuances of the Father's direction is a person God uses. Then, God multiplies our impact as Jesus multiplied the boy's bread and fish. God expands our feeble strength. He makes us adequate to face anything. Then, we are abundantly satisfied, as were the hungry people who ate the miraculous fish and bread.

Competent ministry that leans on God is like that—it blesses and nourishes those who give it and those who receive it. To experience this supernatural energy moves us beyond resisting an overly demanding life to the radiant joy of being used to fulfill a lofty purpose for God.

That kind of living makes it possible for us to live beyond expectations—ours and others. It leads us to a high level of satisfying spiritual fulfillment where we enjoy the joys of commitment, creativity, imagination, and achievement.

Key five—free yourself from stoic self-pity

It easier to be gloomy than hopeful. Our U.S. national psyche is so scarred by negativism and skepticism that we even undermine optimism in children and youth with absurd advice like "Don't get your hopes up" or "Don't get too big for your britches" or "Don't expect to rise above your upbringing."

It has even become common for mature adults to respond to another's greeting, "What a beautiful day!" by saying, "It won't last" or "The TV weatherman predicts a storm for this afternoon." Such negative responses carry over into ministry, so we frequently expect the worst and get it in some self-fulfilling ways.

Conceivably, this might be a reaction to keep us at arm's length from life's hurts. Such reasoning supports the fallacious idea that a minister's spouse and family will never be disappointed if they don't expect too much. These sullen moods place a lid of limitation on everything we do. There must be something better.

New lives for old. To remedy these feelings we must consider the central reality of Christianity and then see our part in it. New life for old is the Gospel's thrilling message. Miraculous conversions are possible. Ailing marriages can be healed. Shattered lives can be restored. Addictions can be broken. And love cures hate. This means, of course, that Christ-quality lives are available regardless of yesterday's scars.

Christianity is God's good news even though some contemporary disciples act as if it is bad news. Like being able to see the smallest letters on the last line of an eye doctor's chart, corrective lenses may be needed to see God's supernatural in the minutiae of life. But, whether we see it or not, the last line of letters on the doctor's chart is always the same. Christianity's bottom line is always dependable too — God works in the details of life.

To resist the infection that self-pity always brings, we must apply Winston Churchill's admonition to ministry, "Never give up. Never, never, give up."[6] It's reliable counsel for every believer — there is nothing to go back to and nothing to give in to.

Follow Mother Teresa's advice. An unbelievable cure for self-pity can be discovered in Mother Teresa's solid advice: "Keep giving Jesus to your people, not by works, but by your example, by being in love with Jesus, by radiating His holiness and spreading His fragrance everywhere you go." She continues with this "aha" sentence: "Accept whatever He gives and give whatever He takes with a smile."[7]

Try turning duty into delight. Affirm that God is greater than our pessimistic moods and our most confusing frustrations or the tempestuous turbulence around us.

Key six: become a person of quality and depth

Ministry, if we allow it, easily becomes a dull, routine, discouraging struggle, or irrational image building. Becoming a quality person in ministry, on the contrary, means you are pleasing to God and at peace with your soul and useful to the people you serve. It means excellence of character that only Christ provides. It means your own spirituality is genuine and growing and natural. It means being holy in a this-world-kind-of-way. It means you are joyously true to God and represent Him attractively with your life and service. It means you are enjoying your marriage and happily involved in your family. It means you give a little more effort than others in everything you attempt because of who you represent.

Live a Christ-saturated life. Becoming a quality servant of Jesus means infinitely more than living up to some human game plan. It is well-lived life—so controllers in the church might think you are doing what they expect, but you know you are living in relationship to Christ that is so much more. It means you find incredible fulfillment in wholehearted kingdom commitments.

In the process, you discover inexpressible joy in living a Christ-saturated life. You do ministry wholeheartedly as unto Christ. Such quality persons in ministry have inquiring minds and a mature dedication to the cause of Christ. They refuse to view ministry as victimization. Such a Christ-indwelt believer prays with the psalmist, "Let me know that You are always present, in every atom of my life. Let me surrender myself until I am utterly transparent. Let my words be rooted in honesty and my thoughts be lost in Your light, Unnameable God, my essence, my origin, my life-blood, my home."[8]

What about limelight? Quality people sometimes intentionally move out of the limelight. Maybe more Christian workers need to hear self-help author Eugene Kennedy's warning, "Standing at the center of things can create whirling currents that sweep everything around us to destruction."[9]

This concept becomes more biblically focused when one says with John the Baptist, "This is the assigned moment for Jesus to move into the center, while I slip off to the sidelines" (John 3:30, TM).

Quality people see to it that Jesus is kept as the centerpiece of their service for Christ. They know ministry is always fouled or frustrated when anyone usurps the Lord's place, even in small ways. This leads to a challenging question: Could it be that some who complain about the fishbowl existence of ministry secretly enjoy being in the limelight?

It's a beautiful life after all. Being a quality person means living an attractive and satisfying life for Christ. The quality Christian leader orders his life by Edwin Markham's poetic lines:

> Ah, great it is to believe the dream
> As we stand in youth by the starry stream;
> But a greater thing it is to fight life through,
> And say at the end, "The dream is true!"[10]

Try this prescription for living such a quality life. Share the good news of Christ as you go. Scatter blessing as you live out the details of your faith. Give a lovely witness with a few kind words to a clerk, waitress, tollbooth collector, or cab driver. Such a Christ-quality life is a delightful way to live that takes us above and beyond any imposed or implied directives from others.

Key seven: commit to a holy character

Anyone can grow a Christ-exalting character with God's help. Often we assume all other believers are involved in a process of allowing Christ to shape them into His image. Such assumptions may be completely unfounded or downright false.

The young pastor's wife asked her more mature mentor, "Why is being holy so important in this work?"

The veteran pastor's wife answered with a question, "Are *you* seeking in every possible way to be like Christ?"

To ask the second question instead of giving an answer is not rhetorical or tricky. Rather, it is a question that presses the issue accurately. Too often those who resist forming a holy character are those who need it most.

Personal wholeness affects achievement. One pastor's wife who lives in the Southwest, commented in a support group, "When I am spiritually dry I become more touchy about expectations of our congregation and my husband." What a valuable insight. Apparently there is some important connection between holiness and wholeness. A whole person usually sees expectations from a different perspective than others. For example, they may see expectations as people crying out for their help.

To enrich your life and increase your effectiveness, abandon all substitutes for a holy character and pattern your life after Christ. Many of us know from experience that a shallow religious professional veneer is never a satisfying substitute for authentic Christianity. But being whole is the source of stamina and satisfaction for everything else. That is why a commitment to allow God to make you like Jesus nourishes every dimension of your life and ministry.

Christ-centered living produces joy. Consider the incredibly rich benefits of a holy life. Authenticity replaces playacting. Spiritual power uproots manipulation. Then important issues stretch your soul, so you no longer feel pressed to live up to unrealistic expectations others devise for you. And as you authentically become like your Lord, you discover amazing satisfaction in your service for Him.

Maybe pastors and their wives need to speak out more about their own inner life discoveries. Maybe we need to share from our experience what we already know about spiritual development. We know holistic spirituality makes ministry magnetic. We know no one can become Christlike by osmosis or by accident. We know personal spirituality provides inner energy that fuels commitment. And it helps us understand that service, selflessness, friendship, and love are the ultimate values of every well-lived life.

Thus, when you are confused by contradictory expectations from so many sources, remember the one who attracts others to Christ is one who pours contempt on all their pride and achievements. That is something quite different than syrupy charisma. Those who effectively attract others to Christ are those who allow the resurrected Lord to mold them into heroes and heroines of this Christian adventure.

Connect with Jesus

Author Chuck Swindoll summarizes the essentials for developing such an attractive character:

> What we need first and foremost are intimate moments with the Savior . . . time spent all alone with Him, watching His model, listening to His counsel, feeling His touch. We need some way to connect our temporal world with His eternal perspective.[11]

The story of Easter helps us unravel our confusing expectations — those we have for ourselves and those others have for us. Remember the first Easter events? As early Christians came to the tomb, nearly everyone expected something different than what happened. In the middle of contradictory expectations and apparent catastrophe, the resurrected Lord shows His early disciples the way He wants them to live. He gives them much more than a lecture about duty and instructions about morality. Instead, He makes good on His promise to provide supernatural power to produce a steadfast character that He can use to build His kingdom (Matt. 28:18-20).

Try giving more attention to the many ways Jesus wants to make you like Him. Think of the miracles at work in you. He forgives when we misuse our influence. He heals scalding memories from our past. He gives us another chance when we goof. The living Lord energizes and fortifies us at the deepest level of our inner life.

Through us, He demonstrates what an incredible impact a holy character makes on others. And at the same time, He shows us the delightful serendipity of how much a Christ-saturated life enriches those who live it.

CONTEMPORARY CHALLENGE
Seven Keys to Empower Ministry

- Be proactive.
- Emphasize benefits and advantages.
- Lower your expectations.
- Get a grip on God's empowerment.
- Free yourself from stoic self-pity.
- Become a person of quality and depth.
- Commit to a Christlike character.

MARRIED TO ONE WHO
MAKES MINISTRY FUN
A Salute to Margi Galloway
by Pastor Dale Galloway

Margi Galloway is my ideal for a pastor's wife because she is free and makes ministry fun! She is free to be herself and to become everything God has created her to become. When it comes to Margi, what you see is what she is. No games, no pretenses; she is genuine, open, and an authentic Christian. Margi is like a rose blooming in unique beauty where she has been planted.

From the day we fell in love, I have admired her, believed in her, and valued her servant's heart for ministry. Yet I am continually amazed at her personal spiritual growth and what she is accomplishing today in ministry. The new gifts that keep developing and blooming are God's special gifts to our shared ministry.

Margi and I are a team in both marriage and ministry in every sense of the word:

- We cheer each other.
- We encourage each other.
- We help each other.
- We compliment each other.
- We cover for each other.
- We are loyal to each other.
- We share everything with each other.
- We complete each other.
- But most of all, we love each other.

Twenty-one years ago, when we launched our New Hope Community Church dream in a desolate drive-in theater in Portland, Oregon it was a very humble beginning. On October 14, 1972 — without people, without money, without financial backing — Margi and I, hand in hand, climbed on top of the snack shack roof at the 82nd Street Drive-In Theater and started a church "for the unchurched thousands." Margi sang and I preached. Oh, yes, before each service together we would clean the junk off the field from the Saturday night before.

Margi was the first person to catch my God-given New Hope vision. During these twenty-two years of ministry together, she has done whatever it took to make the ministry happen. You name it, and she has done it. Her willing heart is an inspiration to everyone and a special blessing to me.

Margi is a public leader

Today, with more than 6,000 members, Margi meets weekly with our ministry staff and plans our Sunday morning celebration services. She knows exactly what I would like to see happen in our seeker-friendly, Christian-nourishing services.

As our worship leader, Margi is extremely gifted in leading our congregation into the presence of the Lord in a way in which even unchurched people feel comfortable and are inspired.

As a women's leader, Margi gives strong gifts of creativity and leadership to exciting events for them. Hundreds of women testify to the impact these events make on their lives.

Margi helps me implement the dream

Around the church on a daily basis, with her office next to mine, Margi often acts as my eyes and ears. Often when I'm off thinking about some lofty dream, she nourishes the reality of what's happening with our staff and parishioners. At times, when I get too far out front with the vision, she tells me to slow down and wait for others.

In recruiting and building the staff over the years, I have learned the validity of Margi's input. I must confess I have not always listened to her intuition. Those have been the times I have made serious mistakes. Today, I never consider adding anyone to the ministry staff without asking her advice and taking it.

Margi loves people

In our church family, Margi is much loved by many. She has the rare ability to give friendship to many people and, in return, enjoys many warm personal friendships. Along with this, her enthusiasm for life is a large contributor to the positive, loving atmosphere of our church. Margi accepts people right where they are.

Margi forgives easily

A priceless gift that Margi brings to everyday life in the ministry and at home is her positive attitude. I have never known her to have a bad attitude for more than a few hours. Whenever she gets hurt in ministry, as we all do, she quickly gets over it and moves ahead.

Margi makes home special

Margi works hard to make home a happy retreat for our family. My testimony and our children's testimony is that we love to be at home.

Birthdays are celebrated at our house, not by the day, but by the week. Margi makes our family times during the holidays unforgettable experiences. Even though both of us work long hours at the church, our children know that when push comes to shove, they have priority in our lives over the church. We have made it a habit to make sure we have family vacation times. Margi excels in being a good listener to the children, and they respond positively to this. We are so thankful that our daughter Ann, age twenty, and our son Scott, seventeen, are committed Christians and really love our church.

A personal note

I find it humorous to see Margi become more task-oriented as the years go by, while her husband is becoming less so. I guess we really have influenced one another as we have worked together in ministry.

The greatest joy of my life is to see what God is doing through this gracious woman and how he is using her life to bless and help so many people in our combined ministry.

Pastor Dale E. Galloway
New Hope Community Church
Portland, Oregon

8

UNTANGLING MODERN MINISTRY MYTHS
Embracing and Using New Realities

◇◇◇◇◇

Lord Jesus, King of Your church,
  Give us minds made wise by Your guidance.
  Give us hearts made warm by Your grace.
  Give us wills made determined by Your salvation.
  Give us lips made courageous by Your truth.
  Help us make the Lord Christ known to the simple,
  seekers, wayfarers, and saints. Amen.

◇◇◇◇◇

WHAT IS THE MOST BEWILDERING contradiction or myth you have ever faced in ministry?" That's the question I asked forty ministers' wives.

At first they struggled with the question—admittedly an issue not raised every day. In our discussion group we defined "myth" as a belief that is accepted uncritically. In the give and take of the discussion the group decided to form a growth exercise around half-truths that shape lots of thinking about ministry these days.

Something like a dentist drilling too deep, a raw emotional nerve seemed exposed. As we went around the group, ministers' wives began revealing and weeping and debunking "myths," "mirages," and "misconceptions" that complicate their lives. Fifteen myths were identified in that discussion:

- The church is losing its grip.
- Church members will always be nice.
- Someone else controls my life.
- I'm expected to be a super-saint.
- The church should be my satisfaction machine.
- Involvement may wear me out.
- Everything is worse in society now
- Ministry cheats a pastor's family.
- Curiosity and gossip will destroy me.
- A grumbler speaks for everyone.
- Detachment is desirable.
- Circumstances determine contentment.
- Key people are permanent.
- Loneliness is inevitable.
- Pastors work harder than persons in other occupations.

WHAT IS
A MYTH?

A myth, by definition, is a faulty deduction or flawed assumption. Thus, myths certainly make an unstable foundation on which to build a life or ministry. In light of this definition, it is important that no pastor or spouse shape his or her life, ravage their contentment, or wreck their effectiveness by mere legends.

In dealing with myths, it is wise to test every half-truth or tradition against Scripture, moral absolutes, contemporary reality, and the potential impact of one's influence. That being true, it is critically important to frequently reexamine all assumptions—our own and other's—to gauge their accuracy against Scripture as well as their congruity with experience.

MIRAGES,
MISCONCEPTIONS, AND MYTHS

Myths, like aggravating, quick-growing weeds, are not unique to the church. They are a part of life which grows out of unsupported assumptions about any subject in almost every setting and occupation.

Ministry myths usually start in some long-forgotten situation and produce more heat than light. The wives introduced in the opening of this chapter felt that many ministry myths imprisoned them as emotional hostages. And they believe that much of the time ministry myths are ingrained in notions that are more folklore than fact.

People who are willing to defend and perpetuate myths attend nearly every church. Members of this curious club come from many levels of the church — lay leaders, common folks in the pews, pastors, their families, ecclesiastic superiors, and even civic leaders. They are often among the best-intended people in the church.

Myths sometimes start as mere exaggerations. Then, like an outbreak of measles, they turn into fascinating legends about embellished practices out of someone's past as they are retold over and over across generations. All these misconceptions usually sound somewhat believable because they contain a remnant of accuracy, fragmentary information, or half-truth.

Myths also start when one person universalizes his own experience and begins to believe his experience should be reproduced in everyone's ministry. Remember the story of the blind man and the elephant — every person's experience is part of the whole but never the whole. For example, one congregation firmly believes a pastor's wife should preach in her husband's absence because one did it once.

These misconceptions often are rooted in so-called traditions that actually grew from an event that happened only once or twice. One woman married to a pastor hit the target when she observed, "Anything the church does more than twice becomes a tradition."

Some myths about persons and practices in ministry are sincerely believed, though untested. This creates legends that are handed down from one generation to another. And they were apparently easier for pastors' families to accept or change when the pace of change in society was slower.

Regrettably, myths are often unconsciously used to sustain the status quo, or as a refusal to acknowledge new environments where ministry must be done in new ways, or as an emotional attachment to an overly comfortable past. Many are accepted as true without considering their human impact, especially for a pastor's wife or family.

WHY WORK TO
UNDERSTAND MYTHS?

We discuss myths here with the hope that exposure to clear reason will lower anxiety and frustration. We have no desire to create more harangues about the state of the church or to confuse women who serve at their pastor/husband's side. Rather, our goal is to relieve frustration and underscore the incredible possibilities in the new realities — to offer a resolution of problems and pressures.

In fact, in discussing these issues, we seek to restate our recurring theme once more: We salute the devotion and affirm the commitment of all ministry couples. We wish to encourage positive progress as readers see new challenges that grow out of a reexamination and modification of traditional myths, attitudes, and assumptions.

We must realize that no outside force, agency, or organizational structure will help anyone do this. Consequently, each clergy couple must accept the challenge to determine what is lasting and what is passing. They must determine for themselves the difference between the vital and the trivial. They must choose what to hold with tenacity and what to relinquish.

Though working through these issues may be demanding, time consuming, or even frustrating, it is worthwhile because it leads to strengthening your own faith and expanding your influence in the church. And the most captivating, magnetic qualities for Christian leaders — authenticity and integrity — will grow out of the process.

Our myth list, for reasons of limited space, is illustrative and not exhaustive. Our choice of assumptions is thus somewhat arbitrary. Every reader can easily think up his/her own list.

MYTH: THE CHURCH IS LOSING ITS GRIP.
"Nothing is like it used to be, I think the church is losing her saltiness."

Reality: Every generation must take ministry to the front lines of their setting and culture.

This myth assumes the church must get back to some special golden hours in her past, whenever that was. This well-accepted, lofty legend calls the church backward and not forward. It aggrandizes a time that may not have really been as special as we remember it being.

Throughout history, many long-forgotten Reformers mistakenly tried to revitalize the church by taking her back to a specific season. Their largely ineffective goal was to restore some golden era that more closely resembled the time and practices of Luther or Calvin or Wesley. In reality, however, the real Reformers applied the principles of faith to the problems of their time.

That means a hard question needs to be asked and answered. If the historic greats lived in our time, would they deal with the same issues in the same way? Perhaps God wants the church in every age to go forward rather than backward. That means the authentic spirit of the contemporary pioneer takes the church forward by asking what Jesus wants done in His world and church now. It is the commitment of the pioneer to the realities of faith applied to the contemporary setting that needs to be renewed rather than a return to another time and another place. Isn't that exactly what Luther, Calvin, and Wesley did in their time? They called the church forward rather than backward—forward to become a vital New Testament force for righteousness in their own time and circumstance.

A similar regression to the past on a lesser scale sometimes happens in a local congregation when they long to get back to when Pastor So-and-So was there. Or they may decide to go back to the '50s or the '60s or the '70s without much serious thought about why.

Though well-intended, going back to a glorious past never works well because the past cannot be repeated and the present has never happened before. And at the same time we can be sure that everything significant in the church did not happen yesterday, last year, or in the last century. The same God who gave the church a glorious past wants to give her a productive present and an exciting future. One church leader accurately remarked, "The Holy Spirit is Jesus in the present tense."

For a pastor's wife, the past should be viewed as a time from which to draw strength but not to duplicate. The principles and commitments that Bible women, great women of history, and strong spiritual women of the last generation used to guide their lives must be rediscovered and lived out in the present. Those principles and commitments must be dressed in contemporary clothing, applied to current issues and used to overcome obstacles that are unique to our time.

It is doubtful that if Susanna Wesley lived in our time she would order her life now the way she did then. However, studying her life story makes one believe she would see to it that the Christian faith was real for herself, her family, and the people of her parish—in whatever generation she lived. Consider this paraphrase for modern pioneers from Eugene H. Peterson: "God's grace is a lever that uses obstructions as fulcrums to move mountains."[1]

MYTH: CHURCH MEMBERS WILL ALWAYS BE NICE.

"Church people are sometimes almost cruel in their reactions to our family."

Reality: Human beings sometimes disappoint you.

All God's children do not always act like angels. Don't expect it. Anyone who ministers to human beings will sometimes be disappointed and shocked by those they serve. Of course, everyone agrees that complete honesty, integrity, and no doublespeak are how believers are supposed to behave. But injustice and unfair dealings are frequently found in the church. And if lack of fairness is going to be your crutch, you will find yourself hobbling throughout all your ministry.

As beginners, most clergy couples start ministry assuming they will work with saints. A surprise soon sets in, however, when they discover that church members are seldom better or worse than the common run of people. In fact, some churches successfully evangelize large numbers of dysfunctional folks who bring big problems to church with them. For these reasons and more, the church is usually a microcosm of the entire population. Consequently, everyone in the church will not always treat you fairly—they probably can't or won't.

What does this mean for a pastor's wife? It means to expect duplicity and be surprised by those who do not practice it. It means that gossip should be out of order in the church, but no one should be shocked when it shows up. It means some Christian people are more unprincipled than we could imagine. It means you should not be surprised by anything, but nothing is gained by repeating over and over, "Christians don't act that way." Physicians are not surprised by sickness, and pastors and their spouses should not be surprised by sin. The reality is, believers shouldn't act the way they do but they sometimes do.

You can help preserve your own sense of balance if you do not expect too much. Better to be surprised by goodness than to be disappointed by its absence. It is freeing to keep reminding yourself that the Father is in charge of judgment. He promised He would fairly determine rewards—and He will.

An experienced pastor's wife in Maine found peace for herself when she said, "I always try to give the people as much slack as I want them to give me on a bad day." Perhaps the best way to practice the golden rule is to pray, "Help me to be merciful to others even as You are merciful to me."[2]

MYTH: SOMEONE ELSE CONTROLS MY LIFE.
"We want to control our own lives like everyone else."

Reality: Either you take charge of your life or it will be out of control.

As long as a clergy couple thinks some sinister force controls their lives, they will experience continuous confusion and chaos. The problem is generally not someone else's control, but no control. Though we think that others have charge of our lives, the supposed controllers likely think only occasionally about our problems. Nearly everyone, including lay church leaders, have difficulty trying to see anything through another's eyes—especially a pastor's wife's concerns or priorities.

They do know, however, that their own problems are sometimes about to sink them. They may be desperately trying to hold an empty marriage together and to make a living for their families. They may even feel alienated from their kids and worry about their own health. They may sometimes be aware that you need their help with housing, salary, and affirmation, but the emotional and financial needs of their own families have a higher priority.

This myth of someone else being in control shows when a clergy couple says, "Can't they see what they are doing to us?" The likely answer is "No, they can't see because they never thought about it."

This myth comes into full bloom when a clergy couple says, "If only we had fifty dollars more a month, our lives would be so much less complicated. Why can't they see that?" The reality: They should, but they don't. Most people outside the ministry don't understand your pressure points.

Most people, even spiritually motivated lay leaders, are busy trying to keep their work in balance, to make ends meet, to keep their families together, and to enjoy a quality life. They do not have much time, energy, or imagination left for thinking about what is happening in the pastor's family or marriage.

These realities mean a pastor and spouse need to take control of their own lives. In an ultimate sense, no one else can determine the quality of your life or the degree of your satisfaction. This means a clergy couple needs to plan for their future, finance their needs, center on keeping their family in loving relationship, keep their home and vocation in balance, and live a Christ-saturated life.

Some useful alternative to the myth has to be found that will allow you to take control of your destiny. The question is how to change the control myth in our heads.

Officials in the congregation will usually respond positively when you state your needs in clear but nonaggressive ways. Sometimes a clergy couple has to provide income supplement for their family—but nonclergy families sometimes do that too. I know a young doctor who took extra work at a hospital emergency room in the beginning hard-scrabble days of his medical practice. I know a young professor who worked two nights per week as an auditor at a motel when he started his teaching. And all of us know two-income families that take extra work to maintain their chosen standard of living.

Take charge of your own life, now.

MYTH: I'M EXPECTED TO BE A SUPER-SAINT.

"Why can't they accept my humanness?"

Reality: Our ideal is Christlikeness.

What do we mean by "ideal," and by whose standards? These days there is no such thing as the ideal pastor's wife, if there ever was. But people in the church sometimes slip back into old ways of thinking. And so do we.

In place of making indignant comments, carrying placards, and lobbying for your rights, why not be your own best self for God—genuinely Christian, happy, involved, obedient to the will of the Father, and involved in satisfying ways in the church? These qualities produce an attractiveness that helps free others to be their own best selves, and often draws people to Christ and to your husband's ministry. Then everybody wins.

The real issue is not to buy into anyone's stereotypes—not even your own—about the ideal pastor's wife. The more satisfying way to deal with this is to be an authentic Christian and not a mere appendage to your husband's ministry. Henry Ford wisely observed, "You can't build a reputation on what you are going to do. It's what you do that matters."

People inside the church and outside the church will accept and even love you for being your own best self. And such a life always pleases God. The priorities for such a life are "Thee first" rather than "me first."

**MYTH: THE CHURCH SHOULD BE
MY SATISFACTION MACHINE.**

"The church's decision-makers never think of my feelings about anything."

Reality: God has not assigned you a happiness machine.

Try unplugging your mental satisfaction machine. Too many clergy couples are overly concerned about what ministry can do for them. The real issue, however, is what they can do for ministry. God never intended for the church to become your satisfaction machine. Satisfaction is a by-product of effective service.

Many in ministry long for, and some expect, heavenly working conditions, congenial church members and neighbors, lay leaders with enormous energy and lofty commitments, no conflicts, no consequences of people's sin, and God's blessing all rolled into one. For some hard to understand reason, some pastors and their spouses expect the whole world to care for them — sort of an imperial standing with the divine rights of a king or queen among the people of God. Someone called this "a craving for celebrity status." God has something else in mind. He intends for pastors and spouses to experience something significantly superior to a monarch's sovereignty. He offers anointing for service.

When we think about this myth on a deeper, logical level we realize that some of the strongest churches are made up of new converts who are not accustomed to churchly ways nor are they interested in treating us as anything special. By the very nature of the pastoral relationship with people, a minister is to be a servant and never to be a member of a "let's pretend" royalty.

In our hearts, we know satisfaction never comes to us when we stalk it. But when we start in the opposite direction it often follows us. Try selfless service, take on kingdom responsibility, embrace the cross, and fulfillment will follow you all the days of your life.

In ministry, satisfaction comes from the strangest sources at the most unexpected times. But let's keep remembering that church was never intended by its Founder to be anyone's satisfaction machine. Genuine satisfaction comes as a serendipity of selfless service.

MYTH: INVOLVEMENT MAY WEAR ME OUT.

"I would be worn out if I got too busy in the church."

Reality: Active involvement in the kingdom produces personal spiritual conditioning.

Elsewhere in this book, we have strongly recommended that a pastor's wife set her own pace and determine her agenda for involvement in the life of the church. Over and over we defend her right to choose her areas of service and the intensity of her responsibilities. But to please Christ and to be a balanced Christian, every believer, including ministers' spouses, must do some significant and satisfying kingdom service.

It is easy, however, to conclude that helping others makes you tired and wears you out. Such a notion is a lie of the enemy. Written into the creation of our soul is the reality that lasting fulfillment comes from being involved in a cause that is bigger than we are.

Far too many Christian leaders are so spiritually inactive, they have no stamina to face special demands that come their way. The Gospel is a cause which gives us the wonderful weariness explained by a woman in the civil rights march to Montgomery, "My body am tired, but my soul am rested."

Lately we are coming to understand that pastors and spouses need to give their lives away in order to find meaning. However, to serve as Christ served means we do more than a job. All this requires a supernatural energizing if one is to serve effectively. Such enablement comes as we try to put Richard Foster's beautiful prayer into practice: "Teach me to see only what You see, to say only what You say, to do only what You do. Help me, Lord, to work resting and to pray resting."[3]

MYTH: EVERYTHING IS WORSE IN SOCIETY NOW.
"Why is ministry so hard these days?"

Reality: Bad times provide great opportunities for the Gospel.

Every generation seems to think their world is worse than earlier generations experienced. Of course, we have carloads of evidence to make us believe things are desperate and getting worse. But because the whole world seems bent on destroying itself does not mean that your church cannot be a fellowship of salt and leaven and light in your location.

Surprisingly, surveys show there is a high satisfaction rate among women married to ministers. Apparently some families are enjoying their work. Some ministry marriages are thriving. Some churches are helping lots of people find the Savior. Somebody must be doing something right. Eugene Peterson gives wise advice about our contemporary situation: "Hope is a sturdy virtue that doesn't collapse under despairing opinion polls."[4]

While no thoughtful person would underestimate the spiritual and moral warfare around us, the worst of times have often been the time when God gave revival and blessing through His faithful remnant. If we believe that God sometimes uses secular desperation for His own purposes, this could be our golden hour.

Lately I have come to realize that whether these are the best or worst of times, these are the only times we have for serving God. None of us has the choice to serve in the last century or the next generation. Wishing it were easier does not make it so, nor do we defeat the enemy by retreating from the front lines. If we want our lives to count, wishing or worrying or deserting are not real options.

Thus, this is the only time we will ever have to come out of our shell and maximize our opportunities and achieve something useful for God. In all of human history, no one has ever faced our unique challenges. Before we were born or knew anything about today's difficulties, God had plans for people like us to take the Gospel of Jesus Christ into the problems of the twenty-first century. Fulfilling that mission Christ has planned for our setting produces meaning beyond our comprehension.

MYTH: MINISTRY CHEATS A PASTOR'S FAMILY.

"Our children don't have the same opportunities other families have."

Reality: Ministry can enrich your family.

This widely discussed myth suggests that pastors' children are disadvantaged or cheated because of a life in ministry. Let's admit it. Raising a family is a challenge for anyone these days. Regardless of occupation, we all face the pressures of secularism, modernity, and sin. But raising great ministry families can be done.

At least four important issues need to be considered:

• **Uniqueness.** Distinct advantages and unique challenges are always present in ministry families. But these issues are no better or worse than those of other families, just different.

• **Family priority.** God is not obligated to take care of a pastor's family that is neglected so the parents have more time or energy for ministry. Parental neglect, even for lofty reasons, is still parental neglect. And neglect harms children, robs parents, and cripples society.

• **The family of God.** In most settings, the people of God will help a pastor and wife raise their children by being an extended surrogate family to them. This relationship can be much like the three-generational families that were common before the population became so mobile, when all lived nearby and child rearing reached across generations to children from their grandparents, uncles, aunts, and even cousins. The church will love your family like an extended family, if you allow them to do so.

• **Consequences.** Poor parenting and good parenting produce lifelong consequences whether parents are in ministry or not. Pastors would do everyone a great favor if they built guidance for Christian parenting into their ministry strategies. Clergy couples could also be of tremendous help to the church by modeling godly parenting.

All four of these issues impact the privileges and the effectiveness of raising a family in ministry.

MYTH: CURIOSITY AND GOSSIP WILL DESTROY ME.

"People always criticize us."

Reality: All talk is not destructive.

Criticism often causes frustration and even anger, even though it probably won't do you much lasting harm. But thousands before you have lived through gossip and curiosity without suffering permanent damage. Try thinking of people's talk about your family as an expression of their interest in you.

Try to differentiate between injurious gossip and inquisitiveness. Common people, for some mysterious reason, are curious about how public people live. Such curiosity is what makes a TV program like "Lifestyles of the Rich and Famous" so popular. This is what makes people pay to take cruises along the intracoastal waterway in the Fort Lauderdale area to see where celebrities live. This curiosity makes tabloid journalism immensely profitable. Interestingly, when otherwise normal people are asked why they have this curiosity, they reply, "Because!"

People have a similar interest in their pastor and his family. As a result, church members sometimes seem overly inquisitive or even snoopy. Apparently they are curious to know if their spiritual leaders are flesh-and-blood human beings. One pastor's wife, obviously pregnant with her third child, laughingly said, "Some church people think we get our children from a mail-order catalog."

In the confusion swirling around this myth, our own concepts about curiosity, meddling, criticism, and interference get mixed up in our attitudes toward the people we serve. Admittedly, it may be difficult to realize that being inquisitive is different from being a scandalmonger. But such interest and curiosity from those you serve should be expected, and sometimes even welcomed.

Why not let people in the congregation know you are grateful for their attention? View their interest as flattering. Since the public spotlight is never completely turned off, you must learn to live with it or maybe even enjoy it. Laugh about it. And show love to people in the process.

When people's interest turns to criticism, as it sometimes does, look inside at your attitude and look outside to see if their talk contains even a small degree of truth. If the answer is yes, correct yourself. If no, pass it off as being the work of a misguided friend or a busybody. It is usually senseless to try to run down a rumor because it is so elusive. Living your life in a way that pleases Christ silences most reasonable critics, and the others won't be satisfied no matter what you do.

Like an airline pilot's checklist, use these six questions to make criticism useful:

(1) Consider a critic's intention — is it to help or harm?

(2) Does the criticism contain an element of truth?

(3) Will careful consideration of the criticism draw you closer to God and/or closer to your mate?

(4) Can you use this criticism to clarify your mission, goals, and purposes?

(5) Can you use this specific criticism to positively impact your perspective about yourself and your practice of ministry?

(6) What does the critic need from you?

Charles Spurgeon offers wonderfully realistic counsel on this issue: "Get a friend to tell you your faults or, better still, welcome an enemy who will watch you keenly and sting you savagely. What a blessing such an irritating critic will be to a wise person. What an intolerable nuisance to a fool!"[5]

MYTH: A GRUMBLER SPEAKS FOR EVERYONE.

"Our church is a seedbed of negativism."

Reality: A minority must not be allowed to rule a church.

"Since I always want to please everyone, one complainer spoils my day and saps my stamina" is how a Southwestern pastor's wife reacts to this myth. What a pity, but how true. For some almost irrational reason, we are overly concerned about the vocal few. Too often a critical minority hold a church and pastor hostage with their outspoken, controlling ways. Every pastor and spouse can cite examples of sabotage by an abusive minority. Their loud opinions gives them more visibility than they deserve.

The vote was 94 percent positive among 400 people in a congregational meeting to build a new sanctuary. To have received that level of support on such a costly project was miraculous. But the pastor and key layleaders wondered aloud if they should proceed with a 6 percent opposition rate. How easy it was for that leadership team to get out of focus. Finally, someone reminded them that 376 people carry much more clout than 24.

Admittedly, looking beyond the outspoken critics is hard to put into practice. But it must be done. In a Midwestern college town, a pastor's wife underwent months of psychotherapy because of the emotional strain caused by an anonymous letter criticizing her parenting skills. Though she was 97 percent sure the letter expressed only one individual's opinion, she allowed herself to believe many people thought she was an inadequate parent. In this downward emotional slide, she gave control of her inner health to one coward who was afraid to sign the letter.

Logically, one negative expression must be balanced by many in the congregation who admire their pastor's ministry and home. Too often we allow a pesky minority too much control, and award a pure cantankerous attitude by giving it too much attention.

A murmurer told an emotionally strong pastor's wife, "Many people at church think your stylish dress is too revealing and too expensive. We don't think you should wear it."

She replied, "I think that's your opinion and you are stirring up an inconsequential issue!" Then she verbalized her own freedom, "And you might like to know that my favorite pastor bought this dress for me for my birthday."

Though she might be considered too outspoken, she has the main issues worked out in her mind. Remember a disquieted few do not speak for the whole church, even when they think they do.

If a troubled minority are allowed to control us and hinder progress, our lives in ministry will be miserable and reactionary. But when we view the majority of church people as loving, positive, and eager to do right, we start seeing the critical few for what they are—individuals speaking their own opinion. And even though we want them to feel heard and accepted, we must be guided by a higher authority.

Five affirmations will keep us from being overwhelmed by idle words from the unhappy vocal minority:

(1) Remember no one person speaks for everyone.

(2) When anyone says, "They are saying . . ." they usually mean, "I am saying. . . . "

(3) Minority reports often come from recreational talkers who do not expect to be taken seriously.

(4) Measure your life by purposes achieved, triumphs won, lessons learned, and good done—rather than by what people say. Don't squander your life by responding to cynicism, faultfinding, and gossip.

(5) The majority of the people do right most of the time, so you can usually ignore or discredit rumors that the sky may be falling and people are about to declare war against you.

Keep reminding yourself that the minority are exactly what their name says. Most often, they speak for themselves, sometimes for their friends, occasionally for the many, but rarely for the entire congregation.

MYTH: DETACHMENT IS DESIRABLE.

"I wish people would accept me more."

Reality: Satisfaction in ministry starts with relationships.

"Keep your distance" is what church leaders from past generations sometimes advised beginning ministry couples. The advice: "Be careful not to be too close to anyone. Don't do anything to cause jealousy among your church members over the attention you may be paying someone." But this message is like telling a parent to be careful not to love their children too much or telling a young bride and groom to limit their love for each other. Since ministry is relational, through and through, such an artificial detachment undermines effectiveness and confuses parishioners.

The importance of agape relationships with parishioners shows in the story behind the hymn, "Blest Be the Tie That Binds." The song started in tears when pastoral relationships were about to be severed. Dr. John Fawcett, the much loved pastor of a small church at Wainsgate, England, had accepted a call in 1772 to a larger church in London. When the departure day arrived, church members who were like family to the Fawcetts gathered around their pastor and wife. In a genuine outpouring of affection, the people begged them to stay.

The pastor's wife looked at her husband and said in a quavering voice, "I cannot bear this. I can't go."

"Neither can I," exclaimed the pastor, "and we will stay. Unload the wagons and put everything back in place; we are not going."

In commemoration of that event, Pastor John Fawcett wrote

the text of the hymn which we still sing with such enormous affection:

Blest be the tie that binds
    Our hearts in Christian love;
The fellowship of kindred minds
    Is like to that above.

We share our mutual woes,
    Our mutual burdens bear;
And often for each other flows
    the sympathizing tear.[6]

There is also another important facet that needs to be considered. Keeping close to common people has its rewards. So much can be learned from ordinary people who may argue they have nothing to give us. But our spiritual development and ministry can be strengthened by common people who genuinely know God. Though untrained and uncredentialed, many of them cherish the grace of God and know life, so they often have the wisdom and ability to communicate spiritual lessons in anecdotes, yarns, and parables. They offer us depth and insight as we tune our ears to discover the significance of their lives. The wonderful insights they are ready to teach us about godliness and spiritual reality can only be learned around their tables, in hearing their prayer petitions as we pray together, or by sitting on their front steps. Who would willingly detach themselves from such richness?

MYTH: CIRCUMSTANCES DETERMINE CONTENTMENT.

"Everyone moves up economically in our church except us."

Reality: Attitude and commitment determine contentment.

Contentment is not the same as being unwilling to work for needed change. The Apostle Paul shared his discovery about contentment right in the middle of his efforts to change the world for

Christ. Listen to his testimony: "Not that I complain of want; for I have learned, in whatever state I am, to be content. . . . I can do all things through Christ who strengthens me" (Phil. 4:11, 13).

Don't you love the way Paul puts his "I can do" affirmation right next to his teaching about contentment? We can do the same thing in our walk with God.

Pastor Larry Lott in Kansas City does it often when he leads his African-American congregation in a rousing cheer at the end of the Sunday worship service, "I can do . . . I can do . . . I can do . . . All things . . . all things . . . through Christ who strengthens me!"

The problem with contentment in ministry is that two small words, "if I," are too often used to set contingencies on contentment. "If I" lived in a different area. "If I" had better health. "If I" had a better education. "If I" had more money. "If I" had more time. "If I" had children who were more responsible. "If I" had a mate who understood my work better. The enslaving problem: the "if I" list is endless, and enslaves us to nonactive acquiescence.

At the bottom line, contentment is an inside job. In fact, those who expect external events to bring them contentment are generally disappointed. Ministry contentment is doomed if we expect it to come from other people or wait for more favorable circumstances to make us happy. One of the toughest parts of confronting this myth is to break the assumption that material possessions bring satisfaction and happiness.

It is much more satisfying to live by this fact of life — contentment is a choice, and it has almost nothing to do with the circumstances of our lives or what other people do.

MYTH: KEY PEOPLE ARE PERMANENT.

"Everyone seems to be threatening to move away."

Reality: Expect people to move and be surprised if they don't.

Wishful thinking makes us want to believe that the best church members are going to be long-termers. Like children in our homes, however, church members are more often only with us for a limited period, then they move to other places. Few stay for a lifetime.

In a congregation of about 125, a pastor's wife in Indiana observed with discouraging regret, "Last Sunday, I heard four families tell others they would be moving soon. Their comments put a dark cloud over me and struck terror into my soul—I simply cannot see how the church could function without them."

In North America, mobility is a reality that causes frequent personnel shifts in every church and community. But it works two ways. Some leave your orbit of ministry and others move into it. Thus, we must adjust to personnel changes in our churches—all the lay leaders often change in five years or less.

What can be done? Rather than resisting this reality of mobility, a pastor and spouse can improve what these changes do to the church by upgrading their assimilation skills. Be open to new people. Accept them gladly. Urge them to become involved in Christian service as soon as they are spiritually ready to accept assignments. Welcome new people in public services, and have a public commissioning ceremony for those who leave for new assignments. Create a positive response to this inevitable reality.

Always be quick to recognize and treasure the grand richness Christian friendships bring. Flavia, the greeting card designer, summarizes this issue so well: "Some people come into our lives and quickly go. Some stay for a while and leave footprints on our hearts, and we are never ever the same."

MYTH: LONELINESS IS INEVITABLE.

"I feel lonely in a crowd at church."

Reality: Well-used loneliness draws us closer to Christ.

If we allow it to happen, ministry can isolate us into becoming the most lonely people in town. But we can overcome loneliness, use it for our spiritual development, and at times even embrace it as a friend.

One hurting pastor's wife asked, "Does Jesus know about my

feelings of loneliness?" You can be sure He does, when you consider how much separation and isolation our Lord experienced
near the end of His earthly ministry. Some of His deepest experiences of isolation took place when He was in the middle of a
crowd or with the trusted Twelve.

The events of His last days in human form were filled with
isolation and loss. Trusted friends defected. He was arrested without cause after Judas gave Him a kiss of death. Religious leaders
fraudulently accused Him. Guards spit on Him. The mob clam-
ored for His crucifixion. And He finally endured the repulsive
death on a cross alone, while others watched and He cried with
deep anguish, "My God, why have You forsaken Me?" The fact
that such an influential life could come to such a terrible end
illustrates the awfulness of sin. All those shocking scenes show us
the loneliness Jesus endured for those He loved.

Perhaps that is an important lesson of ministry — some degree
of loneliness goes with the territory. But other loneliness is rooted
in the absence of meaning, relationships, and fulfillment. As a
Salvation Army officer said recently, "We need to fear being bored
out more than burned out."

Three mature laywomen of faith once taught me that everyone is sometimes lonely. After preaching on ways to make loneliness contribute to our spiritual development, I was mildly am-
bushed by these three retirees who regularly came on Monday
mornings to prepare the church's bank deposit. They were eager to
discuss the sermon from the previous day with me.

Apparently a self-revealing comment in my message made
them think I thought loneliness was unique to pastors and their
families. Almost in unison, they said, "Everyone is lonely. The
only difference between people is what to do with it." Then they
started sharing ways they remedied their loneliness.

Christian medical doctor and counselor Paul Tournier's insightful discussions help us see that loneliness can bear good fruit,
if we allow it to do so. He discusses several kinds of loneliness
with differing results and impact.[7]

• *Perspective loneliness.* Loneliness can help us clarify our perspectives. An example is Jesus' wilderness solitude, where He purposefully refocused the present moment so He could more clearly
see the distant dream. Sometimes the Christian worker does

him/herself a great favor by using solitude for assessing the meaning of life and ministry. One learns valuable insights in the closet of his/her soul.

● *Stand-by-a-principle loneliness.* This kind of isolation must sometimes be suffered for a great cause. Our Lord's awful agony in Gethsemane (Matt. 26:36) and on the cross was loneliness for a cause, even though in those terrible moments He was tempted to doubt His Father's faithfulness (27:46). We may see the good of this kind of loneliness only after an unhappy experience has passed.

● *Self-induced loneliness.* This kind of loneliness comes when we refuse to let anyone else into our heart and thoughts — the opposite of self-revelation. It is the all-too-common absurdity of refusing to be known, of keeping to our own thoughts, insisting on our privacy, and then wondering why nobody reaches out to us.

Most often clergy couples suffer this kind of loneliness when, thinking no one outside the ministry could understand their situation or their pain, they withdraw from the caring laity of their churches.

As a result, laypersons think this withdrawal is a personal need for privacy, so they leave the minister and his family alone. This starts a vicious cycle that makes the pastor and his family even more lonely. You can clutch privacy so close to your chest that it closes your heart from welcoming those who love you the most.

● *Geographic loneliness.* This is the loneliness we feel when we are removed from our biological extended family and from home community roots. This loneliness comes when the grandparents do not get to see the children often enough. It may occur when a member of the older generation needs more care and attention than one can give across miles. Frequent phone calls can often bridge this gap. One extended family I know writes round-robin letters.

Everyone needs a soul friend, but in those dry periods when no one seems available we can count on the Lord to be with us in every detail of ministry. It is important to keep alert to the reality that some, though not all, feelings of isolation and loneliness are a product of our own thought processes. We can think ourselves out of the inner dark places just as we thought ourselves into them.

Then too great causes can be bridges out of loneliness. An

important principle the great Christian causes teach us is that the more we give ourselves away, the richer and more fulfilled we become. This is the exact opposite of secular, material giving. If you give someone courage, your own courage increases. Give someone love, and you get love in return. Give hope, and your own hope flourishes.

A beginning pastor's wife wrote H.B. about her loneliness. Up until this time she had never felt totally isolated from what she calls "spiritual friends." Things changed when she and her husband moved to their first pastorate following seminary. Listen to her empty heartache: "I was beginning to wonder if it might be easier to pass through the eye of a needle than to find a friend for a new pastor's wife. It was several months after beginning our ministry and I was starting to feel the loneliness that occurs in the midst of smiles and small talk. Everyone in our new church was kind and thoughtful, but I had not found a special friend—someone to share a special Scripture passage with or someone to call and just say, 'Pray! It's a tough day.' I did not have a confidante to share my deepest hurts and longings with. I found myself for the first time feeling all alone."

While continuing to be open to finding a soul mate, this same pastor's wife observed: "Our Lord's memory of His own terrible loneliness is the motivation behind His words in the final chapter of Matthew, 'And surely I am with you always, to the very end of the age.' That helped me see my situation and my help. Jesus knows how it feels to be completely alone and He has promised never to leave us alone. Now, I may feel lonely but when I am reminded of the reality of Jesus Christ, my loneliness disappears in His presence."

Her insightful letter continued: "I continue to pray for an earthly spiritual friend that will be the minister of God's comfort to me in my lonely times. Until then, praise God for His promise to be with me always."

Though it may be impossible to prove by statistical surveys, I think more humility and more community will go a long way to lowering our loneliness. This humility admits that a higher Power directs and energizes our lives. And a commitment to community means we know we need each other and we want to live the servant song:

Brother (sister) let me be your servant.
Let me be as Christ to you.
Pray that I may have the grace
To let you be my servant too.[8]

MYTH: PASTORS WORK HARDER THAN PERSONS IN OTHER OCCUPATIONS.

"The church has made my husband into a workaholic."

Reality: Men view work differently than women.

A pastor's view of work is an interesting and often misunderstood factor that shapes his time commitments. Many men in every occupation define themselves by their work. The main issues surrounding work issues in ministry are:

(1) *Schedule writing.* A pastor controls his own schedule and calendar if he wants to do so.

(2) *Schedule adjustments.* A pastor can often arrange his schedule to make room for family, but emergencies sometimes require him to cancel family time. Such emergencies should not happen regularly. These realities create stress in a family which usually sounds like, "Oh, Dad, why can't you change your schedule like you did last week?" or in emergency situations, "You always put church first."

(3) *Incomplete ministry.* A pastor's work is never completely finished—the end of every day leaves something undone. The unfinished nature of ministry seems to encourage workaholism in many pastors.

(4) *Perfectionism.* The nature of a pastor's work encourages perfectionism, so some jobs are done over and over, hoping to make them a little better.

Pastors sometimes face confusion in the meaning of their work because so many outside and some inside the church don't know what ministers do, and thus question whether or not they work. Frank Pittman, in his book *Man Enough,* defines the positive effect of work on men: "Work keeps us busy, it gives us structure, it defines us as functioning, contributing, worthwhile citizens. It makes us a part of the team, a community of fellow workers—even

199

if we do our work in isolation."[9]

Women married to pastors soon see that the work of ministry is a mixed blessing for them and their children. It produces positive acceptance and even admiration in the congregation and community. But a negative disconnectedness can also accompany it, causing a wife to feel isolated and/or angry. She wants the ministry to be important to him, but at the same time she feels that church comes between her relationship with her pastor/husband and before closeness to his family.

Pastors probably don't work any harder than most men who are thoroughly involved in their occupations; it just seems so to their spouses. Perhaps it is easier to hold the church responsible than it is to sort through the key issues together. But these issues need to be faced openly, because most men view work much differently than their wives do.

DEALING WITH
MYTHS AND REALITIES

Our choice of myths for discussion in this chapter, as we said earlier, has been selective. Our criteria for choosing myths for this discussion are issues we hear over and over again in correspondence and conferences. Now that you have read this list, what can be done with the myths? Here are some ways to understand and improve them.

Try to understand the origin

Where and when did the myth start? What is the myth's real message? If it has a valid message, respond positively to the issue rather than warring with preposterous details. Since many myths contain enough truth that they are hard to refute or resist, it is important to try to understand their initial meaning to see if it has relevance to your setting and to your way of doing ministry.

View traditions as significant but not restricting

A practice of ministry is not automatically valid because it has been around for years. Neither is it worthless because it has been done for a long period of time. A young medical doctor, a pioneer member of a newly formed independent church, was asked to write the creedal statement for a new congregation. As he tried, with his nontheological mind and limited understanding of the history of Christian thought, he said, "I simply can't write a statement of belief without lots of influence and reference from past creedal statements." And he was right; some traditions are valid and timeless, and should not be considered to be imprisoning constraints.

Live beyond the myths

See to it that you enjoy a Christ-quality life that is radiant and focused and joyful. Most people will then be so attracted to the magnetism of Christ shining through your life that they will not spend much time judging you by the myths.

Many ministry couples resist what they consider to be myths without replacing them with biblical principles for living. As a result, they live a reactionary existence which makes them miserable and volatile and keeps the church in constant turmoil.

Take your faith to the cutting edge of society

Throughout the Christian era, women and men of faith have taken daring risks for the Gospel. Admittedly, terrible forces in the modern environment seem to militate against the work of Christ. But try to take heart. God is still in control, and He wants human beings won by ordinary people like us. Given our Master's mandate, given the confusion of our times, and given the need of our world, why not believe that the Gospel was as much designed for the new century as for the last century? Pray often, "Keep me ready for the new things You have planned for my life and for the ministry I share with my spouse."

Confront the myths. Untangle the snarls. Overcome obstacles so you can enjoy a contemporary ministry that will help save the world and bring satisfaction in your inner world. Build a life on the values of Christlikeness, and search for lasting values and worthy achievements.

CONTEMPORARY CHALLENGE
Overcoming Ministry Myths

- Every generation must take ministry to the front lines.
- Human beings sometimes disappoint us.
- Either you control your life or it will be out of control.
- Christlikeness is our ideal.
- God has not assigned you a happiness machine.
- Active involvement in the kingdom produces spiritual stamina.
- Bad times provide great opportunities for the Gospel.
- Ministry can enrich your family.
- All talk is not destructive.
- A minority must not rule the church.
- Satisfaction in ministry starts with relationships.
- Attitude and commitment determine contentment.
- Expect people to move.
- Well-used loneliness draws us closer to Jesus.
- Men view work differently than women.

MARRIED TO A WOMAN WHO USES THE REALITIES

A Salute to Charleen Anderson
by Pastor Leith Anderson

We never met. Charleen and I have known each other all of our lives. Our first date was the month I turned fifteen. There is a special glue to a relationship that has so much in common. We grew up in the same church, know the same childhood friends, remember the same childhood places and events, attended the same college together.

My father was pastor of the Brookdale Baptist Church in Bloomfield, New Jersey for nearly thirty-five years. Unlike some pastors' children who speak of frequent moves to distant parts of the country, our family experienced no such relocations. My father was pastor of the same church long before I was born and long after I was married, had children, and became a pastor myself.

Because Charleen and I experienced the same church and had the same pastor and youth leaders, she spent so much time in our home that we both entered pastoral ministry with the same concept and expectations.

But there are ways in which she was far better suited to the role of pastor's wife than I was suited to the role of pastor. She has always had a strong relationship with God and a clear sense of the Lord's direction in her life. When I was a teenager, I struggled with Christianity and with being a pastor's son. When we started to date, I found in her a relationship to Jesus Christ which was powerful and attractive. She was wholesome and uncompromising in her standards, yet vibrant and exciting as a person. While we did not know the term at the time, Charleen "discipled" me — she drew me to God, taught me about Christian living, nurtured me in faith, and redirected my life.

Through college and seminary, I had no intention of becoming a pastor; I planned to teach sociology of religion. But that was OK with her. She married me, not my profession. She never pushed or tried to persuade. Her constant word was that we could live anywhere, I could take any job, and we would love each other and live for God in that place and position.

While a seminary student, I became youth pastor in a Colorado church. She moved easily and comfortably into her new role as a pastor's wife in a multiple staff church. A couple of years later came one of the most painful experiences of my life when the church voted me out during a congregational business meeting. I was devastated. She was amazing — supporting me without condemning the church, ready to move on to whatever God had next. Strange as it may seem, that same church voted me back in as senior pastor two months later, and we were there for ten years. Again, she adapted with love, taking on her new role in the same church.

It can be hard to adequately describe someone you know better than anyone else. Perhaps that is because there is so much to say and there is a fear that telling only part will leave the listener with an inadequate picture.

As a pastor's wife, I am grateful that she has mostly been my friend and lover. Our relationship to each other is not set in my occupation. I have never doubted that I could do something else or go anywhere else and her love and our relationship would be the same. Yet, as a pastor's wife, she has been great. Over twenty-five years I have never once known her to break a confidence or engage in gossip or do anything harmful to anyone in the church or community. She is outgoing and warm. She is easy for people to love.

I have delighted in her willingness to serve as a Christian, rather than as the wife of a pastor. For years she led a children's choir, but when changes came, she stepped aside with grace. As a teacher of two-year-olds in Sunday School, she has made hundreds of little friends and won the love and respect of large numbers of parents. In a large, multiple-service church with thousands of people (and many other Andersons), there are many who have received her friendship and ministry long before they ever realized that her husband is the senior pastor. For years she has led a Bible study and ministered to the wives of professional athletes from Minnesota teams. As a result, she knows some famous people very well, and has significantly impacted their lives; but I doubt that more than a handful of people at Wooddale Church know anything about this ministry.

In other words, she is to God a faithful disciple, to me a marvelous wife, to the church an effective Christian. I doubt she would have done anything different if she had never become a pastor's wife, but all she has done convinces me that she has been the best that any pastor's wife can be.

Pastor Leith Anderson
Wooddale Church
Eden Prairie, Minnesota

How to Be
Yourself
and a
Minister's
Wife Too

It's OK to Be Different If...

Making Life All You Want It to Be

◇◇◇◇◇

Loving Father,
   Clear my vision so I see myself as I am.
      Help me to be different where it makes a difference.
   Open my eyes to ways I can be uniquely useful to You.
      Keep me from rebelling against circumstances I can't change.
         And help me practice the art of Christ-centered dependence.
Amen.

◇◇◇◇◇

On January 1, 2000, headlines in leading magazines and newspapers about pastors' wives might read:

STEREOTYPES TUMBLE EVERYWHERE

MINISTER'S SPOUSE BECOMES MAIN BREADWINNER

PASTORS CONFUSED BY WHAT WIVES WANT

CAREER SPOUSE KEEPS MINISTER FROM TAKING
   NEW CHURCH

PARISHIONERS TREAT ME LIKE EVERYONE ELSE
   AND I HATE IT

CLERGY COUPLES PURCHASE THEIR OWN HOMES

I LOVE BEING SPECIAL IF IT IS TO MY ADVANTAGE
FEMINISM OVERSTRESSES CLERGY MARRIAGES
WIVES PERPLEXED BY WHAT PASTORS DESIRE
MINISTER'S WIDOW LOSES STANDING AT CHURCH

"I HATE BEING MARRIED TO A PROFESSION"

As champions of women's rights march across Western culture, calls for equality have created massive change and caused baffling confusion at many levels of contemporary life. As a result, many couples are unsure about how to relate to each other at home, at church, and in the community because traditional attitudes and informal rules are being altered so rapidly. Even wholehearted male supporters of women's rights are mystified. The plot is even more confusing when these issues impact women of faith who are married to ministers.

SOCIAL CHANGES AFFECT CLERGY COUPLES

Women's roles have changed dramatically over the past thirty years. And like all social ferment, those changes have not always been orderly, predictable, or even rational. No one knows when this metamorphosis will slow down—maybe never. And no one knows who to praise or blame.

Consider women's reactions to the changes. Some have become outspoken "libbers." Others experiment with selective feminism. Some resist change completely because they like being treated as special ladies in traditional relationships. And still others do not have a clue as to how these issues affect them.

Meanwhile, these changing concepts have reshaped ideas about ministers' wives' roles in church, culture, and community. Questions about increased individuality of women sometimes perplex pastors, church members, and even ministers' wives themselves. As a result, many clergy wives are rethinking their aspirations for themselves, their hopes for their families, their expectations for their husbands, and their relationships with the congregations their husbands serve. They feel like Ziggy in Tom Wilson's cartoon who remarked, "It's not easy being me . . . sometimes even I have trouble doing it!"[1]

Argument, hypersensitivity, renegotiation, anger, passive resistance, or debate concerning these issues are the order of the day in many places. Change always meets resistance. But our challenge, in place of resisting or ignoring this in-progress revolution is to use it as a window of opportunity to develop new understandings and to enrich our life together.

Improvement and progress can come from all this. It can lead to a wholesome new balance that is realistic about fulfillment, responsibility, privilege, and obligation. Pastors' wives can use the present revolution as an opportunity to deepen authenticity, test reality, and increase meaning in their relationships.

No couple in ministry, no matter how much they try, can shelter themselves from these changes. No congregation, no matter how resistant, can think about a pastor's wife like it always has. No family of churches or denomination can continue business as usual in relationship to the minister's mate and family. It's time to listen with our whole heart to what these issues say to us, and to do something about it. Following are some suggestions that can help.

RECOGNIZE MINISTRY AS A WAY OF LIFE

These changes between women and men have a profound impact on clergy marriages because ministry is a way of life more than a profession. Though pastoral work should be both a calling and a profession, it is also a total immersion in a great cause. Ministry is always with us around the clock, continuously on our minds, and invading our free time. Like parenting, ministry never leaves us — day in and day out, year in and year out.

Face the fact that ministry is a way of life and then come to happy terms with the realities that requires. Ministry has different values, satisfactions, intensities, salary, work schedule, and family commitments than any other occupation. Ministry produces different fulfillments. Make the list as long as you want; ministry is different from every other profession, occupation, and, to some degree, ministry always involves spouse and children. Nobody planned these differences; that's just the way it is. This fact can be accepted happily or with kicking and screaming, but it is still true, and will likely be true for the foreseeable future.

Ministry and marriage are intertwined

Ministry shapes a clergy marriage in a thousand different ways, even as a marriage shapes ministry. A pastor's feelings and his own marriage experiences seep into his preaching, devotional life, and relationships with other people. For a pastor, marriage and ministry are as much a part of each other as the heart and mind are connected in the human body. Every couple chooses the intensity of this connection, but it always exists to some degree—and some couples even find ways to make it enjoyable.

Ministry limits choices

Being a pastor dictates the city and state where his family lives, and frequently determines the house in which his family resides. Such housing usually determines where the children go to school. Other controlled choices include salary, outside interests, church attendance, time commitments, educational choices, leisure time, and spiritual vitality. And while everyone has some terrible story about an outdated parsonage and a limited small town, I met a pastor last week who is going to a new church building with a modern parsonage for his first assignment; the house is nicer than any he has ever lived in, and the church building is better than his home church.

Ministers work with amateurs

Unlike medicine or law or architecture, the pastor works regularly with well-meaning amateurs—laypersons—who often have strong opinions about how a minister should do his work. They also have a powerful say about the size of his paycheck. But these amateurs usually love God, and want to see something significant happen in their churches. What they lack in training they often make up for in motivation.

Nearly all of these factors about ministry as a way of life impact the minister's spouse and children. To be in ministry means a pastor and his family must see ministry as a way of life that shapes everything.

MINISTRY NEEDS
SUPERNATURAL ENABLEMENT

Ministry can never be done with human energy or ingenuity alone. Sadly, this divine enablement is too often overlooked, assumed, or neglected. But if ministry is to be effective, care must be taken to welcome the One who stands ready to go with us into every aspect of our work for Him.

The Whiteheads, a husband and wife writing team from the Institute of Pastoral Studies in Chicago, sharpen our awareness of the availability of this enablement: "Throughout the New Testament we see God's power moving through Jesus to arouse hope, heal illness and confront destructive patterns of domination."[2] Ministry always needs this power. Two precise points must be acknowledged: this gigantic empowerment is needed, and it is available.

This supernatural dimension is the main distinction between ministry and other vocations. Such a supernatural partnership is the cornerstone for productive pastoral ministry, and contributes greatly to a satisfying clergy marriage. Let's remember, God's enablement is just a prayer away. Consequently, a minister and his spouse and family can count on faith, grace, empowerment, love, and hope to enable them to serve effectively and joyously. Jesus' presence in our marriage and ministry generates divine energy and supernatural strength.

YOU ARE FREE TO
BE YOURSELF IF . . .

You can be as unique as you want—if you are seeking to live a Christ-centered life. Kallie, Sarah, Arlene, Meagan, Mona, Sonya, and Linda were shown in chapter 1 to be fully human and at the same time uniquely committed to Christ. Those seven women represent an extraordinary company of contemporary saints in the making who help us see that unique, even maverick, perspectives on ministry are acceptable to God and the churches when we are genuinely Christian.

Some congregations, by tolerating such incredible differences and sometimes even going so far as to cherish them, are considerably more accepting than many critics think. The secret is obvious—if you are an authentic Christian, you can be different or even maverick. It is OK to differ considerably from the norm if you are growing deep spiritual roots and producing authentic fruit.

The main point—an abiding commitment to develop one's best self under loving obedience to Christ—is far different than passive resistance or outspoken rebellion about involvement in ministry. Though it may not be a genuinely Christian poem, Edgar A. Guest's last verse of "Myself" offers important insight about authenticity for pastors' wives:

> I never can hide myself from me.
> I see what others may never see,
> I know what others may never know,
> I never can fool myself—and so,
> Whatever happens, I want to be
> Self-respecting and conscience free.[3]

God wants you to be your best self, a useful servant of the Gospel, whether you are a beginner starting ministry at the threshold of the new century, in life's prime enjoying mature service, or walking toward the sunset while still busy in the loving employ of Christ.

Oswald Chambers offers guidance for tending our personal fires of devotion and causing people to see far past the ways we are different:

> Our Lord's first obedience was to the will of His Father, not to the needs of men: His obedience brought the outcome of the saving of men. If I am devoted to the cause of humanity only, I will soon be exhausted and come to the place where my love for

God will falter; but if I love Jesus Christ personally and passionately, I can serve humanity though people treat me like a doormat.[4]

Though few parishioners will ever treat you like a doormat,
the focus of all service must be "the love of Christ constrains us"
(2 Cor. 5:14).

TENDING
THE FIRES

Since fires of commitment tend to go out or burn low, an abiding
devotion to Christ requires that we continually stir up the coals,
fan the flames, fuel the fire with prayer, and keep close to the holy
flame in Scripture. Tending the inner flame can be accomplished
in a variety of ways.

Start with conversion

This is the initial meeting with Christ, where one's life is so
radically transformed that the Bible calls it a new birth. This new
birth produces a new life in Christ, so it is the beginning of
everything that genuinely matters for time and eternity. It is a new
start and never a completion. It provides God's forgiveness for sin,
it calls us to make wrongs right, and it gives us a whole new way
of living. Then we have new values, new interests, new priorities,
and new relationships. No pastor's wife can function adequately or
joyfully without being born again.

Commit to mutual support

Like a pendulum moving from one extreme to another, the reaction of some contemporary pastors' wives is to reject the long-held
and widely accepted idea that they are to be supportive to their
husband's ministry. Unfortunately, this quiet revolt probably
would not happen if the same couple were in another line of work
because nonclergy career couples routinely support each other's
occupations in many different ways. But how can it be done more
satisfactorily by a clergy couple?

Commit to a team effort

Mutual support is an essential ingredient of married life — the attitude that "We are in this together." Such support shows up in mutual child raising, shared responsibilities, career changes, and relationships with extended family. Human beings need the support of their spouses, and without it, a marriage is impoverished. Thus to withhold support in a clergy marriage causes injury to the relationship and to the emotional well-being of both partners. Ideally, emotional support flows both ways in every clergy marriage.

Cherish your mate's uniqueness

Serious discussions about strengthening clergy marriages have apparently resulted in a new awareness by pastor/husbands of the needs of their wives. These changes seem to have made many pastors more willing to discuss these issues, more ready to listen, and perhaps more ready to make significant changes. As a result, many pastors are more aware of ways to cherish their wife's special uniqueness. This developing openness allows minister and spouse to enjoy a more emancipated approach to their marriage, more joy in their parenting, and more fulfillment in congregational relationships.

Make the home a laboratory of faith

Marriage and family are the most obvious source of mutual support. Ideally, home is the place for love, acceptance, and faith formation. Though a pastor's wife often takes the heavy responsibility of family care and homemaking, husbands should view home and family as a laboratory for faith development and a place of enormous satisfaction. Home should be a place where children are enjoyed and where children and wife affirm a pastor even as he cherishes them. Increasingly the minister's home must become a fortress of refuge and strength.

Provide emotional stability

The need for mutual emotional support between husband and wife is closely connected to home and family. Traditionally, the pastor's home has been a place where he could vent his disappointments and hurts. It was a safe, accessible, nonjudgmental setting where his wife served as lover, confessor, and burden bearer. Often this led to extreme stress for the wife because she was expected to silently bury in her own inner world the knowledge of the damage troubled people had on her husband's well-being and work.

Increasingly, this emotional support is becoming more two-way, with spouses offering each other a sounding board. They become soul friends in the expansion of their faith and the growth of their ministry together. Affirmation, confidence, and faith in spite of troubles are all needed to make it work well for all members of the family.

Communicate thanks

As a way of life, try expressions of gratitude like these: Thanks for the dinner. Thanks for being the best spouse anyone could ever have. Thanks for the fine job you are doing with the children. Thanks for the important work you are doing in your Sunday School class. Thanks for opening your heart and soul to the church—they love you for it.

Try putting your name or his name into the heart of these lines from an unknown writer:

> I love her because of what she does to me when I am with her. I love her because she has always believed in me. She closes her eyes to my faults, yet sees the good in me that even I did not know was hidden there.
>
> She hears what I say and often smiles, but she also senses my deeper aspirations and echoes them in ways that will keep me loving her forever . . . (author unknown).

Most churches are pleased for a pastor's wife to be as unique as she wants to be when they see that she is supportive of her husband and that he supports her efforts with similar devotion. Beware, however; this idea has a positive trap built in it—couples committed to being mutually supportive never intentionally behave in ways that cause their spouse personal or professional embarrassment.

Keep open to divine direction

When we are open and sensitive, the Lord often sends us to people and situations where we are especially needed.

Gail Magruder needed someone to express God's love to her during the Watergate hearings. As Colleen Evans, a Presbyterian pastor's wife, saw James Magruder's face on TV, she felt directed by God to search for a piece of paper to write Gail, his wife, a note. That is what she did. Though they had never met, Colleen's note simply said, "If you ever need to talk to someone, we will be willing to listen." The Magruders responded to her simple invitation, and a friendship blossomed around the Lord Jesus. All of us can cultivate an increasing willingness to seek and follow divine nudgings like that.

Clergy couples, accustomed to seeking guidance when considering a move to Alaska or Alabama, sometimes hesitate about asking for direction for routine events of daily ministry. Why not rethink this omission? The God who cares for sparrows is interested in your enjoying triumph in the details of your ministry. To find full adventure in this work, keep alert to what God is doing in every circumstance. Then even when spiritual growth—yours or the church's—seems as slow as a snail's pace, you will know that God is still at work in you.

Seek God's direction in the details of your ministry. He wants you to be fulfilled. He wants to optimize your unique personhood for His glory. And though you feel like you live a public life on center stage, He wants you to find joyous satisfaction in all you do. One pastor's wife said, "I asked God to take me out of the limelight, and He taught me to enjoy it."

Define your role in terms of Christlikeness

Satisfaction in being a pastor's wife comes when one turns her life into the life she wants it to be in light of what God wants. Christlikeness always produces a beautiful life that is satisfying to the person living it and an inspiration to those who observe it. To achieve this, you must do the right things for the right reasons in ways that earn you the respect of people. Or, to put it more simply, take Christ into the details. Here are two elements in this process.

Resist anger. Anger always hinders Christlikeness, as well as the cause of Christ. Merely seething in quiet hostility or shouting in loud anger usually changes nothing. On the contrary, anger frequently shrivels the soul and hardens attitudes among those who might be open to solve problems. Such behavior easily becomes a vicious cycle where several people start acting like third-graders fighting on the playground — lots of shouting, no sense of direction, too much displaced anger, and no solution. Nearly every church has had an angry, unpleasant scene at one time or another. What started out so well turns into an emotional brawl or standoff. Anger always destroys relations and often corrodes commitments.

Perhaps we would accomplish more if we worked to accurately clarify the church's mission for ourselves, to get a new understanding of self, to develop an increased openness about what God really wants us to become, and to deepen our awareness of the needs of our spouse.

Find your special place. God has a special niche for you. Finding His special purpose starts with asking, Why am I here? What can I do that nobody else can do? What does God expect of me today? Answers to these questions almost always move one from duty to delight, and from expectations others impose on you to guidance from God.

The best way to work through the hodgepodge of perceptions is to shape your role by the life style of Jesus, by the gifts God has entrusted to you, by what is needed in the parish, and by what your husband and children seem to need most. It means proactively defining the pastor's wife's role in the setting where you find yourself, always asking what your Lord wants you to do in this place. It means accepting your own abilities, talents, and interests, and using them for the advancement of the kingdom. It means being open to new assignments the Lord may have for you in your present setting.

All of this is much more than negative reaction, more than lashing out at systems and expectations, more than an intolerant smirk at what the former pastor's wife did or said. Rather, it is honestly seeking to be an authentic disciple of the living Christ who functions joyously and effectively in a particular setting of ministry.

A pastor's wife wrote these insightful paragraphs after being in ministry at her husband's side for six years:

I think my role as a minister's wife has dramatically changed, because I have changed. It's been a hard and painful road. No one could have prepared me for this, except personal growth or development groups. But, had they been available, I'm not sure I would have gone, since I was so positive I knew it all.

Now I know my "role" is what I make it, in terms of myself, my Christian and personal growth needs, and my need to serve Christ in a Christian community—His church. Above all, my "role" is no longer a role. It is authentic and real and comes from within. That difference makes all the difference.[5]

So while you have every right to reject criteria others impose on you for being a pastor's wife, you must establish serious personal Christ-centered criteria on yourself—standards that make room for God's purposes in your life and in your husband's ministry. Build a life that is energized by Christlikeness.

Pursue spiritual adulthood

To grow up in Christ, one must commit to living out the Apostle Paul's advice to first-century believers:

Let your roots grow down into Him and draw up nourishment from Him. See that you keep on growing in the Lord, and become strong and vigorous in the truth you were taught. Let your lives overflow with joy and thanksgiving for all He has done (Col. 2:7, TLB).

This extravagant Scripture promises nourishment, strength, vigor, joy, and thanksgiving—more than enough for every need you will ever encounter anywhere across a lifetime of ministry.

Times like our own require us to press on to spiritual adulthood. It's time for more Christian leaders to take full responsibility for becoming spiritual giants. The goal, far from becoming a withered up, self-righteous scold, is to become fully unique, spiritual persons who genuinely know God and make a difference in their world. Growing up spiritually is something we all need to do for the sheer joy of knowing we are part of the answers for the church and world rather than part of the problem.

Nourish fulfillment in each other

Helping your mate find fulfillment is among the most important gifts you can give another, and it is a great gift you can give yourself. Living with a mate who thoroughly believes he or she is doing what he or she was created to do is one of life's finest experiences. A sense of being who I am supposed to be and giving myself totally to God's original design for my life is much more satisfying than fancy houses, big cars, an ideal climate, prestigious jobs, and money in the bank. And the potential for such fulfillments is built into most pastorates.

See the big picture

Look past your frustrations and ambiguities. For example, Pastor Joe Ross looked back over his week late Saturday night. He had preached the Sunday before with God's anointing and received enthusiastic acceptance of the people. During the week, his pastoral ministry had taken him to several hurting people and allowed him to save two troubled marriages. He led a weekday Bible study that was well received, and the preparation drew him personally closer to God. Teacher-parent conferences went well that week for his two primary schoolchildren. He and his wife, Alice, had a great day together on their day off, and they rejoiced together over the strength of their marriage. It was a wonderful week in many ways.

But two out-of-the-ordinary events contaminated their peace. Charlotte Kritner phoned to report dissatisfaction among the parents of teens because of a bad mistake made by the youth sponsors. About the same time, Ted Patterson, the church's financial watchdog, was displeased over a $2,000 bill for repairing the flooded church basement.

Alice and Joe had a choice about their reactions. They could rant and rave to each other about the flood, the teen program, and how they loathe being a bull's-eye for church problems. They could talk themselves into a full-blown case of contagious self-pity. And such reactions might even seem justifiable. Sadly, however, the fulfillment resulting from an entire week of satisfying ministry would evaporate in the process. Too much talk about how tough life is almost always annihilates a sense of fulfillment.

To combat such a destructive tendency, why not concentrate on achievements? Why not underscore God's provisions for ministry? Why not remind your spouse that ministry has more joys than pains? Why not recall that ministry offers you many opportunities to help people, and that is what God called you to do?

Don't destroy a dream

A capable woman who lives in the Big Sky country of the western United States is married to a successful rancher who, when he was forty-two, felt a call to ministry. She did not share his feelings and openly opposed the notion of his entering the ministry. She reasoned, "We have a good life. We have security in ranching. Our children are happy here. I did not plan to marry a minister. And my aging parents live only two miles away." Because of her outspoken resistance, he decided to continue with their ranching business and give up his dream. On the surface, their family continues like it always did. But this woman knows she is living with a man with a shattered dream. Maybe her security had too high a price tag. Or perhaps he made some inner compromise with what he thought was a call to ministry. Either way, this couple lives with an unspoken sadness. Neither of them saw the potential satisfaction of ministry because they were so overfocused on the possible sacrifices.

Emphasize possibilities

The time has arrived to say it loud and clear. The ministry offers many immense satisfactions. Those potential satisfactions need to be discussed and recognized. Fulfillments need to be reemphasized on every level of church life. As a way of doing this, every ministry couple must intentionally highlight their own satisfactions to each other as a remedy for blue Mondays and as a light in the valleys of heartache. Like a front-line soldier, the best memories come from heroic action. Like a gallant sailor, never-to-be-forgotten fulfillment comes from the most daring rescue. Like a neurosurgeon, superb satisfactions come from saving a patient in a risky surgery. Ministry, done right in Jesus' name, offers more fulfillment than heroic action, daring rescues, and successful surgeries combined.

Give priority to being before doing

Confusions and frustrations about ministry always increase when we allow others to set the agenda for our service to Christ or for our personal spiritual growth. Often, because we are overly busy trying to do what we think others want us to do, we never quite get around to being gentle, kind, loving, patient, peaceable, honest, content, or even competent. When that happens, the opinions of others or busy activities take a higher priority than intimacy with Jesus.

On the contrary, conscientious development of our own inner self results in effective doing for the kingdom. Lasting achievement for the cause of Christ always begins with who we are, rather than what we can do.

Commit to spiritual self-care

Soul conditioning helps us maximize our potential for kingdom achievement and gives us a quality walk with Christ. It relishes nourishing spiritual food and commits to regular calisthenics for keeping our soul in shape. Self-care uses relevant Bible study to satisfy our quest for godliness, and pushes us to make satisfying prayer a daily joy. It intentionally cultivates the fruit of the spirit (Gal. 5:22-23).

Inner conditioning helps us reflect and refuel and regroup. Such interior fitness gives us a deep-down acceptance that, while a life of ministry does not eliminate disappointments, frustrations, and heartaches, testing strengthens faith.

Specific rules for spiritual conditioning need not be slavishly observed, since everyone is as unique in spiritual needs as in personal preferences of food and clothing and exercise. And like physical conditioning or good nutrition, no one can take responsibility for the spiritual fitness of anyone else.

Pastors cannot do self-care for their wives and wives cannot do it for their husbands. It is important, however, to realize that spiritual fitness is a glorious gift you give yourself. A pastor's wife of forty years' experience advised a beginner:

> Try not to let your husband's faith overshadow your own. It is
> true that you learn from his devotion and from others, but your

225

spiritual life depends on your personal relationship with God. True communication with God develops through long periods of serious meditation and devotion.[6]

To keep spiritually fit, you must feed your faith in every possible way. Spiritual self-care requires energy and exercise and tenacity, but the results of growing a great soul are worth every effort. The benefits include listening to Christ's counsel, feeling His nearness, and living His kind of life.

CONTEMPORARY CHALLENGE
Helps for Tending the Inner Flame

- Start with conversion.
- Commit to mutual support.
- Keep open to divine direction.
- Define your role in terms of Christlikeness.
- Pursue spiritual adulthood.
- Nourish fulfillment.
- Give priority to being before doing.
- Commit to spiritual self-care.

MARRIED TO A YOUNG MOTHER WHO IS DIFFERENT (SHE LOVES THE CITY!)

*A Salute to Janet Benefiel
by Pastor Ron Benefiel*

My wife, Janet, is an unusual woman in many ways. Anyone who knows me at all will tell you that it takes a very unusual woman to put up with me. She is bright, articulate, congenial, creative, industrious, and thrifty. And if I am not mistaken, that list is a fairly unique combination of characteristics.

Janet is a wonderful homemaker, gracious hostess, respected voice and active leader in our church fellowship, and a terrific mom. We have three children — Leanne is eight, Robyn is five, and Timothy just turned three. Our family translates into home and mothering responsibilities that mean a full-time job.

Janet feels called to the city

Even beyond her unusual ability to do the usual things well, Janet is an unusual woman to share with me a calling to minister to the city. The church I have pastored for the past twelve years is in the mid-Wilshire District of Los Angeles. It is an interesting, adventurous, challenging, stretching place to serve in the kingdom. With all its diverse cultures and urban social dynamics, it is any sociologist's dream. But living in the heart of L.A., while being a sociologist's dream, probably does not show up on any list as one of the most sought-after places for most middle-class American women to live, especially when it comes to the matter of raising a young family.

But Janet truly is an unusual woman when it comes to her sense of mission to the city. Her presence and the presence of our family in mid-Wilshire L.A. is not merely the result of following the call of her pastor-husband. Far more, it is something she has embraced for herself. It is her calling as much as it is mine. It is something we share together before God.

Janet serves in the city

As you might imagine, there are extraordinary opportunities as well as unique challenges that "come with the territory" in a place like L.A. One of the things that I have come to appreciate about Janet is her ability to grow with the opportunities and challenges of life in the city. Naturally, there are many times when she finds herself outside her "comfort zone." But she has an amazing talent for adapting in ways that are consistent with our reason for being here.

Crime is a problem in our neighborhood. But rather than fearfully withdrawing, Janet has become actively involved in the local "neighborhood watch" program, attending meetings, joining marches against crime, and hosting neighborhood events of the organization in our home. Amazingly, it seems as though the primary result of living in a high-crime area is that Janet has gotten to know her neighbors better. Not that she is in any way naive about the potential problems of crime; rather, she chooses to be informed and proactive instead of withdrawn and reactive.

When Los Angeles broke out in rioting in the spring of 1992, most of the businesses around us were burned or looted. It was a terrible time. I certainly would have understood if Janet had responded by wanting to move out of the city. Many people did leave for reasons I understand and respect. But for Janet, there never was the thought that maybe we should think about leaving. If anything, the riots merely showed how much the people of our city needed the Lord and the incarnational presence of the people of God. Janet is sure God led us with our family to live and minister in L.A., and that we were not yet finished with the work He has called us to do.

Janet has a gift of compassion

Another thing I admire about Janet is her compassionate spirit. She is a very giving person and models sharing and giving before our kids.

Many of the children who live adjacent to us are Central American immigrants living in crowded, four-story apartment buildings with no play space. I often come home late in the afternoon to find our backyard full of Spanish-speaking children happily playing. They know they are welcome.

Some time ago, Janet decided we should open our home to a teenage girl from El Salvador who found herself temporarily in the difficult position of being in a strange land with no place to stay. For eight months, she was part of our family until circumstances allowed her to return home. For Janet, far from being an inconvenience, the decision to open our home was the natural overflow of her compassionate spirit. It was not only an opportunity to help someone in need, it was an opportunity to enter the world of a Central American immigrant teenager — a learning experience for all of us, especially the children.

Janet is my soul mate

Our life experiences together over the past dozen years have reinforced our shared calling before God. They have also worked together to develop a strongly held set of shared values — values we understand to be in line with those of the kingdom of God. Having these shared values has become increasingly important to us. It means that as my relationship with the Lord and my understanding of His call in my life continue to grow and develop, Janet's relationship and understanding are growing as well.

It means that much of what we hold to be valuable in life we find in our relationship with God, with each other, with our children, and with the people of our faith community as we share the love of God with the people of the city.

In all of this, I have come to value more each day the love and companionship of a very unusual woman — my wife, Janet.

Pastor Ron Benefiel
First Church of the Nazarene
Los Angeles, California

10

WHAT BEVERLEY AND BONNIE TAUGHT US ABOUT MINISTRY

Trusting Your Own Good Sense

◇◇◇◇◇

THIS BOOK WAS INSPIRED by two special ladies. For Neil it was Bonnie; for H.B. it was Beverley. We want to share things Beverley and Bonnie taught us about ministry. We served in different parts of the country, pastored different-sized churches, and have been shaped by different experiences. Together, we two couples have more than fifty years' experience in pastoral service and nearly seventy-five years in various forms of ministry. What a roller coaster ride and what a joy.

H.B.'S RECOLLECTION OF THEIR MINISTRY TOGETHER

Beverley and I were married between my junior and senior years and her freshman and sophomore years in college. We met early in my junior year. I had come off a turbulent event in my life, and she had arrived in the Los Angeles area from a small community in Central California. When we were married on August 23, 1957, I was twenty and she had just turned nineteen. We got married so young because I had been kicked out of college, and when I finally got back in I couldn't play sports, I couldn't sing in the choir, I couldn't represent the school. I couldn't do anything. So we just got married. There wasn't anything else to do. And when we got married, the last thing Beverley wanted to be was a pastor's wife, and the last thing I wanted to be was a pastor.

We had not planned for ministry. In fact, for four generations on my mother's side of our family, every offspring had either been a pastor or married one. I was determined to break that tradition, but it was not to be.

After a year in graduate school in Southern California, Beverley and I packed off to Kansas City, Missouri, with a three-month-old son, to attend seminary. We had no money, no place to live, and an apprehensive view of what would happen next.

In fact, as I reflect on all that transpired during those long years in Kansas City, earning my seminary degree, I can remember Beverley saying as we were driving out of town headed for our first church in California, "I really never thought this day would come."

In many ways, those words characterized our preparation for ministry. It was like walking through a dream—a bad dream.

Seminary training, for some, is a wonderful experience, but for us it was anything but a "fun time." We needed money. We didn't like Kansas City. We immediately saw too much of the political structure of the church. I worked three jobs to make ends meet. Bev was sick, for really the only time in our marriage, with mononucleosis. We were California kids in an ecclesiastical setting we didn't understand or enjoy.

But as is God's way, His grace was sufficient, His patience was long, and we made it. We were somewhat bruised and confused at the turn our lives had taken, but delighted to know there was a place for us to serve and people who wanted us to be their pastor.

On a personal note, many look back at a chapter in their lives much like we do at our seminary days and say, "Boy, it was tough, but we made it and now we are better for the experience." Not so with me. I look back at that experience much like one does a root canal. It's over. It was helpful. I didn't enjoy it. I thank God I don't have to do it again, but we learned the faithfulness of God through the experience.

When Beverley and I arrived at our first assignment, she was twenty-three years old. I remember the first time someone called her

"Sister London." She was unaccustomed, at her young age, to such greetings. She told me she was looking all around the church for my mom. She was too young to be "Sister" London, but ready or not, she was in fact "Sister" London.

I complicated our situation with extreme expectations for Beverley. In all fairness, it was not totally my fault because I had really had only one role model of what a pastor's wife should be. That was my mom. This may seem difficult for some ladies to fathom, but many weeks my mom made a hundred personal visitations on folks in my dad's parish. She would get me off to school and then "head out" to visit families of our Sunday School children, new prospects, shut-ins, and whomever. She was quite a lady, but to my disadvantage, I thought that was what all pastors' wives did with their time.

I was so wrong. Determined as I was to take the church world by storm, I had great expectations of how Beverley could help me with this challenge. I'm not exactly sure how to describe her response, but it might be like an age-old saying about snowballs and hell freezing over. In other words, Beverley would not be like my mom, nor would my success or failure in the ministry rise or fall on the intensity of her day-to-day involvement in the life of the church.

Now it's thirty-four years later. In November 1991, we left the pastoral ministry and began a new chapter of our lives at Focus on the Family in Colorado Springs. I can honestly say I love my role as a vice president at Focus on the Family. To serve as a "pastor to pastors" at this stage of my ministry is a dream come true. But the reality is that everything pales in comparison to pastoral ministry. There is no greater joy or privilege than investing your life and gifts in a congregation of people. How blessed I have been to be allowed the journey God has given me and to have Beverley as my wife for these thirty-seven years.

I want to share with you lessons for ministry I have learned from Beverley as we ministered together. There were highs and lows, hits and misses, successes and failures, but the end result is we have had the satisfaction of helping so many people draw close to Christ.

Lesson 1: "Let me find my place"

I have noticed as I travel about and communicate with clergy families that many wives are forced to assume a role predetermined by others.

Beverley is a musician, not a Bible teacher or a Sunday School worker. Her gift is music and supporting the music leadership of the church. She did it as well as anyone I have known. She could literally create the mood in a service by her preludes and offertories. In a day when the role of the organist is dying out, she may be one of the last of a special breed. She would often say to me, "Please don't ask me to do what I can't do. Let me do what I can do best." I did. And the churches we served were willing to trust our decision. Pastor, let your wife find her place.

Lesson 2: "I love the church, but I love you and my children more"

Notice that Beverley didn't say we were at a higher priority than God. She simply said my first responsibility is to you (H.B.) and to our sons, Brad and Bryan. Beverley was and is a great wife and mother. Though at times the "family thing" seemed to be a conflict for me, it was never a conflict for her. If push came to shove for her, our family always came before the church. Today our children and their families love the church and are active in it, and we all have pleasant memories as we look back at the various stages we enjoyed together. I firmly believe that a woman's wholehearted commitment as a wife and mother is infinitely more important than one's stature as a church woman. Such a priority models a sense of priority that other women in the church need to see.

Lesson 3: "I will be honest with you"

It makes no sense whatsoever for a pastor's wife to sit at the feet of her husband, thinking he is invincible and does not have feet of clay. Face it folks; we are all mere mortals in spite of the success we have achieved. In fact, some of our most visible colleagues who have achieved greatness have clay feet of gigantic size. Success can do that to anyone.

Paul's words in Ephesians 4:15, "Speak the truth in love," apply especially in the life of a pastor's wife. Because the wife has a vantage point and perspective of the ministry she shares with her husband, she is obligated to take advantage of it. It may be the length of a sermon. It could even be the way the pastor/husband relates to members of the opposite sex or even his own children.

Honesty is essential. Don't bug, don't nag, don't badger; establish the ground rule that each of you in the relationship has permission to "speak the truth in love." That also means to recognize the positive aspects of one's ministry. Accentuate the positive with genuine affirmation.

Lesson 4: "I want to be a part of the solution, not the problem"

In many instances the pastor's wife complicates a troublesome matter in a church community. How? It can happen in many subtle ways. For example, a pastor's wife can need recognition so badly that competition exists with the husband for approval or affirmation of the congregation. Another way to compound a problem is for the pastor's wife to "take matters in her own hands," to "stand by her man" to the point of greater confusion. There is a time to speak and a time to remain silent. Blessed is the pastor's wife who learns this lesson well and early. One thing I have admired about Beverley is her restraint. That did me so much good in ministry. My style was to fight every battle. She helped me learn to choose my battles, to lower my voice, and to control my body language. I'm still learning.

My denomination used to choose and reaffirm the tenure of a pastor with a congregational vote where a ballot was given to every member of the church fifteen years and older. At the appointed time, the members would vote on the future of the pastor in that local congregation by writing "yes" or "no" on a piece of paper. The vote needed a two-thirds majority for the pastor to continue. I freaked at these votes. It felt demeaning and insensitive. But it was the way things were done. Weeks before, I would begin to grumble about the process and build up in my mind the worst possible scenario.

I was always both agitated and humbled by Beverley's reaction to the whole thing. She never lost a moment's sleep or gave the "vote" a second thought. Her response was, "If they don't want you here, why would you want to stay in the first place?" To this day, I still think her reaction was a bit simplistic, but she felt if we had nothing to be ashamed of, we had nothing to worry about. She often reminded me that it was God who called me into ministry. He would sustain me. And He did.

I cannot remember a time in our ministry when Beverley became a point of dissension or division. Did everyone accept her? No, and everyone has a right to their opinion. But she was always part of the solution and never contributed to the problems.

Lesson 5: "I will follow where you lead"

This was not a kind of blind submission that did not include prayer and discussion, but our relationship was like Ruth's commitment to Naomi: "Where you go I will go, and where you stay I will stay. Your people will be my people and your God my god" (Ruth 1:16-17).

We served in four churches during our thirty-one years in pastoral ministry. At times I could sense that Beverley was not overjoyed with our assignment, but she found positives in every location, and we established a comfortable home. We were determined to bloom where we were planted. Not one time did Beverley ever say to me, "Let's leave" or "Why don't you look for another church?" We stayed until God gave us clear signals about our next assignment.

Bev and I really tried never to look over God's shoulder for the next step along the way, but rather to look Him in the eye—to see His love and His will for us. Each step we took, our gracious Lord had gone before us, and each place we served has left us with precious memories. In every environment where we found ourselves, Beverley made our home a pleasant place to return to.

Should a pastor's wife have a major part to play in determining the direction of her husband's ministry? By all means. Should she make that decision for him? Never!

I would not for a minute say that Beverley was seen as a spiritual giant or carried an awesome burden for the churches we served. She was not viewed that way. She was a great mom, a faithful wife, and a dedicated servant of the church. She made it easier for me to pastor. She took pressure off me in so many ways that uncomplicated my life. She supported me. She corrected me. She affirmed me. She loved me. She made me proud to be her husband.

As we reflect on how God has led us to His new place for us in His vineyard, Bev is happier than she has ever been. That's a gift from God—not just to her but to me.

Beverley is unlike any pastor's wife I have ever known. To me she is the finest pastor's wife. As I experience the church in so many different settings, I wish there were more pastors' wives like her, but then again I'm glad there was only one.

All that I have been saying to you is to be yourself. There is no one else in the whole human race with your kind of style and your kind of grace. Strive to be the best at being yourself you can possibly be. In the end that will be your success.

To Beverley I say, "Thank you. I would not have made it without you. I love you very much."

NEIL'S RECOLLECTION OF THEIR MINISTRY TOGETHER

Bonnie and I had finished college when we met during my first semester in seminary. A year or two ahead of H.B. and Beverley in seminary, we both relocated from different parts of the country to Kansas City during the summer of 1956. Bonnie moved from Portland, Oregon, to become an administrative assistant to key church leaders in our denomination. And I, after a year's experience as a green associate pastor in a tolerant, middle-sized church in Flint, Michigan, resettled in Kansas City to begin preparation for pastoral service. Both of us worked in different offices at our church headquarters where friends and mentors played Cupid for us.

After a year of courtship, we married in September 1957. One month later, I started ministry service as a student pastor in Gladstone, Missouri. Thus we have been ministry partners for all our married life with the exception of that first month.

Launching ministry in the mid-'50s was unlike starting now. In those days, we had no frame of reference regarding women's rights, for expecting a congregation to provide a minimum standard of living, for understanding the pros and cons of bi-vocationalism, or for dealing with the astronomical educational loans beginners face now.

Consumer church mentality was largely unknown among the laity. And the volunteer work force was larger because many women were not employed outside their home.

When we started, most people had some family member who had been involved with the church somewhere. Divorce was much less common, and no one talked about child abuse or sexual harassment.

Neither did anyone tell us that a strong clergy marriage was a wonderful gift we could give ourselves. We were not trained to know that relationships in a congregation mattered as much as anything else, that burnout should be expected if we did not provide self-care, that a soul friend or mentor would enrich our ministry, or that we should not move from an assignment until we accomplished something important for God.

In those beginning years, we were unseasoned and naive and had ineffective people skills. Sacrifice was expected, so we gave it. Hard work was required, so we did it. Isolation and loneliness were facts of life, so we toughed our way through. And even though personal spiritual formation was assumed, it was not taught; so we stumbled through times of testing and valleys of disappointments without much inner strength. In spite of our many inadequacies, we found fulfillment and fun in pastoral ministry, and we would gladly do it again.

Along the way, twenty years of ministry were invested in pastoral service. But even when involved in other roles, I was always close to the pastoral scene in my affections and priorities. Even when I was a college department head and academic dean, I taught future pastors, led continuing education for 5,000 pastors, and produced pastoral resources like magazines, audio cassettes, and books. And I once served as college chaplain for six years.

Now, as the G.B. Williamson Professor of Pastoral Development at Nazarene Bible College, I help prepare second career adults for various forms of ministry. Though teaching and preaching are my first loves, Christian publishing and serving as a resource consultant in many settings also brings incredible satisfaction.

Along this journey of service, Bonnie and I raised two fine sons—Todd and Scott—who grew up believing they were privileged to be preacher's kids. In every church, people loved our family and honored us with being colaborers in the Gospel.

In our pastoral partnership pilgrimage, Bonnie taught me many things about ministry. Of course, I should point out she had a head start on me because her parents were a wonderfully effective pastoral team. I was raised in a committed layman's home, so the perspective of those who sit in the pews was bred into me. Though Bonnie vowed never to marry a pastor, she consented to marry me, and we have had a joyful journey.

Though we have differing gifts and perspectives, Bonnie and I are a willing team in ministry. Her talents and class and sensitivities make people overlook many of my obvious weaknesses. And though I do not wish to leave an impression that everything is always perfect in our relationship, we love each other and enjoy most of the tasks of ministry. We've been through more than we could have possibly imagined at the start, but we feel extraordinary exhilaration as we look back.

Though Mark Twain did not have ministry couples in mind, Bonnie and I believe he was right about ministry when he observed, "One who has had a bull by the tail once has learned sixty or seventy times as much as a person who hasn't."[1] We believe many useful lessons can only be learned on the playing field of ministry, and we learned many of ours the hard way.

Lesson 1: "I can be both an enabler and a professional person"

Our sons, people in our churches, and I all view Bonnie as a friendly enabler and helpful nurturer. Bonnie is a great mother and grand-mother, a devoted wife, and a sensitive woman of God. In our pastorates, she was always available to people, listened to their concerns, and ministered to them as needed. At the same time, she cooked, cleaned, sewed, did crafts, and performed a miraculous economic balancing act with limited income at home.

Though some people in our churches might have been willing to see me leave, they always loved Bonnie for good reason. They knew they could count on her kindness, affirmation, and caring. Over the years, she made her share of hospital calls, taught Sunday School classes, sang in the choir, stood with me as dying people changed worlds, loved people, and welcomed new babies.

A high point of our week was standing together at the close of a worship service to greet the people, to receive their kindnesses, and to hear about their victories and valleys. Never pushy but always available, Bonnie offered people guarded confidentiality, a shoulder to lean on, or a friend to cry with.

Bonnie is also a professional person. She does everything with excellence and competence. At age forty, she earned her master's degree and has used it in several ways since, especially teaching English to grown candidates for ministry and making them enjoy it.

Since we married, she has typed and proofed every word I have ever written for publication. She keeps our checkbook balanced, is mastering the new world of computers, and keeps a comfortable home. Though nurturing and being a professional person rarely come in the same person, Bonnie has both qualities in abundance. She loves God, family, people, and quality, in that order.

Lesson 2: "You need a refuge at home"

Pastors' homes can easily become something like a busy hotel lobby, overrun with official guests and people who "just drop in" at inopportune times. If allowed to get out of control, these occurrences disrupt family equilibrium and keep a pastor from recuperating from the stresses of ministry in the safe privacy of his home. Of course, these strains originate both from people who have emotional, physical, and spiritual needs, and with pastors who carry around the spiritual responsibilities of ministry.

Though all of us need to live close to people, we found there is a great difference between Christlike hospitality and encouraging continuous invasion.

The refuge at home idea, because of my background, was a hard lesson for me. I was raised in a home where we often took in strays and drifters who were welcomed to stay for extended periods of time and they often did. Our guests included traveling evangelists between revivals and camp meetings, long-lost relatives who turned up periodically, and mere acquaintances who were down on their luck. Occasionally, we had people from two of these categories at the same time.

During any calendar year, my parents might have kept three or four different evangelists who stayed for a week or two each. Occasionally they stayed for longer periods and even brought their families. During the Great Depression, one pastor and his young family of three children, starved out of a little church in Canada, stayed for six months. That little family was homeless, though we did not know what to call it then.

Throughout our years together, Bonnie's idea about home being a refuge proved right. It provided me a refueling and renewing place—a sanctuary of calm and peace. Bonnie shielded me from problems the other policy would have caused our family. As a result I was energized to do many ministries I could not have accomplished otherwise. In every place, no matter what the parsonage was like, Bonnie made us a home and saw to it that it was an attractive shelter from the storm.

Lesson 3: "Marriage and ministry are not in competition"

From the beginning, Bonnie freed me to give myself fully to ministry. Like starting any business or profession, she realized that ministry takes long hours and hard work, a point many clergy couples miss. She knew that if I was fulfilled in my work I would likely be a better husband and father. And she was right.

She also understood that books and professional resources were necessary tools for a pastor, just as a carpenter needs a hammer and a trucker needs a truck. So books were high on our list of expenditures and still are.

As part of an emotional and spiritual commitment to the work of Christ, she gave me away to ministry and expected I would be given back in full measure to her and our sons. And that's what happened—when I was free to do ministry with every fiber of my being, I also felt eager and responsible to be with the most significant people in my life. This made home a magnet at the end of every day.

This is an important principle for a married couple in any vocation. If vocational demands are incessantly resisted and resented by either husband or wife, an occupation loses its meaning and attractiveness. Then the employed person feels it is necessary to give in to mediocrity in his work or, unconsciously, to give even more time to his work so he can avoid the conflicts at home.

Of course, in ministry there is always a danger of being out of balance or becoming a workaholic. As we say elsewhere in this book, balance in ministry is among the most pressing problems ministers face. But alongside the balance issue, every clergy couple needs to realize no pastor will be happily effective if he has to continually defend his time investments to his wife.

Though I seldom have had the time issue in balance as much as I wished, I kept trying because I did not have to defend my time use to Bonnie. It was easy for her to tell the children, "Dad has to go to work" instead of "The church is taking too much of our family time." And that idea was not especially novel to our boys because other fathers in our neighborhood sometimes worked late too.

And about our marriage — we could have grown a great relationship sooner if we had understood the full picture earlier. Like many ministry couples, we thought at the start that marriage and ministry had to compete for time, commitment, and energy. Now we know a solid marriage is worth any price because effort invested in a good marriage enriches ministry and at the same time serves as a model for a quality Christian home to families in the church. In troubled times like ours, modeling a good marriage may be among the most important ministry we offer our congregation.

Now to everyone who will listen, especially our students in training for ministry, we advise that a good marriage is a magnificent gift one can give himself and his ministry. From experience, we have learned that a healthy marriage and an effective ministry, growing side by side, make both better and much more fun.

Though we did not have Mother Teresa's writing to read in our formative years, we enjoy sharing this message with pastors' wives and their husbands. She said:

> My own mother used to be very busy, the whole day, but as soon as evening came, she moved very fast to get ready to meet my father. At that time we didn't understand; we used to laugh; we used to tease her; but now I remember what a tremendous, delicate love she had for him. It didn't matter what happened that day; she was ready with a smile to meet him.[2]

The anticipation of being together at home with our spouse and family at the end of a day is among the most powerful satisfactions and motivating anticipations life offers. We always tried to make it special and recommend that you do too.

Lesson 4: "Being an authentic Christian makes me a better minister's wife"

God created stretch points for everyone in the Christian life. However, we sometimes mistakenly think those concerns come to us because of ministry. Not Bonnie. Years before we met, she came to personal faith through the influence of her parents, who were well-adjusted Christian models. They were so much more than professional ministerial Christians. Therefore, obedience to the will of God, faithful stewardship, meaningful Christian service, and personal spiritual formation were part of her way of life and character long before we started in ministry and long before our sons were born.

Bonnie found opportunities of useful service in every ministry assignment we had—not as a pastor's wife, but as an authentic Christian. Sometimes she filled in when we had a gaping lack where no one else was interested or qualified—but only until we found someone. She shook hands, listened, entertained, listened, took women to lunch, loved the senior adults, and listened some more. She resisted serving on boards and committees, so it did not appear that she was speaking for me or trying to assume authority in the church. Some of her most enjoyable service was team-teaching a young adult Sunday School class and leading Bible studies for women's groups. Now, for the last eight years, she has taught grammar, spelling, reading, and love for ministry to second-career adult ministerial students.

As part of her Christian witness, she kept the spirituality spring at our house. She shielded what came into our home, what was read, said, and viewed on TV. She worked hard to keep prayer, Bible reading, attitudes, church attendance, and mealtime prayers attractive and vital. She inspired us, cherished us, and set limits for us. As a result, the three Wiseman men—our sons, Todd and Scott, and I—owe her a great debt for being an authentic pattern of faith.

As keeper of our home and lots of other things, as an inspiration for our devotion to Christ, and as an enabler for everything we dreamed, Bonnie helped our family and congregations live by this insightful Shaker poem:

> *Life is mostly what we make it,*
> *Filled with sunshine or with storm;*
> *Just whichever way we take it—*
> *Sad and cheering—cold or warm;*
> *Come what may, we need not borrow*
> *Grief or trials, great or small—*
> *Troubles of the brewing morrow,*
> *Which may never come at all.*[3]

I can't imagine ministry or life without Bonnie, and I pray I never have to. Bonnie Wiseman is one of a kind.

MARRIED TO A WOMAN WHO SHARES AND SHAPES MY DREAM

A Salute to Kay Warren
by Pastor Rich Warren

The greatest gift God has given me, next to my salvation, is my wife, Kay. My life has been enriched immeasurably and my ministry has been far more effective because of her.

In 1979, God gave me a dream of starting a new church as soon as I finished seminary. But that dream would have never become a reality if it hadn't been for Kay's deep commitment to doing God's will, her willingness to sacrifice, her love for people, and her faith in an idealistic husband. It takes a team to fulfill a dream!

We were not always a team. Because we are so different, our first years of marriage were very difficult. But since neither of us considered divorce as an option, we were forced to learn how to love, listen to, and adapt to each other. The payoff has been personal growth, greater ministry, and a genuinely satisfying relationship. I can't imagine my life or ministry without Kay.

Kay has been my greatest encourager

She has helped me maintain a clear perspective when facing impossible problems or unjustified criticism. Kay has practiced Ruth Graham's approach: "It's God's job to humble my husband. It's my job to love him!" When everyone else laughed at the size of my vision for the church in those early years, Kay was a true believer.

Kay is a woman of faith. With no money, no members, no building, and no guaranteed support, we left the security of Texas in a

U-Haul truck for the insecurity of beginning a new church in one of the most expensive locations in Southern California. Not once has Kay ever questioned or doubted that God would provide for us in our years of ministry.

Kay has been flexible and willing to change. This has been an absolute necessity for a church that grew from just our family to over 8,000 attending each weekend thirteen years later. Can you imagine the changes we've gone through in the short history of Saddleback Church? Our church met in fifty-six different facilities over the years before we were finally able to move to our permanent property. Adapting to change is not one of Kay's natural abilities; instead, it is a trait she has allowed God to develop in her character.

Kay has a servant's heart. She's always been willing to do whatever ministry was needed, serving in dozens of different capacities in our church with enthusiasm. Today our lay ministries have grown to the size that now Kay can focus on the area that God has gifted her most: teaching the Word.

Kay is a woman of the Word

She hungers for it like no other person or pastor I know. Not content to merely learn God's Word, she insists on personally applying it to everyday life. Her reputation as a competent Bible teacher is deserved. When she teaches, it is with integrity, humility, and sensitivity to the hurts of her audience. Like Paul, she "not only shares the Gospel but [her] life as well."

Amazingly, in spite of the enormous time and energy required to grow a church from scratch, Kay has kept our family a priority. The Warren clan is a wild bunch. Being the wife and mother is demanding and exhausting, but never boring. My three kids and I idolize her. I don't know how she does it all.

Kay accepts the loss of privacy

One difficult aspect of ministry that we've encountered is the decreasing amount of privacy we have as the church has grown. With 23,000 names now on our church roll, approximately one out of ten people we meet in our community attends Saddleback Church. We can rarely go anywhere without being recognized. Neither of us is comfortable with this, but Kay says, "Ministry means life in the public eye. This brings both problems and privileges. You must choose to focus on the benefits."

There are two characteristics that make a genuine ministry team: First, you must have a common goal. Kay and I have dedicated our lives together to the goal of reaching, teaching, encouraging, and sending out people to serve in God's kingdom. Second, you must have deep, regular communication about your common goal. Working toward the same goal doesn't make you a team unless you are communicating with each other. So Kay and I make sure we get plenty of time together to talk. As a result, my wife really is my best friend.

Kay compensates for my weaknesses

The value of team ministry with my wife is that we compensate for each other's weaknesses: I'm a visionary; Kay is a detail person. I'm good with crowds; Kay can sense an individual's need. I can be overconfident; Kay is cautious. The balance that comes from blending our personalities has made us both more effective for God.

You might conclude that I'm married to a superwoman. Actually, as Kay says, "God loves to do extraordinary things through very ordinary people." I've observed that the reason God uses my wife is that she never stops growing. Her own growth — spiritually, emotionally, and intellectually — is a constant challenge to me.

I feel confident that one day my wife will stand before Jesus Christ and hear Him say, "Well done, thou good and faithful servant!"

Pastor Rick Warren
Saddleback Church
Mission Viejo, California

11

A BILL OF RIGHTS FOR A PASTOR'S WIFE
Finding Significance in Shared Ministry

◇◇◇◇◇

Father, In our ministry we need Your help
to enjoy ministry insightfully and wholeheartedly,
to cherish relationships joyously and courageously,
to treasure our marriage lovingly and authentically
as a lifelong adventure. Amen.

◇◇◇◇◇

*L*EADERSHIP MAGAZINE did ministry couples an important service of building self-awareness with its 1992 survey that indicated current trends in clergy marriages. The study deals with the pastor's home and with relationships in the minister's family. That survey shows that 94 percent of pastors feel pressured to have an ideal family. Eighty percent of pastors in the survey indicated their spouse felt pressured to become an ideal role model.

In the actual marriage relationship, 55 percent of pastors were very satisfied with their marriage and 31 percent were very satisfied with family life. But only 25 percent of pastors' spouses were very satisfied with family life. Time pressures were the number one challenge facing clergy marriages — not enough time together, not enough time to talk, not enough time to work out difficulties, not enough time to love one another, and not enough time for emotional and physical intimacy.

Closely related to these issues was the assessment of their fears. The question, I thought, was highly significant: On the whole, do you think being a pastor is a benefit or a hazard to your family life? Of those surveyed, 40 percent said hazard and 60 percent said benefit. While everyone can rejoice with the 60 percent, these responses mean that 40 in 100 ministry couples believe they face some kind of risk. On a similar point, psychologist Archibald Hart's survey indicated that 80 percent thought ministry reflected negatively on the life of their families. Many said they would not enter the ministry again if they had a choice.

ONE WIFE SPEAKS FOR MANY

Now, after more than three decades of pastoral ministry, Bev and I can look back a bit. Recently, while we were talking about the message of this book, I said to her, "You know what it's like to live under all that pressure in the pastor's home. We've been in it together all these years; help me understand the stress points you felt."

• **Always present.** First, she mentioned that the ministry is so constant—it just never stops. "You're always talking about it," she said. "When you're with people socially, you talk all the time about the church. When you come home, you want to talk about the church." Many pastors are constantly on the phone talking to someone about church life. The church can easily dominate every aspect of your life if you are not careful.

• **Mistress mentality.** Beverley said, "I felt like I never had you to myself. I was sharing you with somebody." In talking to so many pastors and pastors' wives, there is almost a mistress mentality that develops. The church seems to seduce a pastor to give it more time, more energy, more affection. Then the spouse feels left out and jealous—for good reason. The wife thinks the mistress takes too much time and attention away from her and the children.

• **Achievement addiction.** The third thing Beverley suggested, which I buy totally, is that my Type A personality and my tendency to be a workaholic kept me from taking time to give our boys all they needed. I'm guilty, and I know it. I have talked with our two sons about this.

When I came out of seminary, I was enamored with numbers and recognition. I felt driven to compete. I was sure I had to have ten more the next Sunday than I had the last Sunday or I was a failure. And in many ways I was a failure to my family and was not a whole person.

• **Worship deprivation.** Another lack was a failure to worship together. We seldom had opportunity to worship together even in our own church. Bev played the piano or the organ, and I was in the pulpit doing my thing. We were doing our best to help others worship, and they did. But we never had the wonderful experience of coming together as a couple and a family in worship situations — to sing together, to sit together, and to be fed together by the preaching of the Word of God.

• **Private space.** Beverley pointed out that our private times had to fit in with what was going on at church. I'm talking about the quiet times, the away times, and even our times of intimacy. The *Leadership* survey agreed with our conversation. It suggested specific reasons why intimacy is not as frequent as many wished: 70 percent faulted the pastor's busy schedule, 54 percent the spouse's busy schedule, 35 percent frequent night church meetings, 25 percent children at home, and 17 percent stress from the congregation. This means that if you are going to find quality time for togetherness, solitude, and intimacy, you will have to plan it, guard your date book, and be intentional about how you schedule church events.

In our most frustrating moments, we agree with the pastor's wife who was quoted in *Newsweek:*

> Clergy ought to be celibate . . . because no decent, right-minded man ought to have the effrontery to ask any woman to take this lousy job! . . . I, myself, am happy, basically because I love my husband but I'm afraid it is often in spite of the church. All this seems too far away from the ideals of our youth and the teachings of Jesus.[1]

She could be right. But love of spouse and family, the ideals of Jesus, and commitments from our youth help us keep going and improving and growing.

A BILL OF RIGHTS FOR A PASTOR'S WIFE

At this point, let me speak to pastors' wives and walk into territory you may feel I don't fully understand. But please let me share my perspective to see if it helps you drastically improve your fulfillment in your work for Christ. My only right to speak about these issues stems from a deep desire to be helpful—to share my perspective as a pastor/husband who wants to come alongside ministry couples with inspiration and caring and encouragement. I want ministry to become a joy and an adventure for you. I want you to find wonderful ways to increase your fulfillment.

Try being yourself

You must be your best self, but be yourself. Resist the pressure to live a fictionalized role you put on like an article of clothing to please someone else. Playing an empty role makes it easy to allow a church to make you into something you don't want to be. Then you find yourself becoming someone you don't recognize or like. Please don't let that happen.

Ask yourself these questions often: What gives you satisfaction? What makes you feel you have maximized your greatest potential at the end of the day? How can you best express who you are through your personality and your unique abilities?

You must find a level of happy acceptance of yourself—a unique pastor's wife significantly different from any other minister's wife who ever lived. Resist letting your husband, children, or church family push you to become someone you don't want to be. It can happen so easily, and then you will likely feel used by others or angry at yourself for becoming someone you don't even know.

Jill Briscoe offers a wholesome, balanced insight when she writes:

Eventually, with my husband's help, I was able to face the pressures and say, "If you will let me be who God has gifted me to be, then I will really be able to contribute, and that includes letting me exercise gifts that don't fit the role here. But if you don't allow me to do that and you insist on me doing things that I am not gifted to do, I will be no good to anybody and we will all end up being frustrated."[2]

Use your best gifts most often

The biggest mistake is trying to be all things to all people so you end up being harried and exhausted. You need to do what you do best. Leadership expert Bobb Biehl suggests you delegate what you don't do well, and not feel guilty about it. If there's anybody in the church who can do what you do 80 percent as well, you need to let them do it.

Ladies, you know your highest level of frustration often comes when you are asked to do something you are uncomfortable doing. Of course, you must grow and attempt challenges, but some of you will never be comfortable leading a Bible study or entertaining or even teaching teens. But there is a golden growth opportunity that comes when you stretch to improve what you do best. There is always a sense of satisfaction in that. What do you like to do? What do you do best? Follow Peter's wonderful advice, "Each one should use whatever gift he has received to serve others, faithfully administering God's grace in its various forms" (1 Peter 4:10).

Make your priorities obvious

People need to know what your priorities are. If you want to be a "taxi driver," then inform the congregation of your availability. Let them know you are willing to take people to the doctor's office and sit there for half a day. And if you want to keep their kids while they go on a weekend getaway or marriage encounter, that's fine too. But if your priority is to be a wife and a mother and live your life for the greatest good, then you must speak up kindly but convincingly. People have a right to know your priorities. But they will never know unless you tell them, and you can't tell them until you know.

One pastor's wife told me about her husband's first interview with a decision group looking for a new pastor. She said the interview did not go well until one of them looked her way and asked, "Do you play the piano?" When she answered "Yes," the interview vastly improved and they began to warm toward her husband and ultimately called him—all because they needed a pianist. She always thought they wanted a pianist more than they wanted a pastor. For all the years of that pastorate she felt ambivalent toward the church.

Early in a new assignment, set the parameters of priorities. Your husband can help by making it clear how you feel about your role in the church. Don't let the church squeeze you into their mold, and don't overreact so they think you are too good to be a servant. A delicate balance is needed.

The whole issue has to be squared with Jesus' call to seek first the kingdom of God and His righteousness. That sounds like both an inner priority and an outward commitment.

Don't attempt to control the church

You are not the last word on every issue—maybe not even the first. So often when laymen talk about pastors' wives, they say to me, "Why does she have to express her opinion on every issue? Why does she think she knows everything?"

I'm not sure why this happens, but one may be the fact that you want your husband to succeed so much that you take matters into your own hands. What I have found is that if you insist on having the last word or being the only one who can do what needs to be done, in time they will let you do it. Then when you need people, they will not step forward.

Why not give them an opportunity to grow, even if they sometimes fail? Work alongside of them. Be a happy affirming helper rather than the one who has all the answers and influences all the decisions.

Listen more and talk less

Hurting people need redemptive, active listeners. The most helpful pastors' wives are those who feel and express compassion and caring. They listen; they don't need center stage; and they don't

255

offer simple answers. For some strange reason, many Christian leaders mistakenly think their credibility lies in their ability to solve problems for everyone. It does not.

Those who help others the most are often those who just listen. They do not condemn. They do not put people in their place, nor do they compromise. Instead, they are listeners who allow others to come to their own conclusions about issues of consequence. Some of the most memorable counseling relationships are those where we have been quiet, listened intently, and allowed those who are hurting to discover the direction they should take for themselves. So often as those people leave you, they say, "Thank you. You have been so helpful. How will I ever thank you?" Insight comes to the person in need, and affirmation comes to the helper, when we are willing to listen thoughtfully and redemptively.

Nurture change agents

Spend quality time with those who can make a difference. To be a "change agent" means you seek out people within the congregation who have potential to impact the church, the community, and the world—other ladies whom you can teach fine things about ministry and about being wives and mothers. If you can leave a few ladies in each church who have the same compassion and priorities and desires to serve within their hearts that you have, you will have left a lasting legacy. Move past restrictive relationships into meaningful friendship with persons you can mentor.

Second Timothy 2:2 applies to women as well as to men in the church. To paraphrase the passage a bit, "As pastors' wives, entrust to reliable, faithful, teachable, committed women those things you have learned so in time they will be able to disciple others." Take time to spot several women in your church who have not been tainted by politics, negativeness, or cynicism, and work to mold them into energetic and inspired Christian women.

Show visible love to your husband

Stand beside him in every way. No cutting sarcasm, please. Hold his hand in view of the congregation. Walk with him across your church grounds and parking lot. In your conversations, let people know that your husband is both special and human. Let them know you love him. Support him. Pray for him. And thank God for him. So many unfortunate situations that ruin ministry marriages could be avoided if the pastor's home sends out the right signals.

In every possible way, say by your words and attitude, "I love my husband and he loves me. He is off limits to outside interference. Though our relationship may not be perfect, don't mistake our being human for a lack of love and loyalty to each other."

A pastor's wife shared her pain in a letter not too long ago: "I have no respect for my husband because he's letting people push him around. He's wrecking our family. I will probably stay with him because we would go bankrupt if he lost his job. I detest this whole charade." I wonder if a new commitment to love would help this situation.

There is so much that woman is missing—such richness in love, togetherness, and respect. You can do better in your relationship. Keep showing the church that you love one another and you care for each other. Even as your mutual love energizes your lives, it will spread a model of marital wholeness to the congregation.

Talk about advantages to your kids

Never tell your children they have to do something because they are the pastor's children. Give better reasons for your family standards—there are many. Don't expect perfection, but help them know that while they have unique demands, they have special privileges. Help them see the benefits in being a pastor's son or daughter, and how they have a positive part in your family's shared ministry. Try to raise them feeling that the church is important to them, so they will not begrudge or blame the church when they grow up. I get so many letters from pastors' kids who hate the church and anything it stands for because of what it did to their parents. Avoid that at any cost. Cultivating their faith may be the most important ministry you will ever accomplish.

Work to maximize the advantages. In most pastors' homes, if the wife does not take the initiative, days off will be haphazardly observed and vacations will be hurried and unplanned. Even if your husband is not good at it, you can schedule vacation days and date nights. It is a way of helping him know he belongs to you and the children. Help him keep you as a priority by planning happy times together with you and the children. You are God's gifts to each other.

Find a prayer partner as a soul mate

Seek to be a part of, or even establish, a pastors' wives group who hold each other accountable. Get beyond the hype and fantasy and be honest with one another. I think every young pastor's wife needs a mentor who has been around the track and knows how to read the danger signs. And even more mature pastors' wives will grow in such a two-way mentoring group.

This relationship will create some risk for you, but you need someone beyond the ladies' Bible study group to lean on. Finding that person will not be easy, but be willing to search until you find such a relationship.

Take a worship break

Take a busman's holiday to occasionally worship at another church. Go somewhere every few months where you don't have to critique anything, where there are no expectations, and where you are not expected to play any kind of role. Just drink in the inspiration and worship. Instead of a shopping weekend, take a worship weekend. Get away and read. Listen to music. Be refreshed in your soul.

Sometimes you will even need to seek the support of another pastor in times of crisis. Charlotte Ross, a pastor's wife, offers a scenario when that might be necessary:

> She had found the lump a week before. It was low, on the right side of her breast. A visit to the doctor had confirmed its presence. Without hesitation, the doctor, a member of the congregation, made the arrangements for her to enter the hospital. Today she had been x-rayed as an outpatient so that the surgeon would have as much information as possible. The specialist in the radiology department had questioned her gruffly. Then he had said, "I don't see how anything so extensive could just show up!" With that he had dismissed her.

His words had frightened her. When her minister-husband picked her up outside the hospital, she fought to keep her self-control. She knew he was frightened too. That night when the house was dark, she stretched on the bed in the spare bedroom and sobbed. She felt utterly alone. There was no pastor, except her own husband, to whom she could talk about her fears and no close woman friend to share her feelings of rage, dread, and helplessness.[3]

That frightened woman needed someone other than her husband to help her find spiritual sustenance at such a trying time in her life, and her husband needed someone to help him sort through his own anxieties. They both needed a pastor and so will you.

Don't spiritualize everything

People will come to you seeking answers to questions dealing with life and death. You do not need to feel less of a pastor's wife if you can't answer with chapter and verse, or even out of your own experience. I heard Chuck Swindoll tell a story that makes a case for leaving all the reasons to God, and not feeling as though everything has some major spiritual application.

Swindoll tells about a Christian school where children were highly regimented. Everybody marched in line, and the children had to raise their hand to respond to the teacher. The headmaster was a real taskmaster. The children and teachers feared him for good reason.

One day the headmaster walked into the third-grade class and started asking questions. The children were afraid they were going to give wrong answers. He asked, "What is furry, has a long tail, climbs trees, and collects nuts for the winter?" Nobody replied. After a long wait, he finally said, "If you're not going to answer, I'm going to choose someone." He pointed to a little third-grade girl and said, "You answer. Tell me what is furry, has a long tail, climbs trees, and collects nuts for the winter."

The girl was quiet for a minute and then said slowly, "Well, it's probably a squirrel, but I'll say Jesus Christ."

I mean, you just don't have to have full-blown, spiritual answers for everything. Sometimes God doesn't seem to make sense. As Dr. James Dobson wrote:

> When we are young and health is good and we have not yet encountered disease, disappointment and sorrow, it is easy to believe that life will always be rather carefree and happy. But every person who lives long enough will eventually experience difficulties that are not easy to understand. At those times, the pieces simply will not fit, and God just doesn't make sense.[4]

You know there will always be these people whose kids are the ones that fall off the swing and they always have the flat tire on the way to church and their husbands always lose their jobs. They live in a vicious circle of crises. And they want a logical explanation. The reason may be they're careless or dysfunctional in many ways. Or there may be no answers. Life has many unexplainable ambiguities. Don't blame God or put all the responsibility on His shoulders. Sometimes a hug will be your only answer to troubled souls.

On the other hand, don't cover all your actions by saying, "God told me" or "This is the will of God." Sometimes it is better just to admit that it is your desire or your own best judgment, or your ignorance, but don't blame God.

Schedule vacation days and date nights

See to it that your husband puts important family dates on his calendar. Don't leave it up to him. If there's any wonderful ministry you can do together as husband and wife, it is to help your marriage and family succeed.

Get the details into his schedule. Write them in: This time belongs to us. This time belongs to the kids. These are the three days we're going to be away. Most pastors follow through on what is written in their date book.

Don't be bizarre or eccentric

Don't call undue attention to yourself by being weird or unusual. I know you need to be yourself, but there are limits. Many pastors' wives undercut their husbands' effectiveness because they have some need to "stand out" or want to be different or make a statement or just want to be outrageous. Try not to create such a sensation by who you are, what you do, or how you look so people leave the church parking lot commenting more about your oddities than they do about their worship experience. "Too much" or "too little" often causes the problem—too much or too little make-up, too much or too little jewelry, too much or too little feathers in your hair. Genuine Christlikeness is the most impressive characteristic anyone can have.

Please think carefully about what you do and its implications. Little things like what people see when they enter your house or ride in your car make a statement about you and your life style. If you need a shovel to clean McDonald's cartons and wrappers out of your car before someone can sit in the passenger seat, then you might want to rethink your behavior patterns. To be vocal in your opinions to a point of not caring what you say, how you say it, or to whom you say it can be counterproductive or even damaging to your ministry as a colaborer with your husband.

Paul called for ladies in the church to be women of "decency and propriety" (1 Tim. 2:9). And I think 1 Timothy 4:12, though the words are especially addressed to youth, apply to all persons in ministry roles: "Set an example for the believers in speech, in life, in love and in purity." Whatever it means to you to be submitted to the lordship of Jesus Christ, try it and I guarantee it will temper or destroy any eccentricity that might hinder the cause of Christ.

Be a keen and accurate observer of the church

Alert your husband to the red flags you observe in the congregation. Keep aware of the trends and the winds of change. It is hard for him to read the signals at times. Often you have an uncanny ability to spot trouble with a capital "T." Take permission to ask, "Have you thought about this?" "I wonder why that person said this?" "Are you sure that you've given attention to this?"

As a pastor's wife, you have a totally different perspective of church and family life than your husband or any church member. As you walk among the congregation, you feel things, hear things, sense things that no one else can. Also, as you move around the community, you meet people in the market, at school, at the hairdresser, at the Little League games who will give you helpful insights into the church and community you serve. Be faithful to these moments. And share them with your man — this could make the difference between your husband's effectiveness or failure.

Try to see things as laypeople view them. Be honest about your expectations of others and the real pressures they face every day. The spiritual level of the church does not rise and fall alone on the quality of your husband's preaching or pastoral care, but by the way the people are equipped and encouraged to live out their faith in the real world. The more successful laypersons become "more than conquerors" in their day-to-day activities, the greater influence your church will have in the community. And that is also reflected in the Sunday services.

Please be a sentry on the wall of your church, protecting your husband's integrity and the church's authenticity — subtly, simply, and surely — just as you protect the emotional and spiritual needs of your family.

Encourage your husband to find an accountability partner

Most men have few close friends. Wives really need to encourage their husbands to find an accountability friend. Only three out of every ten pastors can name a close friendship with another man. Every pastor needs a covenant partner, other than a wife, that he can talk "pastoral stuff" with and someone who understands the burdens he carries.

Don't be jealous of this. Encourage it. Perhaps you could even make a specific suggestion about who this man friend should be. You might invite a couple over for a meal or a visit to start developing such a relationship.

Men are loners, and much of the depression we find in pastors of all ages stems from the fact that they have no one to help them hold their arms up when they are weary. Moses had Aaron. Your husband needs an Aaron or a Barnabas — someone with whom he can just be human, but who also understands his divine calling.

Laugh a lot

Learn to laugh at yourself and your situation. Most of us take life too seriously. All human relationships are filled with laugh opportunities. You cannot carry a heavy load all the time.

Sitting across the table from a pastor and his wife a few days ago, I was struck by the fact that she knew as much as her husband did about the attendance, the spiritual temperature, and the ministries of the church. It was as though they were copastors. I could see that she became super serious when we talked about all the "church" things. And when I left the table, I wondered if they ever just talked about normal husband and wife issues or if they ever laughed at themselves.

If that's your desire—all this serious stuff—more power to you. But I sense that most clergy wives do not want to be a pastor. Remember, as a pastor's wife, you are in a position to keep it light, to keep laughter at the table, to plan big birthday parties, to celebrate anniversaries, and to do spontaneous things that are fun. In the pressure cooker you live in, there must be those times when the steam is released. If it doesn't happen, there will be some kind of explosion somewhere.

You also have opportunity to make sure your husband doesn't start seeing himself as the world's savior and thinking he must single-handedly solve all the ills of society. This can be done by refusing to let him get away with being "Rev. Father" or "Pastor Husband." At home, the clerical collar must come off and the old sweatshirt must go on. Remember, genuinely holy people are not spooks.

Don't bug your husband

Pick the time to make your point, and then move on. Every woman has her own unique ways to get the full attention of the man in her life. Use yours. But remember, an emotional splinter in the finger does not need an amputation to correct it. Just never let him off the hook where you and the kids are concerned. Your home and your marriage energize and stabilize his ministry.

Stay attentive to your husband's needs

Don't back away. There will be times when your husband, under the weight of the struggle, will become sullen, aloof, and depressed. It may not be a pretty sight, but that is not a good time to withdraw or punish him emotionally. It is likely the time he needs you most. Try doubling or tripling your affection and support.

Please try to understand that next to you and the family, his ministry is the most important thing in the world to him. It's his calling, his life, and usually the way he identifies himself. By your words and your actions please do not minimize his role in God's scheme of things. Tell him often that you are proud of him. A kiss on the cheek or a candlelight dinner will do wonders for both of you. Try calling him at the office to tell him what a great husband and father he is. Tuck a love note in his study Bible or in his briefcase. Or pack a mushy card in his suit bag when he has to travel.

Commit to self-care

Take care of yourself—spiritually, emotionally, and physically. John advised Gaius in 3 John 2, "I pray that you may enjoy good health and that all may go well with you, even as your soul is getting along well."

Pastor Bill Hybels of the great Willow Creek Community Church near Chicago talks about gauges that are spiritual, emotional, and physical. If you see those gauges, like gas or heat gauges on your car, reflecting potential problems in any areas of your life, you must get help and correct the problem. The letters I receive at Focus on the Family are filled with incredible imbalance. Use these questions as examining gauges:

- Are you eating right?
- Are you getting enough exercise?
- Are you emotionally stimulated by the right things?
- The Bible says to "watch your life" (1 Tim. 4:16). If you don't care for your wholeness, nobody else will.

Keep your perspective

Pray, "Lord help me see how things look to You." And then live by Ecclesiastes 3:1-8:

> There is a time for everything, and a season for every activity under heaven: a time to be born and a time to die, a time to plant and a time to uproot, a time to kill and a time to heal, a

time to tear down and a time to build, a time to weep and a time to laugh, a time to mourn and a time to dance, a time to scatter stones and a time to gather them, a time to embrace and a time to refrain, a time to search and a time to give up, a time to keep and a time to throw away, a time to tear and a time to mend, a time to be silent and a time to speak, a time to love and a time to hate, a time for war and a time for peace.

Continue to mature spiritually. A well-balanced godly woman is her pastor/husband's greatest asset. Solomon wrote in that great tribute to a godly woman, "Her husband has full confidence in her and lacks nothing of value. She brings him good, not harm, all the days of her life" (Prov. 31:11-12). The world, your family, and even the church will sometimes disrupt your equilibrium. They don't mean to; they just will by the nature of things. That's why I urge you to guard your time with the Lord. Have a time and a place to meet your Heavenly Father on a regular basis. Always have a good book going—maybe two. Meet with your prayer partner regularly. Have your own unique ministry. Monitor your home for signs of apostasy. Satan would take great delight in breaking down communication in your household. Remember, you are the "keeper of the springs." Don't let anything or anyone bring pollution into your life or the life of your family. You and those you love have been "created to be like God in true righteousness and holiness" (Eph. 4:24).

Care for your finances

The North American clergy family is not being overpaid. In fact, many live below the poverty level. There is nothing as debilitating as financial pressure—like being locked into a small, steel jail cell with little chance for escape. The pressures will be relieved by controlling spending, shopping wisely, and earning more money. Drive the old car. Minimize the use of credit cards. Shop creatively. Take a low-key, part-time job. Encourage those in your extended family to invest in your ministry like they do for missionaries. If you're not a missionary, I don't know what you would be called. Don't buy impulsively; talk it over before any purchase of consequence is made. And keep all financial surprises to a minimum.

YOU CAN DO IT
WITH JOY

By now, you know you are not a superwoman and no one wants you to be. Our intent is to hang beautiful mirrors around so you can see how well you are doing. Everyone needs to know that many pastors' wives are living beautiful lives of service and meaning.

But if you don't like what you see in the mirrors, don't run. Start making realistic choices where changes are needed. Think about the beauty and the opportunity and the grace that is possible, and then rejoice in your potential and privileges.

We care about you. We believe in you. The role you play in the church of Jesus Christ cannot be overestimated. God needs you more than you know.

Neil and I have been blessed with wonderful partners in ministry. Though our lives have not always been trouble free, we have experienced most of the things you have in our various stages of ministry. We survived and thrived and we would do it again.

I love TV commentator Andy Rooney's insight:

> If someone bases his happiness or unhappiness on major events like a great new job, huge amounts of money, a flawlessly happy marriage or a trip to Paris, that person isn't going to be happy much of the time. If, on the other hand, happiness depends on a good breakfast, flowers in the yard, a visit from a friend or a nap, then we are more likely to live with quite a bit of happiness.[5]

Let me paraphrase Rooney's ideas for ourselves: "If happiness depends on living with a dedicated spouse, being involved in a great cause, lots of affirmation, and a church full of friends, then we are likely to live with quite a bit of happiness."

Above all, live by Psalm 32:8: "I will instruct you and teach you in the way you should go; I will counsel you and watch over you." That commitment by our Lord provides guidance, direction, assurance, and protection. With that kind of help you have magnificent opportunities for Christian greatness in your own home, church, community, and especially in your marriage.

12

QUESTIONS EVERY PASTOR'S WIFE WANTS ANSWERED
Answers for the Present Dilemma

◇◇◇◇◇

Jesus, Lover of my soul,
   Help my mate and me
      communicate Your wisdom,
      radiate Your love,
      depend on Your power, and to
grow in effectiveness across a lifetime. Amen.

◇◇◇◇◇

*I*N MINISTERS' HOMES EVERYWHERE, conscientious women of God are working through questions about marriage, parenting, and ministry roles. They want answers and solutions to help them live full lives. It's amazing that nearly identical questions are asked again and again at conferences in so many different settings. And many of the same issues frequently come up in letters to H.B. London at Focus on the Family. Thus there is good reason to believe every question and letter probably represents hundreds of others who do not ask or write.

Clergy homes are under siege like never before. We all realize it. Bewilderment, ambiguity, and assault on Christian values are common. Many churches are out of balance and dysfunctional.

267

Thus every question represents a need for information, or a cry for help. Some questions represent desperate distress dealing with a specific issue in a particular family. Generally it is easier to cope when we know others have faced the same problems.

We asked pastors who wrote salutes to their wives throughout this book to help answer these questions. Thus, the reader has several perspectives. Our thanks to these contemporary Christian leaders, as the Apostle Paul says, "for their work's sake."

If a ministry couple is helped to find deeper appreciation of their partnership, we will be gratified. If someone finds new purpose and deeper meaning in his/her service for Christ, then this chapter will have served its purpose.

1. How do you face tough times and troubled people — common problems in contemporary ministry?

I won't pretend we have never complained to each other when tough times, painful circumstances, or unkind people have come or had to be dealt with. But Anna has never wavered from a posture of complete partnership in facing these demands of pastoral work. She has never suggested that we do something else. She has a sense of call to ministry that makes it infinitely easier for me to be faithful to my call. — Jack W. Hayford

2. I heard a speaker at a recent pastors'/wives' conference say our marriages could be a source of rich ministry. I'm confused by the potential conflicts between marriage and ministry.

Please avoid competition between marriage and ministry at any cost. It always has dreadful results — one or the other suffers, and it is so unnecessary. Too often we dwell on the downside of ministry marriages without realizing the upside. In a broken and dysfunctional world, a Christ-saturated ministry marriage has a modeling influence that extends beyond the pastor's home into the church and community. A ministry couple's healthy, stable marriage creates an attractive spiritual and emotional magnet that draws people to them. Many couples with problems in the church and community are attracted to wellness wherever they find it. They look for model marriages they can emulate. Let's remember, a good marriage nourishes all aspects of a pastor's ministry. And as a serendipity, a pastor and his wife's life together are enriched in the process. — HBL

3. How can we maintain or improve motivation to continue when the work is hard and slow?

Left to our own response and reaction, the ministry has too many demands and the work is endless and difficult. But we are not left to ourselves. Ministry by definition is a partnership with God. We are never alone in our efforts for God and for His people. To be used of God to make an essential difference in someone's life may be hard work, but it is the most satisfying work in the world. Think of the realities and potential in our work. God revives churches through us. God wins people through us. His cause always triumphs, like it did at the Exodus, at Calvary, on the first Easter, and last Sunday. But He always works His achievements of redemptive ministry to people through ordinary, yielded human beings like us. — NBW

4. How does a young woman with heavy family responsibilities and an outside job develop a life of prayer?

Anna learned to pray without ceasing during the first five years of our ministry when three of our four children were born — there wasn't a lot of "protected time" for devotions then. She became as effective at home interceding over a kitchen sink as in a sanctuary. There is a kind of prayer in motion which is available to even the busiest Christian. — Jack W. Hayford

5. How can I be sure I'm a people person?

I appreciate your obvious concern — it is an important starting point. Many who think of themselves as people persons are really people users. They manipulate people. They slap individuals on the back and greet everyone in a crowd because it is the thing to do. Then too they reason that someone important might see them doing it and be impressed. They ask "How are you?" without listening for an answer. In Christian organizations and church staffs, they use people to accomplish their purposes, but seldom value people for their real worth to God and the kingdom.

Churches, like other people groups, seldom love a leader unless the leader loves them. But when they feel loved and accepted, they almost always automatically return the favor. On the contrary, "things"-focused leaders relate to persons in a kind of professional way, and those they lead suspect a subtle friendlessness beneath their thin veneer of friendliness. Pastors and their spouses who use people are among the loneliest persons in the world. — HBL

6. How can I know if I'm focused on people instead of programs or the institutional aspects of the church?

Here are a few questions I use to keep clearly focused on people and their needs.

- Am I reflective about relationships?
- Do I need others to need me?
- Do I welcome the opportunity to share myself with people?
- Do I give time to persons who are different from me?
- Do I enjoy people who could never do anything for me?
- Do I spend time with common folks — the kind that fill most churches?
- Do people feel accepted by me? — HBL

7. I get out of focus very easily and start emphasizing trivial concerns. Do you have suggestions to help me keep the big picture of ministry in mind?

Since ministry always revolves around relationships, work at cherishing people. Allow positive people to strengthen you. Let up on your criticism of others because you have never walked in their shoes or seen things from their viewpoint. When people ask about your family or health, or ask for your opinion, respond with appreciation and quickly turn the conversation back to them. Ask them to tell you about their family and their interests. Express spiritual concern about them and those close to them. Learn to love people in spite of their idiosyncrasies, and they will love you in return.

One pastor's wife commented sadly, "Ministry is difficult for us because we are basically 'things' people." She continued, "Things are easier to control because they are always the same. People, however, are unpredictable, often inconsistent. I guess you can say people frustrate and surprise us." Though she is right about human predictability, people stand at the center of ministry. And everything else in ministry is important only when it serves people.

Every individual who attends anyone's church needs someone to cherish them, to value them as important to the cause of Christ, and to give them a sense of meaning and belonging. No one enjoys attending a church where they are seen only as a part of the crowd. No one wants to attend a church where they are loved only in theory. — NBW

8. Is ministry harder now than it used to be?

For many reasons, every phase of ministry now seems more complicated than it used to be. Anyone who lives at the epicenter of a congregation finds their stamina and vision tested often. It is incredibly easy for a pastor and his family to become spiritually drained because so many count on them. A Colorado pastor's wife once observed, "Too many people wanted a piece of us this week. We feel used up and unready for Sunday." Anyone who serves in ministry can easily identify with those feelings.

To have energy to meet all these spiritual demands, the pastor's wife must find ways to nourish her own faith. Personal prayer, Bible reading, public worship, and close contact with spiritually vigorous people are absolute requirements. Do not be surprised if these resources do not come from your husband, because he is so busy giving support to others. — HBL

9. What about shared limelight in pastoral ministry between the pastor and his wife?

During a question and answer period at a conference, Margaret was asked, "Is it difficult for you to 'stay behind the scenes' and allow John to spend so much time in the public eye?" Margaret replied, "No, I feel that there is room for only one star in a family, and John is our star." — John C. Maxwell

10. How did you and your wife develop a Christian home?

Anna has a solid, good-sense genuineness that is at the heart of why our home and family has always been a pleasant, predictably nice place to be. I think our four kids would say I was a pretty good dad, but I know they believe they have a great mom. As a result, all four of them are committed to Christ and serving in Christian ministry in some respect. Our oldest son, a chemist, is a Bible teacher at his church, and our other three children are in full-time pastoral work. They are all happily married and all raising kids in a way that is clearly forming a new generation of solid-stuff Christians. I attribute the realization of this fact, of course, to the grace of God. But I also know it's direct fruit of the homey, loving, practical wisdom of my wife. She was there all the time, raising good kids through her credible, effective, "plains-proven" good sense and godliness. — Jack W. Hayford

11. Does every assignment offer potential for satisfying ministry?
Yes, I believe it does. In our book *The Heart of a Great Pastor,* we explain how every assignment can be holy ground. Journeying together in ministry has potential for pastors and their wives to discover beauty and meaning in every place. But they must intentionally recognize the possibilities, look at the opportunities, and count the joys. It takes close attention and testing our own stereotypes to make full use of moment-by-moment potential.

By the same token, our troubles must be clarified and understood before we can solve them. But most of them can be solved. I plead with you not to stoically accept what you can change. Our problems in ministry must be diagnosed and analyzed, but they must also be remedied. An overpowering accumulation of old problems is what so often destroys ministry and clergy marriages. — HBL

12. Do you share details of your family or marriage in your preaching?
Yes, and I have a story that I like to tell about that. Margaret and I are avid readers, and for the last several years she has been reading my books and magazines before I do. She often makes comments in the margins, and that helps keep us discussing common issues after I read the material and her comments.

One day in my office, while reading a book on marriage, I came across some warm personal comments from Margaret. Her comments motivated me to cancel my afternoon appointments and make a "pastoral" visit to my wife. The next Sunday I related this story to them from the pulpit. The next week the church office received over 200 calls from wives requesting the title of the book. The following Sunday I shared with them that it wasn't the book that was so great, but Margaret's comments.

I love sharing my heart with people. Often that helps them grow as much as any other one thing I could do. —John Maxwell

13. How do you keep your children sold on your ministry location?

We live in Los Angeles in a high crime area, but this area is all the children know. The decision of whether or not it is a good idea to voluntarily raise our family in mid-Wilshire Los Angeles is one that we have had to look at carefully from many different angles. Admittedly, there are aspects of life in L.A. that we would not choose for our children, but we feel providentially assigned here.

• Is that fair to children?

We think so. Janet has taken the lead in helping our children see the positive side of the city by taking advantage of its culture and diversity to introduce them to the wonder of the many worlds that have come to reside here.

• Is that enough?

No, there is much more. Going deeper than the question of what we really want for our children has led us to an appreciation for the spiritual opportunities our children have here. We want our children to know the Lord and what the mission of the church is in our world. We want them to know how the church responds to a sinful, hurting world. We want them to be able to experience firsthand how the church responds in love to people who are homeless or outcast or discriminated against. We want the values and priorities of the kingdom of God to be planted deep in their souls.

Living and serving in Los Angeles offers all that and much more. We have come to value for our children the experience of growing up in our city. And Janet and I believe Los Angeles offers opportunities for children to grow up in the midst of ministry challenges. —Ron Benefiel

14. Do you and your wife work together in ministry?

We share ministry in many ways. Margi has an office next to mine. In ministry we have learned that we become so much more working together than we could ever be by ourselves. Yet having said this I must also say that Margi has become a strong Christian leader in her own right. —Dale Galloway

15. We hear so much about ministry authenticity and integrity. How can I build these factors into my life?

Let's admit it—moral integrity, absolute veracity, and unquestioned authenticity are in short supply in our society these days. The French writer Arsene Houssaye observed an important truth for us in ministry: "Tell me whom you love, and I will tell you what you are."[1] His statement sounds a lot like the teachings of Jesus.

Duplicity and petty double-dealing have infected many churches and clergy marriages. Though duplicity is frighteningly common in the secular world, when it shows up in a pastor or his spouse it sends a garbled message to the people of God and to the world. At the same time, it also confuses neighbors and friends outside the church. They reason, if truth cannot be found in church and among believers, it can't be found anywhere. Meanwhile, the ministry couple dies inside little by little when they lose trust for themselves.

Too often bedrock integrity is an undervalued asset of our witness. But let's face reality: many people are searching for genuineness, morality, and authenticity in leaders, especially among spiritual pacesetters. With amazing accuracy, serious seekers and harping critics quickly spot phonies and are tuned to broken promises. They quickly detect every expression of self-glory. Thousands of grown children of the church have left for good because they have seen truth stretched so far by those who lead the church. The basic requirement is to be who you claim to be.

In your walk of faith, try not to imply a higher level of spiritual maturity than you have reached; neither degrade what God's grace is doing in you. Instead, allow people to see your struggle and growth points. Ask them to pray for your spiritual growth. Share your prayers and Bible reading discoveries.—NBW

16. What's a good way to lower tension?

Learn to laugh, especially at yourself. Try thinking back to the last funny thing that happened to you, or the funny thing you thought about, saw, read, or heard. See humor in your situation and in your reactions. Make fun of yourself. Tell funny stories about yourself. When did you last laugh out loud about something you said or did?

In every minister's life, there are many absurdities that can make us laugh. Too many ministries have too much pomposity. Most of us take life far too seriously.

Of course I do not mean a scoffing laugh about some ridiculous thing someone else did; nor do I mean humor that cuts and burns others emotionally. Neither do I have in mind toxic remarks some ministers and wives make about each other and call it humor. Rather, I am thinking of some funny things you did or said. I mean those things that you thought were incredibly serious but you now know are funny. I have in mind what C.S. Lewis suggested: "In my own experience the funniest things have occurred in the gravest and most sincere conversations."[2] — HBL

17. I'm always anxious when I hear a pastor's wife say, "I'm tired of trying to be a role model and an example for others to follow." How can we get by that sense of obligation and the need to make a good impression?

That's easy. Stop trying and start being what you say you are. That will provide a Christ-saturated model for others to follow. Stop showy affectations and become authentically Christian. Be your best possible self for Christ, and enjoy the inner exhilaration it brings. Rejoice in the outer impact it makes on those you serve. Others will then draw strength from you. They will want to be more like you — courageous, loving, loyal, dedicated, selfless, tenacious, committed, and faithful. A wholesome Christian life is a kind of spiritual "show and tell" that convinces others even when we may not be aware of it. — NBW

18. How can we encourage our children in the choice of Christian mates?

I can tell you what my dad did. Some might think it too strong, but it worked for me. My dad told me many times when I was studying for the ministry, "Son, the person you marry will determine the level of your effectiveness." When I talked with him about my desire to marry Margaret, he quickly gave his blessing. He then shared these words with me: "Son, when you started dating Margaret consistently, I made an appointment with her pastor, her principal, and her parents. I wanted to see what kind of a girl had caught your interest. I traveled to where she lived and spent the entire day with those three appointments. I was very pleased with what they had to say about Margaret. I asked them not to tell either of you about our discussion. John, she is a wonderful Christian lady and will be a wonderful wife for you." Dad was right. — John C. Maxwell

19. What's the main secret of your happy marriage?
Although I'm not one for playing games, Joyce taught me the most important game we've ever played since the day we married. It's called "Let's See Who Can Be Nicer to Whom." Let me explain how that works. Joyce usually wins the game. In all seriousness, one of the greatest lessons this lovely, petite woman has taught me, and one of the traits I see in her which I most want to mimic, is that winning a fight is never as important as cherishing our relationship. Even if she knows she's right and I'm wrong, she will invariably let the issue go, because to her "we" is more important than "me." — Ron Mehl

20. Does a pastor's wife impact the laity of a church?
More than any one of us can ever imagine. A paragraph of a letter to Margaret from a layman in our church puts what I think about this matter in perspective:

"Margaret — You have always been such a steady supporter of John. Your spirit, quiet when it needs to be, firm when it needs to be, complements John's spirit so well. Your commitment to him and to his work is obvious. You have so many talents of your own, but you're willing to put them on the back burner so that you can be the wife that John needs in his ministry.

"It's also been a blessing to see you properly model the role of the wife in a marriage. You probably don't want to be, but I'm sure you are an example to many of the wives in our church. A lot of them reflect your behavior as their husbands reflect John's behavior and teaching. John does a great job as a leader, but your job in many ways is tougher and even greater. Often it's easier to teach and demonstrate leadership than to teach and demonstrate 'followership.' You have been able to show us how a wife can be submissive without being less of a person, without losing her identity, and without being any less valuable to God and His people. Thank you for letting God make you the blessing you are for the rest of us. I want you to know that I'm always praying for you and your children." — John C. Maxwell

21. What is your wife's spiritual impact on your life and ministry?

Of course, it is loving and giving. But it is much more. Psalm 16:8 says, "I have set the Lord always before me: because He is at my right hand, I shall not be moved." In our home, it isn't uncommon for the boys and me to wake up in the middle of the night for cookies and milk and find that Joyce is in the living room on her knees, covering us in prayer. I know that's one of the main reasons for the peace and stability, not only in her life, but in our family life as well. — Ron Mehl

22. Are you and your wife always together?

One of our greatest secrets is that we both have personal interests. We respect one another, and each of us, in our way, has freed the other. Because of this there is a greater desire to be together when we are together. Exploring our interests and differences makes for more and better conversation when we are together. Naturally, we share many things in common, but individuality is our strength, deeply embedded in trust. — Tommy Barnett

23. How do you and your wife handle criticism?

It's never easy. But even while being criticized by insensitive members for not fulfilling their non-biblical expectations of what a pastor's wife ought to be, Lois would shed her tears in private, recommit her ways to the Lord, and continue loving and serving those who reviled her. She keeps her focus on what matters most in the maturing of our ministry together. — Tony Evans

24. How do I deal with rumors and hearsay?

Don't confuse rumor or gossip with facts. Rumors and notions fuel the fires of unrealistic expectations in many churches. Sometimes one person's opinion is assumed to be fact by the one who speaks or the one who listens. Not so — a mere notion or rumor should be viewed for what it is. It is liberating that one outspoken person's ideas are not always the will of God. Too often church civil wars start when one opinion, even the pastor's, is taken to be the will of the majority or the will of God.

Resist responding to rumors and speculations. People who bring you rumors are often trying to be helpful, but they do not represent the views of the whole congregation. Try to be careful too to keep from presenting your own opinion as fact. — NBW

25. Do you believe a woman should give her husband away to ministry?

I believe that because Marja freed me, early in our marriage, depositing me into the treasury of the Lord, we have this incredible tie that binds us together. Nothing separates us from the love of God or each other. But that happened because Marja has never felt competitive or jealous of my ministry. — Tommy Barnett

26. How do I nourish my own faith?

Nearly any basic discussion of the spiritual formation disciplines gives many ways to feed your faith. You must find your own pace, your own style, and your own commitment for avoiding a dry soul. Keep close to the flame of faith. Read the Bible for soul food, pray to stimulate your faith, and ask for insight to trust and cherish people. Go to church to get as much as possible out of it rather than being the resident critic who goes to be the team's crabby coach.

As eating a well-rounded diet keeps a person physically healthy, nutritious spiritual food must be eaten for strength and stamina. More than a religious duty, a nourishing diet of soul food enables you to do God's work more effectively, with less strain and with more vitality. We suffer spiritual anemia when we try to do ministry without being nourished by God's abundant provisions. — HBL

27. Can I learn to love people when I've been advised not to get close to everyone?

Start by evaluating how you react to people and how they respond to you. Why do you feel driven to be so private about your life? Show an interest in others. Recognize that you cannot be close friends with everyone in a congregation, but everyone you meet is a possible best friend. You can't know which one could be your best friend until you open your heart to people.

Try applying this advice from a secular management specialist to your parish relationships:

> Being a people person is learned just as much as being an engineer, accountant, market researcher, or health and safety expert is. You may not be able to get a degree there, but the congregation you work in is a classroom in human sensitivity just the same, and plenty of homework is required.[3]

Clergy couples in church settings often expect people to love them and accept them because of their position—they even wait for people to reach for them.

But this could be an error because church folk can be just as shy and frightened as people in other settings. Someone must make the first move. The secret—reach out to people and many of them will joyfully reach back to you.

Remember: church systems, ministerial credentials, academic degrees, noble reputations, stately status, or organizational hierarchies never genuinely love you. Only people do that. And in the long run relationships are about all that really matter.

Observe your mentor—Christ Jesus our Lord. Time and time again in the Gospels, He shows Himself to be immensely more interested in people than in things and institutions. And He is our pattern.—NBW

Epilogue
AN OPEN LETTER
TO THE PASTOR'S WIFE

Thank you for reading this far. You have honored us with this effort. We hope you found the book helpful and liberating. We want you to know that whether or not you have agreed with all we have said, we offer it in love. We care about you. You're special to us and incredibly important to the cause of Christ.

We have walked long journeys in pastoral ministry with our wives. We have seen the highs and lows of relationships and ministry fulfillment. We have, like Paul, known what it is like to have a lot and to have nothing in the way of material things. At times, it seemed that the road would never end, and then one day for us it was over. We packed our things, loaded our cars, and drove off to new endeavors — namely, helping pastors and their families like yours.

Our wives loved what they did while they were doing it, but they are content with the way things are now. We probably are the ones who, when the "church bells ring," feel the pang to return to shepherd a group of people. Those days are probably behind us forever, but for you and your spouse, the journey continues.

As you walk along, may we, in closing, say a few things to you personally — as though you will be the only one to read this epilogue. Mainly because you matter a lot — a whole lot.

In our lives and ministries, Bev and Bonnie provided balance in our homes. You will do the same. You will know when to say the right thing at the right time — please say it. Calm your husband down, affirm him, let him know he is loved, help him keep things in perspective. Keep him humble, help him choose his battles, and by all means, be honest with him.

At times, your home will resemble a hurricane, the pace will be so frantic. You will be the calming component. You will make the difference. Let your home become a sanctuary from all the influences and pressures. Help your family understand one another, cheer each other, and truly communicate with each other. You can find a way. God will help you.

Find some time for yourself. We are certain that Bev and Bonnie survived because they did not simply "live the church." They had friends in and out of the church, involved themselves in outside activities that gave them satisfaction, and put their families first. Get away when you can. Take care of yourself. Watch your diet. Stay current in world events. Have pride in your home, be it ever so humble, and continue to remind yourself that you're very special. God loves you a lot, and many times He is probably the only One who really understands your situation. There must be a Sabbath in every life. When and where do you find your rest?

Whether or not you feel called to be a pastor's wife, you are one. As we have attempted to say in this book, nobody else in the whole human race has your style and grace. You are one of a kind—you are unique—you are special. Remember that.

I wish we could promise you blue skies and calm seas from this point on, but we can't. What we can promise is God never fails. We can promise One who knows the end from the beginning, and One who will never leave you alone. We are not saying this to sound righteous or overly religious. We are saying it because in our lives and throughout our ministry we have found it to be true.

Bev and Bonnie send their best. As they have looked over the pages of this volume written to pastors and their wives by two old pastors, they have often said, "Where did you learn so much about being a pastor's wife?" We would simply smile, give them a little hug and say, "Because I married one."

Oh, by the way, have we made the point clear enough? You are special and that God loves you a lot. Hope so—because you are—He does—and so do we.

NOTES

Introduction

1. Ruth S. Peale, *The Adventure of Being a Wife* (Englewood, N.J.: Prentice-Hall, 1971), 2.

2. Cited in Golda Elam Bader, *I Married a Minister* (Nashville: Abingdon Press, 1942), 8.

Chapter 1

1. Cited in Leonard I. Sweet, *The Minister's Wife* (Philadelphia: Temple University Press, 1983), 78.

2. Ibid.

3. Charlotte Ross, *Who Is the Minister's Wife?* (Philadelphia: Westminster Press, 1980), 13.

4. Sweet, 14.

5. Roland Bainton, *Here I Stand* (Nashville: Abingdon Press, 1950), 384.

6. Sweet, 79. See also John Kirk, *The Mother of the Wesleys: A Biography,* 2nd ed. (London: Henry James Tresidder, 1864); and W.H. Withrow, *Makers of Methodism* (New York: Eaton and Mains, 1898).

7. Sweet, 87.

8. Ibid.

9. Ibid., 86.

10. "Ministers' Wives," *United Presbyterian,* 28 April 1898, cited in Sweet, 222.

11. Margaret E. Blackburn, *Things a Pastor's Wife Can Do: By One of Them* (Philadelphia: American Baptist Publication Society, 1898), 5–6.

12. William Barclay, *The Letter to the Romans* (Philadelphia: Westminster Press, 1957), 235.

13. Ibid.

14. Gale MacDonald, *High Call, High Privilege* (Wheaton, Ill.: Tyndale House, 1981), 89.

Chapter 2

1. Charlotte Ross, *Who Is the Minister's Wife?* (Philadelphia: Westminster Press, 1950), 9.

Chapter 3

1. *New Yorker* (7 October 1994), 100.

2. *Parade* (16 October 1994), 26.

3. S.D. Gordon, *Quiet Talks on Prayer* (New York: Fleming Revell Co., 1904), 12.

4. Quoted by John Oertberg, "The Latest Taboo," *Leadership* 15, no. 2, Spring 1994, 80–83.

5. John Locke, *An Essay Concerning Human Understanding,* cited by Rhoda Thomas Tripp, compiler, *Thesaurus of Quotations* (New York: Harper & Row, 1970), 427.

6. Marilyn Norquist Gustin, *The Inward Journey* (Ligouri, Mo.: Ligouri Publications, 1991), 51.

7. Eddie Fox, *The Asbury Herald,* 105, no. 2, Spring 1994, 23.

Chapter 4

1. Adapted from Liz Greenbacker, *The Private Lives of Ministers' Wives* (Far Hills, N.J.: New Horizon Press, 1991), 183–84.

2. Ibid.

3. *Pastors at Risk* (Wheaton, Ill.: Victor Books, 1993). *Heart of a Great Pastor* (Ventura, Calif.: Regal Books, 1994).

4. Charlotte Ross, *Who Is the Minister's Wife?* (Philadelphia: Westminister Press, 1950), 129.

5. Data from Kenneth E. Crow, researcher, *A Survey of Ministers' Wives* (Wheaton, Ill.: National Association of Evangelicals, 1990).

6. The address is 20820 Avis Ave., Torrance, Calif. 90503. Telephone (310) 793-9747; fax (310) 539-0007.

Chapter 5

1. Richard A. Blackmon and Archibald D. Hart, *Clergy Assessment and Career Development* (Nashville: Abingdon Press, 1991), 37.

2. Ibid., 41.

3. Cited in Donald R. Robertson, *Dear You* (Dallas: Word Publishing, 1989), 154.

4. Richard J. Foster, *Prayers from the Heart* (San Francisco: Harper & Row, 1994), 103.

Chapter 6

1. Adapted from William Barclay, *Prayer for the Christian Year* (New York: Harper & Row, 1964), 126.

2. Dorothy S. Hunt, ed., *Love: A Fruit Always in Season* (San Francisco: Ignatius Press, 1987), 110.

3. Stephen R. Covey, *The Seven Habits of Highly Effective People* (New York: Simon and Schuster, 1989), 88–89.

4. Liz Greenbacker, *The Private Lives of Ministers' Wives* (Far Hills, N.J.: New Horizon Press, 1991), 322.

5. John Powell, *Through Seasons of the Heart* (Allen, Texas: Tabor Publishing, 1987), 179.

6. Cited in Allen Cox, *Straight Talks for Monday Mornings* (New York: John Wiley and Sons, 1990), 253.

7. Hunt, 61.

8. Stephen Mitchell, "Psalm 19," in *A Book of Psalms* (New York: Harper Collins, 1993), 10.

9. Eugene Kennedy, *A Time for Being Human* (New York: Simon & Schuster, 1977), 195.

10. *The Bathroom Book,* vol. 1 (Salt Lake City: Compact Classics, 1994), 3-A2.

11. Cited in Ken Gire, *Intimate Moments with the Savior* (Grand Rapids: Zondervan, 1989), xi.

12. "The Sound of Clashing Expectations," *Leadership* 5, no. 3, Summer 1984, 83.

Chapter 7

1. Paraphrased from William Barclay, *Prayers for the Christian Year* (New York: Harper & Row, 1964), 102–3.

2. Alan B. Mangum, *Ministers' Wives Speak Out,* unpublished manuscript, p. 6.

3. Liz Greenbacker, *Who Is the Minister's Wife?* (Philadelphia: Westminster Press, 1950), 58–59.

4. *Colorado Springs Gazette Telegraph* (1 April 1994), 34.

5. As cited in David Mace and Vera Mace, *What's Happening*

to Clergy Marriages? (Nashville: Abingdon Press, 1980).

6. Adapted from William Douglas, *Ministers' Wives* (New York: Harper & Row, 1965), 53.

7. Ibid., 54.

8. Ibid., 61.

9. Ibid.

10. Cited in *Leadership,* Fall 1981, 68.

11. Cited in Briscoe, op. cit., 1.

Chapter 8

1. Eugene Peterson, *Praying with the Early Christians* (San Francisco: Harper Collins, 1994), reading for 2 November.

2. Ibid., reading for 24 February.

3. Richard J. Foster, *Coming Home* (San Francisco: Harper Collins, 1994), np.

4. Peterson, reading for 24 June.

5. Cited in Jill Briscoe, *Renewal on the Run* (Wheaton: Harold Shaw, 1992), 132.

6. Donald R. Robertson, *Dear You* (Dallas: Word Publishing, 1989), 102.

7. Paul Tournier, *Creative Suffering* (San Francisco: Harper & Row, 1981), 47.

8. Richard Gillard, "The Servant Song," in *Sing to the Lord* (Kansas City: Lillenas Publishing Co., 1994), 679. Used by permission.

9. Cited in *The Denver Post,* 18 September 1994, 4D.

Chapter 9

1. *Colorado Springs Gazette Telegraph,* 18 July 1994, B-10.

2. James D. Whitehead and Evelyn Eaton Whitehead, *The Promise of Partnership* (San Francisco: Harper, 1991), 16.

3. As cited in "Dear Abby," *Colorado Springs Gazette Telegraph,* 7 October 1994, D-6.

4. Oswald Chambers, *My Utmost for His Highest* (New York: Dodd, Mead and Co., 1935), 171.

5. Charlotte Ross, *Who Is the Minister's Wife?* (Philadelphia: Westminster Press, 1950), 42.

6. Margaret M. Damp, *Finding Fulfillment in the Manse* (Kansas City: Beacon Hill Press, 1978), 105.

Chapter 10

1. "Points to Ponder," *Reader's Digest,* November 1988, 33.
2. "Points to Ponder," *Reader's Digest,* November 1990, 185.
3. *Simple Wisdom* (New York: Viking Studio Books, 1993), 69.

Chapter 11

1. Cited in *The Minister's Wife: Person or Position* (Nashville: Abingdon Press, 1966), 27.
2. Briscoe, op. cit., 90.
3. Charlotte Ross, *Who Is the Minister's Wife?* (Philadelphia: Westminster Press, 1950), 95.
4. James Dobson, *When God Doesn't Make Sense* (Wheaton, Ill.: Tyndale House, 1993), inside front cover.
5. As cited in *Reader's Digest,* October 1990, 131.

Chapter 12

1. Louis E. Boone, *The Twenty-First Century Manager* (New York: Random House, 1993), 268.
2. Cited in Wayne Martindale and Jerry Root, eds., *The Quotable Lewis* (Wheaton, Ill.: Tyndale House, 1989), 321.
3. Allen Cox, *Straight Talk for Monday Mornings* (New York: John Wiley and Sons, 1990), 135.